Da Capo Press Series in
ARCHITECTURE AND DECORATIVE ART
GENERAL EDITOR: ADOLF K. PLACZEK
Avery Librarian, Columbia University

Volume 26

WILLIAM STRICKLAND

Architect and Engineer

1788-1854

WILLIAM STRICKLAND

Architect and Engineer · 1788 - 1854

BY AGNES ADDISON GILCHRIST

Enlarged Edition

DA CAPO PRESS • NEW YORK • 1969

A DA CAPO PRESS REPRINT EDITION

This Da Capo Press edition of *William Strickland, Architect and Engineer*, an unabridged republication of the first edition published in Philadelphia in 1950, is reprinted by special arrangement with the University of Pennsylvania Press. It includes as a supplement three articles about Strickland prepared by Mrs. Gilchrist following the appearance of the first edition, and the publishers are grateful to The Society of Architectural Historians and to the American Philosophical Society for permission to reproduce these articles.

Library of Congress Catalog Number 69-13714

A Division of Plenum Publishing Corporation
227 West 17th Street
New York, N.Y. 10011

Printed in the United States of America

WILLIAM STRICKLAND

Architect and Engineer

William Strickland

WILLIAM STRICKLAND

Architect and Engineer • 1788-1854

BY

AGNES

ADDISON

GILCHRIST

Philadelphia

1950

UNIVERSITY *of* PENNSYLVANIA PRESS

LONDON: GEOFFREY CUMBERLEGE
OXFORD UNIVERSITY PRESS

Manufactured in the United States of America

FOR
PHILIP STRICKLAND HARPER
GREAT-GRANDSON
OF THE ARCHITECT
WILLIAM STRICKLAND

PREFACE

THE ARRANGEMENT OF THIS BOOK has been dictated by the desire to be acceptable to people interested in the American scene, in history, in biography, in the nineteenth century, in art and architecture, and especially to students of American architecture. Therefore, three chapters, unburdened by footnotes, are devoted to summary discussions of Strickland's life, character, and style. The first section of the appendixes represents the bulk of the research which has been done. It is designed primarily for the serious student of architectural history. A separate account of each building is given with a bibliography, a brief history, and a description which, when possible, includes comment on style, plan, materials, cost, and outstanding features. This is an attempt to give concrete, objective, and factual information about the buildings designed by William Strickland.

Since there is no corpus of Strickland papers, information concerning him and his work has to be gathered from varied and sometimes seemingly unlikely quarters. Newspapers and guidebooks have been fruitful sources. I wish to commend especially the diligence and architectural perception of Cephas G. Childs, who published *Views in Philadelphia* in 1830, and of Samuel Hazard, who edited *Hazard's Register of Pennsylvania* from 1828 to 1835. The fullest account of Strickland's life is to be found in the obituary given by John Kintzing Kane to the members of the American Philosophical Society. Concerning federal buildings, the National Archives in Washington contain a wealth of information.

For information about the Strickland family, the late William Strickland Harper, of Hamden, Connecticut, grandson of the architect; and Philip Strickland Harper, of Chicago, supplied me with many anecdotes and family traditions. Mrs. Ruth Strickland Fleming, of Washington, D. C., granddaughter of the younger son of the architect, graciously showed me the memorabilia of Strickland which are in her possession. Mrs. Bertha Edwards McGeehan, genealogist of Philadelphia, has conducted research on the Strickland family and generously given me transcripts of the references which she has found.

Fiske Kimball, Director of the Philadelphia Museum of Art, has kindly encouraged me throughout and loaned me all the notes and photographs which he has collected pertaining to Strickland. His helpful criticism is gratefully acknowledged.

Special thanks are due to Talbot Hamlin, of the Architectural School of Columbia University, who has been so good as to read the typescript and make valued comments. David Robb, of the University of Pennsylvania, and Sydney Martin, Philadelphia architect, have also read the work in typescript and made excellent suggestions.

Miss Gladys Wiley, formerly of the Tennessee State Library, found much of the Strickland material in Nashville which I should never have seen without her help. I wish to thank her especially for her kindnesses to me while I was in Nashville and for her unremitting interest in seeing that this volume would be finally finished.

Concrete aid was given by the American Philosophical Society of which Strickland was a member for thirty-four years. In 1941, I received Grant No. 518 to go to Nashville. Also in 1941, the Committee on Research of the University of Pennsylvania granted funds which were used to photograph buildings and drawings in Nashville.

I wish to thank for their coöperation the following people who live or work in Strickland buildings: in Nashville, Miss Josephine Farrell, who formerly lived in "Burlington" and made available the Elliston papers; Mrs. Edgar Foster, owner of "Lynnlawn"; Mrs. Meredith Caldwell, owner of "Belle Meade"; in Burlington, New Jersey, Mr. and Mrs. A. Neilson Carter, owners of the "Old Stone House" or "Parsonage"; in Philadelphia, Mr. and Mrs. Robert B. Haines 3rd, of "Wyck," Germantown, who not only gave me complete access to the house but also to the letters and drawings in their possession; Alfred W. Price, Rector of St. Stephen's Church and James Carrigan, the Sexton; Rear Admiral Forde A. Todd, formerly Governor of the United States Naval Home; Paul L. Brogan of the firm of Yahn and McDonnell, present owners of the Musical Fund Society Hall.

Frank J. Roos, Jr., University of Illinois, gave me a copy of the bibliography which he had made on Strickland. William Sener Rusk, Wells College, first turned my attention to the need for a life of Strickland. William E. Beard, of the *Nashville Banner*, initiated me to the vagaries of the Nashville newspapers and kindly gave me the references which he had collected on Strickland's work in Nashville. Professor David Robinson, formerly of the Johns Hopkins University, permitted me to examine the Latrobe letter-books which were on exhibit there in January, 1942. The crucial volume for the year 1818 was not there, and I have not seen it. B. Rhett Chamberlain, vice-president of the Mint Museum of Art, Charlotte, North Carolina, gave me photographs and much information. John E. Reynolds, of Meadville, Pennsylvania, gave me information and a view of the courthouse there. Miss Louise Hall, Duke University, found the reference to the Brandywine Shoal Lighthouse in the National Archives and referred me to the volume of the Practical House Carpenters' Society of Philadelphia. John L. Sanders sent me copies of the Strickland letters which he found during his research on the Capitol of North Carolina. Strickland Kneass, of Strawberry Hill Farm, Boylston Center, Massachusetts, sent me a manuscript written by his father telling of the Beefsteak Club and a copy of a poem by William Kneass, Strickland's friend. Dr. Edward B. Hodge, of Philadelphia, informed me of the Strickland drawing in his office, a view of the "Parsonage" in Burlington, New Jersey.

Miss Edith H. Gates, acting secretary of the Cairo Association of Commerce, Cairo, Illinois, made special efforts to answer my inquiries. The Charlotte, North Carolina,

Chamber of Commerce and the New Orleans Association of Commerce answered my letters promptly and sent excellent photographs.

The following people I wish to thank for answering inquiries and making useful suggestions: Turpin Bannister, Allen Berstein, Mrs. Nicholas Biddle, Vincent B. Brecht, Jean Brownlee, Joseph Carson, A. L. Crabb, William S. Dewey, William B. Dinsmoor, William Gerhard, Henry Hope, Charles T. Ingham, Joseph Jackson, G. B. Kneass, Clifford Lewis, Jr., Roger Hale Newton, Charles Peterson, Margaret Bailey Tinkcom, Samuel Wilson, Rev. Jacob A. Winterstein, and Leon de Valinger, State Archivist of Delaware.

All the members of the libraries and societies where I have worked while gathering material on Strickland, I wish to thank for their courteous help. Especially helpful in Philadelphia were: Gertrude D. Hess and Marie Richards, American Philosophical Society; Henry B. Allen, A. Rigling, and Claire Johnston, formerly of the Franklin Institute; Merle M. Odgers and Hazel Erchinger, Girard College; Catharine Miller of the Manuscript Department of the Historical Society of Pennsylvania; Joseph T. Fraser, Jr., Pennsylvania Academy of Fine Arts; Seymour Thompson and Edith Hartwell, formerly of the University of Pennsylvania Library; Barney Chesnick, Ridgeway Library. Also, in Philadelphia, the following people aided me: George F. Lee, Mariners Church; Leon H. Elmaleh, Rabbi Emeritus of the Mikveh-Israel Synagogue; Rev. Richard H. Tafel and Edna M. Eayre, of the Swedenborgian Church of the New Jerusalem; Alice Farr, secretary, First Unitarian Church; and George Farnum Brown, secretary-treasurer of Laurel Hill Cemetery.

My research in Nashville was furthered by Mrs. John Trotwood Moore, Librarian of the Tennessee State Library (now retired), and her assistant, Mrs. Alexander Russell; by Liston M. Lewis, of the Nashville Public Library; and Mrs. Brainard Cheney, of the Vanderbilt University Library. In Washington, my research was facilitated by P. M. Hamer, National Archives; Captain Dudley W. Knox, U.S.N. Retired, and Mrs. Alma Lawrence, of the Office of Naval Records and Library of the Navy Department; Leicester B. Holland and St. George Sioussat, both formerly of the Library of Congress, and Alice Parker, of the Fine Arts Division. Mrs. George W. Cooke and Clara B. Mowry, of the Providence Athenaeum, placed all their material at my disposal. Miss R. Pratt, of the Sterling Library, Yale University, found the Strickland material, which at that time had not been catalogued. Evelyn J. Snyder, of the Cairo (Illinois) Public Library; Nell B. Stevens, assistant general librarian, Pennsylvania State Library; and William D. Hoyt, Jr., assistant director of the Maryland Historical Society, answered questions which involved research for them. To these and all the many other people whose enthusiasm and interest aided me in this study, I wish once more to acknowledge my debt.

Rexford Newcomb's article on Strickland in *The Architect;* Alfred M. Brooks' life in the *Dictionary of American Biography;* and Joseph Jackson's collection of Strickland material in *Early Philadelphia Architects*, were the cornerstones of this research.

Robert C. Smith of the University of Pennsylvania has checked the illustrations and taken new photographs where he thought necessary. He has also referred me to new material.

The interested encouragement and patient forbearance of my friends and members of my family during these years of my preoccupation with the work of Strickland, I wish to gratefully acknowledge, especially that of my husband, John Mason Gilchrist.

Finally, I must thank Philip Strickland Harper, a great-grandson of William Strickland, whose gift to the University of Pennsylvania made possible this publication. In appreciation of his generosity, I have dedicated this volume to him.

Mount Vernon, New York
February 6, 1950

Agnes Addison Gilchrist

TABLE OF CONTENTS

LIST OF PLATES

(Following page 145)

CHAPTER I

LIFE

William Strickland was born in November, 1788, at Navesink, New Jersey, a son of John and Elizabeth Strickland. His brothers were John and George. John (1791-1835) became a carpenter like his father, and married Jane Hurst on May 9, 1815, in Christ Church in Philadelphia. The youngest brother, who was born in 1797, studied drawing, painting, and engraving with his brother William. In the 1830's, George left Philadelphia and became a clerk in the Patent Office in Washington.

John Strickland, the father (1757-1820), had his portrait painted by Thomas Sully in 1809, and the portrait shows him to have been a man of intelligence and sensitivity. During the Revolution, he is said to have owned a farm at Navesink. He was in Philadelphia by 1790 according to the census of that year. He became a carpenter of repute and in 1811 was a charter member of the Practical House Carpenters' Society. He was carpenter of the Bank of Pennsylvania from 1797 to 1801, a building which was designed by Benjamin H. Latrobe. It was during this time that his son William first came to the attention of Latrobe. The boy who used to play about the unfinished building showed great brightness and a natural aptitude for drawing. Therefore, in 1803 at the age of fourteen, young Strickland was apprenticed to Latrobe to learn the fundamentals of engineering and architectural practice. Latrobe had a high opinion of the quickness and ability of his pupil, but he also found him to be undependable, independent, and difficult.

Early in the apprenticeship, Latrobe wrote John Strickland a letter which augured well for the relationship of the pupil and master. It was written from Newcastle on March 1, 1804, and began:

> My dear Friend—
>
> Your son has bethought himself that he has both a father and a mother alive, and is seized with such a violent inclination to see both, that I have given him a furlough for a few days— You will find him increased in stature and in favor with Man—I hope also with God. I have in fact nothing to say of him, that it would not be a pleasure to me to say of my own son, and indeed there is not much difference in the interest I feel for him and for Henry. I hope you will find him as much improved as you expect.

After some inquiries about a log house that John Strickland was building, Latrobe concludes, "God bless you my dear fellow, and give you and your good wife health."

When William returned from his furlough, he brought the perennial question, did Latrobe have a job for John Strickland. That time Latrobe could answer in the affirmative, "Yes, Clerk of the Works of the Chesapeake and Delaware Canal."

Latrobe was engaged at this time as the engineer for the proposed canal from the Chesapeake to the Delaware which would facilitate travel between Baltimore and Philadelphia. He was so engaged until 1806 when the work lapsed. He was also commissioned to make a survey of Newcastle, most of the work of which was done by his apprentices, or pupils, of whom there were at least four at that time. Robert Mills from South Carolina was the eldest and most conscientious. By 1807, Latrobe trusted him to superintend the construction of the Bank of Philadelphia, after which Mills was on his own and was commissioned to do the new wings of the State House, or Independence Hall, in Philadelphia, Washington Hall, and probably the Dorsey Mansion. Peter Lenox and Latrobe's son Henry, with Strickland, completed the quartet.

In August of 1804, William displeased his teacher who wrote his father that it was necessary to treat him with great severity. He had been sent ahead to open the house in Ironhill, to air the beds and furniture, to rub the mold off the walls, and to be ready for the Latrobes on their arrival, but, instead, he had gone off to Salem on a fishing party and had not returned until six in the evening. Latrobe added that he thought William was spoiled by his mother.

However, Strickland was with Latrobe for another year, until August, 1805, when he absented himself from the office without notice or leave. Latrobe then wrote directly to William that he took it for granted that it was not his or his mother's intention that he should return and asked him to call for his drawings and instruments, to return any keys belonging to Latrobe, and to call for a draft for twenty-five dollars, paid by the Commissioners of the town of Newcastle for the regulation of the streets, work Strickland was doing with Robert Mills.

It is not certain whether Strickland returned or not. The work on the Canal came to an end in 1806, and in 1807 John Strickland was employed by John Holland on the rebuilding of the Park Theatre in New York. William Dunlap remembered that William went with his father to New York at that time. The playbills of the Park Theatre for the winter 1807-08 show how William was employed. He and Hugh Reinagle painted scenery for the new productions which Holland put on that winter. It is probable that Strickland did the drawings of New York which are now in the New-York Historical Society collection at the same time.

By the summer of 1808, William Strickland was back in Philadelphia, for there are several pencil sketches which he did along the Wissahickon then. Also in 1808, he made his first important and independent architectural drawings for the Masonic Hall on Chestnut Street between Seventh and Eighth streets, a Gothic design which was accepted in November. The building was started in 1809 and completed in 1811. Therefore, he began his independent architectural career before he was twenty-one. While the Masonic Hall was being built, he became a Mason, a member of Lodge No. 91, on November 27, 1809.

In 1811, Strickland painted a large oil painting of Christ Church in Philadelphia which was exhibited at the annual exhibition of the Pennsylvania Academy of Fine Arts and of the Columbia Society of Artists. Strickland was a member of the latter society at that time, and later, in 1814, became a member of the Pennsylvania Academy of Fine Arts and, in 1819, a director, a position he continued to hold until 1846.

In 1812, near his twenty-fourth birthday, Strickland was married to Rachel McCollough Trenchard at Christ Church on November 3, 1812, with Dr. Abercrombie officiating. Miss Trenchard was born in Woodstown, New Jersey, in 1789.

Strickland had no certain means of support at that time but did surveying, engraving of landscape and portrait paintings, and theatrical scene painting. He drew a map of the city of Philadelphia for a publisher Charles P. Harrison and another dedicated to the Hose Companies of the city, published by William Kneass. Kneass, an engraver and publisher, was one of Strickland's best friends at this time, and they were associated both in business and in society.

The War of 1812 did not disturb Philadelphians until 1814 when the English were coming up the Maryland coast. Then a Committee of Safety for the defense of the city was established under General Joseph Bloomfield. Strickland, with William Kneass and Robert Brooke, was engaged by the Committee to survey the land for nine miles west of Philadelphia and to make a report on the possible approaches to the city which might be taken by the enemy and on the best situations for defense. This survey and report was finished in September, 1814. Strickland was about to serve in the army as a volunteer when he was asked to help supervise the defenses of the city which consisted of earth redoubts thrown up by the citizens.

During these years before Strickland became established as an architect, he did various engravings for the *Analectic Magazine* and the *Port Folio*. He also did a series of drawings of famous naval encounters during the War of 1812 and engravings of the naval heroes. His patriotism led him to write a popular song called *Decatur's Victory*. Another project of this period was an ambitious design for a National Washington Monument which was shown in the annual exhibition of the Pennsylvania Academy of Fine Arts in 1813. He engraved the illustrations for the book by Captain David Porter of the *Essex*, which was published in 1815 under the title *Travels in 1812, 1813 and 1814.* He made an aquatint for the title page of a book called *The Art of Landscape Painting* and was probably the author of the text and the artist responsible for the illustrations. Also, he made a view of Old Baltimore for W. and J. Coale, an example of which is in the New York Public Library. Correspondence about these prints is in the Historical Society of Pennsylvania and the Manuscript Department of the New York Public Library. Miss Eliza Leslie, later famous for her cookbooks and novels, colored some of these prints, and Strickland's younger brother George colored the rest.

After the war, Strickland's first architectural design was for the Temple of the New Jerusalem, the Swedenborgian Church at the corner of Twelfth and Sansom streets, which was bought by the Philadelphia Academy of Natural Sciences in 1826 and converted by Strickland from a church to a museum and lecture hall with the exterior unchanged. The style of this building was unique; it had a low dome and four-centered arches which gave it a Saracenic appearance.

The architectural competition for the Capitol in Washington set the pattern for innumerable others. The State of Pennsylvania held an architectural competition for the State Capitol and Strickland submitted plans. He was unsuccessful. His former fellow-student in Latrobe's office, Robert Mills, received the second premium. Strickland entered at least three other competitions: he won the first premium for his design of the Second Bank of the United States; second premium for his design for Girard College, while Thomas Walter won the first; and he was unsuccessful with his plan for the Eastern Penitentiary, in which John Haviland won the first premium.

In 1817 and 1818, Strickland had several buildings under construction; the Friends' Asylum in Frankfort, the Custom House which was adorned with a statue of Commerce by the sculptor William Rush, extensive repair of the Medical Hall of the University of Pennsylvania, and a new Medical Museum there.

The year 1818 was a crucial one in Strickland's architectural career. In that year he entered and won the competition for the plan of the Second Bank of the United States. The competition was announced in May by the Directors of the Bank who specified that a Greek order of the least expensive kind was to be employed. The competition was originally to have closed on the first of August, but was extended to the first of September. The results were published in the *Philadelphia Gazette* on Saturday, September 12, and copied in other papers on Monday. This statement said that Strickland won the first premium and Latrobe, the second. Strickland was engaged to superintend the construction of the building. The cornerstone was laid on April 5, 1819, and the work was finished in August, 1824. The Bank was under construction for six years, but because of a delay in allotting the money, the work was not continuous. It is said to have cost over half a million dollars. The Bank was and is one of the finest buildings designed and built in this country. The design is a mixture of late Georgian and Greek Revival. The porticoes were copied directly from the plates of Stuart and Revett, illustrating the Parthenon in Athens. The arrangement of the side windows and the oval entrance vestibule are Georgian in proportion and detail. The ground plan is a mixture of pure utilitarianism, as directed by the proposals for the competition, and Georgian with the central entrance and balancing rooms on either side at both ends of the building, and with a cross axis in the center where the large banking room is roofed by a barrel vault. The exterior design was changed at the last moment and Latrobe was told that the new plans by Strickland were similar to the ones which he had presented, but there is no definite proof that Strickland ever saw Latrobe's drawings. Both are Doric, but the silhouette is different since Latrobe's banking room was roofed by a dome which projected up above the gable roof, while Strickland's barrel vault was lower and the classical gable line of the roof was unbroken. The construction was masonry throughout, in an attempt to make it fireproof. It is an example of the excellent architectural work of the period.

This was an important building and immediately gave Strickland standing as one of the best architects in the country. During the six years that he was working on the Bank, he had at least eighteen other architectural commissions, including designs for four churches, the Chesnut Street Theatre, and the Court House of Meadville, Pennsylvania. Also, during 1822 and 1823, Strickland did some engineering work, first, on a committee of the American Philosophical Society to study the possible routes for the Delaware and Chesapeake Canal, then making a report on the proposed route, and finally making a survey of it with a Mr. Siddall.

Strickland was twenty-eight years old when he won the competition for the Bank which is young for such an important undertaking. It is even more surprising when one remembers that he had designed only four buildings prior to then, none of which was Greek Revival. Strickland himself thought that he received the premium partly because of the good will of some of the members of the Board of Directors, to whom he had recommended himself during the autumn of 1814 when he had been one of the engineers in charge of the defense of the city.

One of the results of winning the competition for the Bank was his election to the American Philosophical Society on September 22, 1820. Strickland already belonged to several societies —the Tullian Club, the Academy of Natural Sciences, of which he was an early member, elected in 1813; the Columbian Society of Artists, and the Pennsylvania Academy of Fine Arts. He was a convivial man and enjoyed especially the social side of the societies to which he belonged. He was more constant in his attendance at the social affairs than at the scientific meetings of the American Philosophical Society, but he served on the Building Committee until he went to Nashville. There were a number of other societies to which he belonged during his life, both social and professional. Of the former, his favorite was the Beefsteak Club which consisted of informal dinners where a group of congenial men gathered together to eat, drink, and be witty. In such surroundings, Strickland's convivial good nature and spontaneous wit showed to best advantage. He was one of the first members of the Franklin Institute and the first recording secretary. He was also a charter member of the Musical Fund Society and a director of the Fund until he went to Nashville. He was member No. 181 of the state in Schuylkill Fishing Club, but he remained a member for only two years, 1822-24. During that time he and his wife attended several of the Club dinners, but evidently his volatile nature was not content with the quiet and sedentary pleasures of fishing, and not even the famous punch was sufficient inducement for him to continue his membership.

One of the events of 1824 was the visit of General Lafayette to the United States. He arrived in August and, after visiting New York and Boston, came to Philadelphia late in September. Strickland had a number of commissions in connection with this visit. He was a member of the committee in charge of arrangements and was appointed to superintend the repairs in the old State House, or Independence Hall, where Lafayette held his levee. Strickland, with his pupil Samuel Kneass, was in charge of the triumphal arches which were erected along the route by which Lafayette was driven from the entrance to the city in Kensington to the State House where the main arch was erected. It was designed by Strickland on the model of the Arch of Septimus Severus in Rome.

Thomas Sully painted the coat of arms of the city on the arch and William Rush carved figures for it.

There was a grand ball held for Lafayette in the Chesnut Street Theatre and Strickland made the design for the painted floor, while John Haviland was in charge of the decorations.

Strickland was so impressed by the event that he wrote the words for a song in honor of Lafayette's arrival, to the tune of *My Heart's in the Highlands*. This was published by G. Blake and Company in Philadelphia and was illustrated by a line drawing of the Triumphal Arch on Chestnut Street.

Strickland was probably present at most of the entertainments in honor of Lafayette, including a banquet at the Masonic Hall and a reception given by the American Philosophical Society at the residence of Nicholas Biddle.

Lafayette's secretary, Monsieur Levasseur, found time to keep notes on the journey which were later published in book form both in France and, in translation, in Philadelphia in which he speaks highly of the Bank which Strickland had just completed.

During the last year of his work on the Bank, Strickland was much engaged by his membership in the new Franklin Institute. Beside being Recording Secretary, he served on a number of committees and designed the seal for the Institute, and during the winter of 1824-25, he also gave a series of lectures on architecture at the Institute which were well attended. One of the young men who listened to these lectures was Thomas Ustick Walter, who later worked in his office. Walter's father was a bricklayer who had been employed in the construction of the Bank.

Strickland received his next important commission because of his connection with the Franklin Institute. He was asked to go to England as a special agent for the Pennsylvania Society for the Promotion of Internal Improvement. The membership of the latter society was largely that of the Institute and Strickland was well known to all the members. The reason for the creation of this society was that the civic-minded Philadelphians realized with dismay that the importance of Philadelphia as a port was dwindling because of the population shift to the West and the better routes of transportation from New York and Baltimore. New York became a formidable competitor because of the opening of the Erie Canal which enabled goods to be carried from the Hudson River through northern New York State. De Witt Clinton's "Great Ditch" immediately bore economic dividends. Baltimore also had advantages as a port for western Pennsylvania and West Virginia because it was located on the Chesapeake and Ohio Canal. Between the two, Philadelphia was losing out and the Society desired to arouse the Legislature of Pennsylvania and also to learn of the improved methods of transportation which were becoming popular in England.

Already in 1825, when Strickland was sent to England, the question of whether the canal or the railroad would prove to be of more value was current and that was one of the specific questions to which Strickland was to learn the answer. He was also to learn of the construction of breakwaters, roads, gas plants, iron smelting, printing of calico, to collect books and pamphlets on these subjects, and to get models of machines. The model of Stephenson's locomotive which Strickland procured is still exhibited in the Franklin Institute.

The Society raised three thousand dollars to pay for Strickland's services and additional funds to send his pupil, Samuel Honeyman Kneass, with him to aid in making the drawings and reports. They sailed from Philadelphia in March 1825 and returned in December, after spending eight months in England, Ireland, and Scotland. The reports which Strickland made were published in 1826 under the title *Reports on Canals, Railways and Roads.* It was subscribed to by Congress, state legislatures, the War Department, colleges, and canal companies, as well as by individuals all over the country who were interested in internal improvement.

Strickland himself was convinced that railroads with locomotives provided a better means of transportation than canals and wrote to that effect. However, since a number of the Society members had large investments in canal companies, his statements were edited in the publication of the report. Nevertheless, the reports provided the first clear descriptions of the construction of railroads published in this country. The Society asked that the reports be written in simple, nontechnical language and the result is that they are readily intelligible and interesting to the layman.

Strickland was well received by the English engineers and found them helpful. One of them, Jesse Hartley of Liverpool, who was in charge of the docks at that port, became a good friend. Strickland named his younger son for him.

The Legislature of Pennsylvania was awakened to the need for improved transportation across the state as the land to the west of the Alleghenies became more settled. A Canal Commission was appointed in 1825, and surveys were undertaken to determine the best route from Philadelphia to Pittsburgh. The ridge of the Allegheny Mountains presented a serious barrier. After it was decided to construct a canal from Columbia to Johnstown to Pittsburgh, there was still a discussion as to the best means of crossing the mountains. The suggestion of the engineers, that a tunnel be dug, was the least expensive and most efficient, but both the Legislature and the people in general seemed to find something ludicrous in a canal going through a mountain, so that project was discarded and, instead, the so-called Pennsylvania Mixed System was adopted. This called for a railroad from Philadelphia to Columbia, canal from there to the Alleghenies, a portage system of inclined rails over the mountains, and then canal again to Pittsburgh. The obvious disadvantage was that the freight had to be transshipped, which increased the cost and the time and made the whole undertaking inefficient.

Strickland was employed by the State of

Pennsylvania as the engineer in charge of the Eastern Division which included the railroad to Columbia and the canal to the Alleghenies. While he was so employed from 1826 until the first of June, 1827, his residence was in Harrisburg. His salary was three thousand dollars a year and he was permitted to undertake other commissions during that time. He resigned from that position because the Legislature passed a bill providing that the engineers should not be paid more than two thousand dollars a year and that they should remain in residence at the site of their work. Strickland wrote the Canal Commissioners that he much regretted that he was forced to resign, but that the exigencies of a large and growing family made it impossible to comply with the new regulations. He had five children then, one a baby just over a year old, and his wife was expecting another child, which explains his references to his family. The reason that he could not remain at the site of the canal was that he had accepted several other architectural commissions which were being executed at that time.

Strickland was wise to resign his position as engineer of the Eastern Division of the Pennsylvania Mixed System, for in the next five years he received his most important commissions in Philadelphia and reached the apex of his architectural career.

His engineering activities did not lapse completely, however, for he was a consultant for the Columbia and Philadelphia Railway, he made a report in 1828 on the Fair Mount Dam, and, most important, was the supervising engineer of the Delaware Breakwater from 1828 to 1841. The Breakwater, which is still in use, was a monumental undertaking which Strickland's trip to England prepared him to see to a successful completion. It was built off Lewes, Delaware, and made a protected harbor for the ships which were going to Philadelphia.

In 1825, Strickland made a design for a monument to Washington to be erected in Philadelphia. It was large and heavy and was criticized as taking up too much space in Washington Square. It was never erected, nor was any monument to Washington placed in Philadelphia, although a cornerstone was laid with great ceremony and an impressive procession in 1833. The Philadelphians would not subscribe sufficient money and the project finally lapsed into oblivion.

One of Strickland's most noteworthy designs was made in 1826 for the United States Naval Asylum, now called The Naval Home. His first sketch, which he sent with an estimate to the Secretary of the Navy, is still in the Archives Building in Washington. The correspondence, also preserved there, indicates that Strickland's younger brother George made plans for the Asylum too, and felt that his brother incorporated some of the features of his design in the accepted plan. He was appeased by being appointed Clerk of the Works at a salary of six hundred dollars a year. Strickland, as supervising architect, received one hundred dollars a month.

The building, when it was designed, was to serve as both a home and hospital for retired seamen. It was, in addition, used for the Naval Training School until 1845 when Annapolis was established.

The plan and the design are successful. There is a central square building with an Ionic portico which houses the public rooms, the auditorium, the dining room, and the officers' rooms. On either side there are wings, three stories in height with central corridors, and the sleeping quarters for the men. At the far ends of the wings, there are the recreation or common rooms. An innovation in the design were the balconies which opened off each floor of dormitories so that the men might get out into the fresh air even when the weather was inclement or when they were not strong enough to go out onto the grounds. The construction of the building was fireproof, the floors were of brick and the ceilings vaulted, or domed. Iron columns were used to support the piazzas, but otherwise the construction was masonry.

Strickland's connections with the Asylum terminated at the end of 1829, but the building was not entirely completed, furnished, and ready for use until 1833.

As far as is known at present, Strickland designed few private houses. Therefore it is rather surprising that he made two sets of drawings for the residence which James A. Hillhouse was planning to build in New Haven. Hillhouse wanted a classic design and finally obtained a successful one from Alexander Davis. Strickland's plans are square, heavy, and dull.

One of the interesting events in Philadelphia in 1828 was the restoration of the steeple of the old State House, or Independence Hall. When the building was first used in 1735, there was no tower, but one was added in 1741 which was used for the staircase and which housed a small bell. The timbers became rotten and in 1781 a low roof was put up instead. In 1828, after the building had been purchased by the City of Philadelphia, City Councils determined to get a new clock, since the old one was inaccurate, and a new bell. Various members of City Councils felt that this would be an excellent opportunity to restore the tower so that the building would more closely resemble its former appearance. The feeling that the building was a shrine was already strong at that time.

Strickland's design for the tower, at an estimated cost of eight thousand dollars, was presented by the committee to a joint meeting of City Councils on February 28, 1828, and—strangely enough—it precipitated a great discussion for one of the members considered it hideous, "a mammouth Chimney—a shot tower," and could find nothing to recommend it. Another felt that in such an important undertaking, Councils should go slowly. However, the committee prevailed and the tower was built during the summer under Strickland's supervision.

Strickland worked on a series of important buildings in the next five years. He was generally called "City Architect" and always referred to with some complimentary epithet. John Haviland, an Englishman who had come to Philadelphia in 1816, shared with Strickland the honor of being Philadelphia's leading architect. Some of Haviland's important commissions at this time were the Franklin Institute on Seventh Street, the Walnut Street Theatre, the Eastern Penitentiary, and the Naval Home in Norfolk. Strickland and Haviland belonged to many of the same societies and must have seen a great deal of each other. Their opinion of each other is not recorded.

Strickland's second theatre design was for the Arch Street Theatre which was built in 1828. Also, in 1828, he designed a church for the First Congregation of Unitarians. It was of marble and a good example of the Greek Revival style with plain walls and a carefully proportioned Doric portico. In 1829, Strickland received two commissions from the University of Pennsylvania, which had been occupying the house at Ninth and Market streets originally built for the Presidential mansion. By this time it was in bad repair and inadequate for the needs of the growing university. It was torn down and two similar buildings were erected on the same plot, one to house the Medical School and the other the College Department.

Another commission of 1829 was for the United States Mint to be erected at the corner of Chestnut and Juniper streets. It was another handsome marble building with Ionic porticoes. It was used until 1907, when it was torn down and Wanamaker's store was built on the site. Strickland's good friend, William Kneass, had been appointed designer at the Mint in 1824 and continued in that office until his death in 1840.

Strickland's merit as an architect was enhanced by his engineering approach to the problems of planning and construction. This virtue was evident in his design for the Naval Asylum and was repeated in his design for the Philadelphia Almshouse in Blockley Township on the west bank of the Schuylkill, between the river, Darby Road, and the Hamilton estate, "Woodlands." There was a Doric portico with unfluted columns, but otherwise the buildings were strictly utilitarian with three stories of plain, roughcast brick, gable roofs, and rows of large windows. The interior plan had central corridors and rooms on either side. There were four long buildings set at right angles to each other to form a court with a well and a bell tower containing a clock in the center. There were workhouses, stores, large kitchens, and wash houses. The buildings were planned to house destitute children, old men and women, the insane and the sick. Since the Almshouse had to house hundreds of the poor and sick, it required careful planning. When it was completed it was found to be adequate for the purpose and some of the Strickland buildings are still in use (1946).

In 1830, the interior of St. Paul's Episcopal Church on Third Street near Walnut was renovated under Strickland's direction. The church had been built in 1767, and the congregation determined to have the simple Georgian interior changed to a modern classic decor with white woodwork and gilt ornament. The interior has been considerably altered since then and the pews removed, but the Doric columns and the altar screen are still in place and indicate that when it was new, it was modish.

From his early days, Strickland designed monuments of which some of the more ambitious had been shown at the annual exhibitions of the Pennsylvania Academy of Fine Arts. The first which was executed, however, and which is still in place is the sepulchral monument to Benjamin Carr in the churchyard of St. Peter's on Third Street at Pine. Carr was an Englishman who settled in Philadelphia in 1797, started the first music store in the United States, and was organist at St. Peter's. He was also a charter member of the Musical Fund Society and very active on its committees and at its public concerts. Therefore, when he died in 1830, the Society determined to erect a monument to his memory and entrusted the design to his fellow member, William Strickland. It is of marble, with a cylindrical base on which are three reversed torches supporting a disc which contains a lachrymal urn. A long inscription was composed by the Society and is carved on the circular base.

One of the great architectural events of the century in the United States occurred in 1832-33; the competition for Girard College. Girard, who was the first American multimillionaire, left the bulk of his estate to the City of Philadelphia to be administered by a Board of City Trusts and, with it, he left instructions for the erection and organization of a school for orphans. The money which was left after the school was started was to be used to pay the taxes of the poor in the city. Girard wished that a plain, serviceable building be erected and he gave minute instructions as to the kind of windows to be used, the size of rooms, and the type of vaulted fireproof construction to be adopted.

The awards were announced on February 18, 1833, and Thomas Ustick Walter, a young man who had just spent over a year in Strickland's office, won the first premium of five hundred dollars. Strickland won the second premium of two hundred dollars, and Isaiah Rogers, of Boston, the third award of one hundred and fifty dollars.

Strickland's design was for a Doric decastyle temple-type building. His drawing and those of John Haviland are still preserved in the Museum at Girard College. Walter's winning drawings were of a simple and unpretentious design, but because of the influence of Nicholas Biddle, who was chosen chairman of the Girard trustees, the present plan was substituted. Biddle, who had rather grandiose ideas about money, anyway—as the history of his presidency of the Second Bank of the United States indicates—felt that the whole two million dollars of Girard's estate might as well be devoted to the college and none to alleviating the burden of taxes of the poor of Philadelphia. Biddle, as a young man, had traveled in Greece in 1806, and was a dilettante Grecophile. However, as Biddle candidly wrote in his diary, he thought the Girard College project furnished an opportunity to build a magnificent building with no worry about money. Therefore, he persuaded City Councils to accept the peristyle plan which he forced Walter to design. This decision caused a lot of discussion, and pamphlets were written criticizing the plan and the expenditure. One was written by Strickland, or by a friend of his with his help. Biddle was successful and his Corinthian temple was completed in 1848 at the cost of over one and one-half million dollars. It is an impressive example of the Greek Revival, but it is not what Stephen Girard wanted, nor would he have tolerated such needless expense for show.

The last of the important buildings in Philadelphia which Strickland designed and supervised during construction was the Philadelphia Exchange, built between 1832 and 1834 at the corner of Walnut, Dock, and Third streets. It is triangular in plan with a semicircular apex since it is built on a plot of ground surrounded by the three streets. Strickland had a good site and he took full advantage of it, especially the vista up Walnut and Dock. At that corner, he placed a rounded portico and a tower. The building is still standing, but markets have been built in the lower floors so the general effect has been lost, and the stonework now needs repairing. The interior has been modernized, and little of the original Strickland plan is discernible. On the ground floor some of the rooms appear to be only slightly changed, and the vaulted ceilings are preserved. On the second floor, the room behind the circular portico which was formerly used as the library for the Exchange maintains its proportions, but that is all. The ceiling is the height of the portico which is thirty-five feet, but since the room is large and spacious with long French doors from the curved wall giving out on the portico, it is not out of proportion.

A number of Italian workmen and master-craftsmen were employed on the Exchange, and the masonry work is excellent. On all sides of the ground floor, there are one-story, recessed columns with capitals derived from those with the water leaf pattern on the Tower of the Winds, in Athens. On Walnut Street, there is a recessed Corinthian portico with a pediment. The rounded portico and the tower also have Corinthian columns. The tower was a tour de force of Greek Revival adaptation. Towers were not used in Greek architecture, but low towers, domes, and cupolas were prevalent in Georgian architecture, an attenuation of the great domes of the Baroque period. In the early nineteenth century, towers and spires were greatly admired for the skyline which they gave to cities. Early writers referring to Philadelphia often commented on the few steeples for the size of the city. The classic gable roof seemed rather tame although it was becoming more prevalent in civic architecture. Strickland took the Choragic Monument of Lysicrates, as illustrated by Stuart and Revett in the *Antiquities of Athens*, for a model and placed an oversized copy of it on the roof of the Exchange. The circular arrangement of the columns of the tower repeated the circular portico of the building. The result was unique, effective, and generally admired. The idea of using the monument was not original with Strickland; it had occurred to Thomas Jefferson who had written to Benjamin H. Latrobe, commending it to his attention. Whether or not Strickland knew of the correspondence, he was, nevertheless, the first to use it in an architectural design.

When the Exchange was finished, it also

housed the United States Post Office and Strickland had his office there until he left Philadelphia in 1845.

In 1835, after the completion of the Exchange, Strickland was busy with a number of architectural drawings and one engineering project. The latter was a survey for the Wilmington and Susquehanna Railroad in which he was helped by his pupil John Cresson Trautwine, who did most of the actual work. Strickland, in his report on the survey, said that he found it comparatively easy to do since he had been over the land before when he was surveying for the Delaware and Chesapeake Canal and he found his former survey accurate.

Of the architectural work that he was engaged upon, one plan was for a private residence for the rector of the Episcopal Church in Burlington, New Jersey, for which he designed a Gothic cottage with hood moldings over the windows and a crenelated parapet above the study, which was a one-story ell at the back. The walls are one and one-half feet thick and the ceilings seventeen feet high downstairs, and thirteen feet upstairs. The kitchen, dining room, maid's quarters, and storage space are in the basement. On the ground floor, there is a central hall and rooms on either side. The unusual feature is that the stairs are tucked away at the back of the house. Strickland had written Hillhouse that he was not in favor of using too much space for stairs and evidently he was still of the same opinion.

Strickland also received two federal commissions that year—one for the Mint at Charlotte, North Carolina; the other for the Mint at New Orleans. His designs were built, but he had nothing to do with the construction of the buildings and it seems unlikely that he even visited them, either during the construction or afterwards. In 1844, there was a fire in the Mint at Charlotte, and while the original plan seems to have been followed in the rebuilding, there may also have been some alterations. The building in New Orleans remains the same on the exterior with a handsome central portico and wings, but the interior has undergone various transformations since after it was no longer used as a Mint, it was a prison and is currently used by the Coast Guard (1946).

That same year, Strickland made ambitious designs for the new building which the Franklin Institute was planning to build. The Institute felt that its quarters on Seventh Street, in the building designed by Haviland, were inadequate and planned to buy the Masonic Hall, which Strickland had designed in 1808, use that building for a museum, and erect a new building for the lecture hall and classrooms. The depression of 1837 put an end to this plan since the Institute was unable to raise sufficient money.

In 1836, when the charter of the Second Bank of the United States expired and was not renewed despite Nicholas Biddle's earnest efforts, the Bank was rechartered as the United States Bank of Pennsylvania and Biddle remained as president until he was removed and brought to trial on the charge of mismanagement of funds in 1844. When the change in charter was made, the directors decided to have repairs and alterations made and Strickland was again employed.

Strickland was probably the architect of the Philadelphia Bank which was built next to the United States Bank on Chestnut Street in 1837. It was a handsome edifice with a recessed, second-story Corinthian portico.

Another important plan which Strickland made in that year was for the Providence Athenaeum. He went to Providence to study the site and learn the needs of the society and he designed a stone building with a Doric distyle-in-antis portico. The exterior is unchanged except for the addition of a wing at the back. The interior has been considerably altered, but the general distribution of space, the small offices on either side of the entrance vestibule, the large library and reading room, is the same, and also much of the woodwork, the doors, and the windows are unchanged.

The Providence Athenaeum is the only known Strickland building in New England. Since there were many excellent native architects, there was little reason to call in a Philadelphian. However, in this instance, Russell Warren, the leading local architect, whom the directors of the Athenaeum expected to employ, was engaged on a commission in Halifax, Nova Scotia. The building committee did not wish to wait until his uncertain return to Providence. Strickland was highly recommended, so he was asked to come to Providence to make plans and give an estimate. This he did in November, 1836, to the satisfaction of the committee.

Strickland's most interesting activity in 1837 was to design the new sarcophagus for the remains of George Washington. The design specified an eagle clutching arrows and a flag perched on a banded escutcheon for the lid, and an inscription on the side. Strickland was present in September when the tombs in the burial plot at Mount Vernon, Virginia, were opened. The remains of both George and Martha Washington were transferred to new mahogany caskets before being placed in stone coffins; that of Martha's was not decorated. These sarcophagi were carved by John Struthers and presented at his expense to Colonel Lawrence Lewis who had inherited the Mount Vernon estate.

John Struthers was an Englishman who settled in Philadelphia about 1816 and became a leading master mason. He was associated with Strickland on a number of buildings: the Second Bank of the United States, the tower of Independence Hall, the Naval Home, the Almshouse, and the Philadelphia Exchange, to cite some of the most important. Since they were excellent friends, it was natural that Struthers should have asked Strickland to make the design for Washington's sarcophagus.

Strickland realized the historic significance of this event. He made drawings of the design, of the entrance to the burial plot, and of the bust of Washington by Canova which is in the house at Mount Vernon. These, with letters from Colonel Lewis and Struthers and a dedication to Henry Clay, were published in 1840.

In 1838, Strickland did no architectural work. Instead he took his wife and two young daughters, Emily and Jane, to Europe. It was an opportune time to go, since after completing the series of lucrative commissions just described, there were few prospects of obtaining new work. Because of a financial panic and accompanying labor unrest, and racial and religious riots, no one had the money or inclination for civic building. In fact, Strickland was architecturally idle for the next seven years until he went to Nashville, except for federal commissions, the most important of which were the residences for the Governor and the Medical Officer on the grounds of the United States Naval Home, Philadelphia.

The Stricklands were away from Philadelphia for about six months. They sailed in January for Liverpool where they visited the Jesse Hartleys with whom Strickland had kept up his friendship. In 1828, he had presented a paper by Hartley at a meeting of the American Philosophical Society. After a few weeks in Liverpool, they went to London, where Strickland did a number of water-color sketches, including two of Crosby Hall. He saw various engineering friends and informed himself on recent railroad and locomotive construction.

They crossed to the continent and went to Paris, where Strickland admired the Venus de'Medici in the Louvre. On their way south, they stopped at Lyons, where Strickland made a sketch of a suspension bridge; and at Nîmes, where he made an expedition to the Pont du Gard of which he made a sketch which he annotated "Drawn on the Spot."

On the way through Italy to Rome, Strickland made some sketches, but the majority of drawings which he made on the trip were done in Rome where everything interested him and aroused his curiosity. He drew Roman antiquities, medieval towers, and Renaissance St. Peter's. His memories of this visit to Rome appeared in a series of eleven articles which were published in the Nashville *Daily Orthopolitan* in 1846. He was critical of the popes as architects, and of archaeological legends. He viewed the monuments with a fresh, keen eye. He admired the engineering skill displayed in the construction of the Coliseum and the Baths. He noted that the stones on the Arch of Septimus Severus were mitered as if the construction were of wood instead of stone. As an old scene painter who was accustomed to using modern tempera, he took a critical interest in the Roman frescoes.

The Stricklands left Rome about the middle of April, going north through Italy and Germany, down the Rhine, and back to England where they again visited the Hartleys and were in London for Victoria's coronation in June. They returned to Philadelphia early in July on the S.S. *Philadelphia.*

One reason they returned before summer was that Strickland, while he was in London, was engaged by John Wright and Company, London brokers who were issuing bonds for the Cairo City and Canal Company, to survey the land at the confluence of the Ohio and Mississippi rivers to determine whether a city could safely be built on that land. Strickland went to Illinois with Richard C. Taylor, a geologist and engineer who had come from England and settled in Philadelphia. They made the survey and a map and report which concluded that if the levees were sufficiently high a city could be started on the peninsula. Strickland was retained as a consultant engineer by Darius B. Holbrook, the president of the company. He and Taylor were listed among the persons in Philadelphia from whom information concerning the company could be obtained.

The project for the building of Cairo was not successful. John Wright and Company failed. A flood in 1840 submerged the site before the levees were completed, the people who had settled there moved away, and the warehouses and factories which had been started were destroyed. When the company failed, the money which had been raised was lost. Charles Dickens, the English novelist, was one of the many people who suffered through the failure. When he went down the Mississippi in his American tour in 1842, he made caustic comments on the site of Cairo, which is supposed to have been the inspiration for the malaria-ridden town of Eden in the novel *Martin Chuzzlewit.*

Another unsuccessful venture which came out of Strickland's trip to England in 1838 was the attempt to gain an American patent for a propeller invented by a Mr. Smith.

The next few years, Strickland was engaged on large projects which never went beyond the drawings. George Burd planned to erect a hotel at the southeast corner of Chestnut and Ninth streets, extending to Sansom Street, but it was not built. The Walnut Street prison had been torn down at Sixth Street and Strickland designed two buildings for that plot. One was for the American Philosophical Society, and the other was for a joint society building which would house six libraries. Neither project was carried out.

Also, evidently just before the failure of the Cairo City and Canal Company, Strickland made a design for a monument in the shape of an obelisk which was to have been erected to the memory of Robert Fulton in grateful recognition of the benefits of steam navigation, but there is no record of its erection.

A more successful undertaking which resulted from the London visit was the publication of *Public Works in the United States* by J. Weale and Company of London in 1841. Strickland was one of the editors, with Edward

H. Gill and Henry R. Campbell, also American engineers. Canals, railroads, gasworks, and the Delaware Breakwater were diagrammed and described. Partly, probably as a result of this publication, William Strickland was elected to membership in the Royal Institution of Civil Engineers in 1842. His friend John Struthers was elected to associate membership at the same time. They both resigned in 1853.

As it became more and more evident that practically no private building was being projected, Strickland determined to get some federal commissions and even tried to play politics to further his chances. Dire necessity probably drove him to his unsuccessful role as a sycophant. His work on the Breakwater was ended. He had no new commissions. The trip to Europe probably broke into his capital. It is likely that he invested in the Cairo City and Canal Company. In any case, he is said never to have been prudent with money. It is not surprising that he used all the influence that he could muster to get government work.

He was most successful in his connection with the Navy Department for which he had been working since 1826 when he began the Naval Asylum in Philadelphia. In 1842, he began making alterations there since the Secretary of the Navy wished the building divided into two separate parts, one for a hospital and the other for the retired seamen's asylum. Later, in 1844, he was commissioned to design and superintend the construction of two houses on the grounds of the Naval Home, one for the Governor and the other for the Medical Officer. These houses are still in use and in good repair.

During these years in the early 1840's, Strickland was practically commuting between Washington and Philadelphia. Two of his letters to John Struthers, written from Washington early in 1844, are preserved and give a notion of the irritation with which he viewed Congress and the tedium which he experienced in job-hunting. Strickland evidently had some connection with John Tyler and his brother Robert. He went so far as to organize a Tyler party in Philadelphia in the summer of 1844 and he wrote the President directly about the plans for Tyler's projected visit to the city. All these machinations came to nothing and James K. Polk from Tennessee was the next president.

The most interesting and ambitious of Strickland's designs for a building in Washington was his project for the War and Navy Department Building. He and the people who were interested in the building were unable to get an appropriation from Congress and the project collapsed.

He provided an estimate for an addition to the hospital building at the Marine barracks of the Navy Yard at Philadelphia. He examined the grounds of the Depot of Charts in Washington and made a plan of buildings for officers' houses. His report and plan were approved by Secretary of the Navy Mason on September 10, 1844.

In desperation, in April of 1844, Strickland had applied for the position of Superintendent of the Dry Dock at New York. The Secretary of the Navy wrote him that should a superintendent be needed his application would be "respectfully considered."

Strickland was one of the few important American architects of the early period who was never employed as Federal Architect on the Capitol in Washington. However, he had various connections with it. During his apprenticeship under Latrobe, he worked as a draftsman on drawings for the Capitol, while Latrobe was the architect in charge. In 1826, when Charles Bulfinch was the architect, Strickland was called in as a consultant on the problem of the acoustics in the Hall of Representatives. He recommended hangings and flat walls to cut out the echo caused by the rounded niches designed by Latrobe. Strickland's report was published in 1830. In 1843, when Robert Mills was the architect, Strickland was again called in as a consultant on the problem of the Hall for the House of Representatives. Colonel J. J. Abert, Chief of the Bureau of Topographical Engineers, made a design for a new wing of the Capitol to house the hall and called on Strickland to make one for comparison. On April 5, 1844, Abert wrote Strickland that the Committee of Buildings of the War Department had given up the idea of a new wing and that the present plan was to convert the library room of the Capitol into a new hall for the House of Representatives. Strickland went to Washington immediately and presented plans and an estimate on April 21 without success. The whole organization was changed in 1851 when Thomas Ustick Walter was appointed architect, and the new wings and the great iron dome are after his design.

Also in 1844, Strickland received a letter from the chairman of the committee in charge of building the capitol of Tennessee, inquiring whether he would be interested in designing the capitol. Strickland did not hesitate to accept this offer and stipulated that he wished to have the superintendence of the building at a salary of two thousand five hundred dollars a year. He had often earned more than that amount, but the prudence gleaned through the lean years since 1837 cautioned him not to ask too much. His offer was accepted and in May, 1845, Strickland and his family moved to Tennessee and took their residence in the City Hotel which was their home until Strickland died in 1854 while he was still working on the Tennessee State Capitol.

Nashville was not established as the permanent capital of Tennessee until 1843. The city then presented the state with Campbell's Hill as the site for the State House. It was a fine plot of land with a low hill, not far inland from the Cumberland River near the Public Square and the center of the city. The building committee was instructed to find an architect, but not to have an architectural competition which some of the committee favored. Therefore, they wrote about in the East to inquire which architects were considered the best and which might be available. The committee learned Strickland was highly regarded and especially recommended for the accuracy of his estimates. They regretted that he was so advanced in years, he was fifty-five at the time, but they concluded that he was well able to undertake the commission to design the State Capitol and supervise its erection.

Strickland came to Nashville and presented his drawings and estimate and description of the Capitol to the building committee in May, 1845. These were accepted and work began immediately, in order that the cornerstone might be laid on July 4 with appropriate Masonic ritual. The Capitol was completed in 1859, five years after Strickland's death. From 1854 until 1857, the work was continued under the supervision of his son Francis and finished by the building committee largely because of the efforts of Samuel Morgan, the chairman. The halls of the Capitol were ready for the legislature in the autumn of 1853, while Strickland was still alive and able to hear the criticisms of planning, expense, lighting, and acoustics.

The design which Strickland first presented was executed in almost every detail, except the stairway. The site was an excellent one, a low hill which gave the Capitol a towering position in the city. He used the Ionic order of the Erechtheum in a portico on each face, gabled on the ends and flat on the sides. The gable roof was crowned with a tower, which was copied after the Choragic Monument of Lysicrates. There is a wooden model of the tower now in the attic of the Capitol which shows that Strickland intended an exact copy, but the tower as built under the direction of his son Francis has eight columns instead of six.

It has been said in Nashville that Strickland died of a broken heart because the building committee insisted on a tower, while Strickland wished to have a low, temple-type, gable roof. Since both early sketches of the Capitol and his first report to the Committee in 1845 have the tower as an integral part of the design, this is obviously only legend. Also, since he had used the same form of tower on the Philadelphia Exchange with success fourteen years before, he was probably eager to try it again.

Tennessee marble was used. In order to quarry and cut it as economically as possible, the state bought a quarry and used prison labor for the rough work. Slaves were bought to work on the building. The free stonemasons protested the use of prison labor and it was finally given up, but not until most of the stone had been quarried rough-hewn.

The building was supposed to be of marble throughout, but Strickland, in the interests of economy and efficiency, persuaded the committee that bricks could be used for the core of the walls and vaulting. The rafters and girders of the roof are of iron. At first, in order that the building be completely fireproof, the window frames and door jambs were to be of iron, but they are now of wood.

The stonework is handsome, although the Erechtheum Ionic capitals are a little coarse because of their size. The interior details are fine, however, especially the staircase and the decoration in the halls of the legislature.

Although there was no competition, other plans than those by Strickland were submitted. His former pupil Gideon Shryock, from Lexington, Kentucky, presented plans and August Heiman, the leading architect of Nashville at that time.

Heiman was a German who settled in Nashville about 1838 and who had a distinguished military career as well as an architectural one. He served as adjutant to the Tennessee Volunteers in the war with Mexico, and rose to be a major. In the Civil War, he fought with the South and died a brigadier general. In the period between the wars, he designed most of the important buildings in Nashville, including the prison, the university, the Masonic Hall, the theatre, and the asylum. He and Strickland were good friends. Heiman consulted Strickland about the suspension bridge over the Cumberland; Strickland often consulted Heiman about the work on the Capitol.

Strickland found many other congenial people in Nashville. One was Gerard Troost, a geologist, whom he had known in Philadelphia where both had been members of the Academy of Natural Sciences. Troost had gone west in 1824 and was professor of geology at the University of Nashville. When the state was looking for decorative marble for the Capitol, Troost was called upon to make a report on the various kinds and qualities of marble in the state.

Another friend was Wilkins Tannehill who had been Mayor of Nashville in 1825 and who at the time that Strickland came to Nashville was editor of the *Daily Orthopolitan* and, later, of the *Port Folio*. For both of these Strickland wrote various articles, the most ambitious being a series of eleven articles on Roman architecture which were based upon Strickland's visit to Rome in 1838. He also wrote an essay on the "Orders of Architecture, Truth, Wisdom and Beauty" which was his most philosophical writing on art. Tannehill was a leading Mason and active in all Masonic affairs and since Strickland was a Mason, he joined Cumberland Lodge No. 8 in Nashville.

Strickland was on good terms with the members of the building committee, especially John Bass and Samuel Morgan. William Stickell, a plasterer who worked with Strickland on the Capitol and on the First Presbyterian Church, became a congenial friend. Berrien Lindsley of the university and Wm. T. Berry, the bookseller, were others with whom he passed pleasant hours.

Strickland must have returned to Philadelphia at least once after work on the Capitol was begun, because on March 30, 1846, he bought a plot of land, lot 47, section D, in the Laurel Hill Cemetery and on April 1, his daughter, Jane Hall Strickland, aged eighteen, was buried there. It is likely that he was also in Philadelphia in February, 1849, when his daughter Emily Maria was married to Charles Augustus Harper in St. Stephen's Church on Tenth Street.

Three of Strickland's six children were married. Mary Trenchard, the eldest daughter, married Thomas Large about 1837 and had at least one daughter whom she named Elizabeth after her mother and sister. Emily married Captain Charles Augustus Harper and the younger son, Jesse Hartley, married a girl from Murfreesboro, Tennessee.

Almost as soon as Strickland arrived in Nashville, he received a commission to design the first Roman Catholic cathedral in Tennessee, which is now St. Mary's, a parish church. It was begun in 1845 and was dedicated October 31, 1847. Strickland is said to have considered it his best design. The interior and the side exterior wall have been changed, but the marble façade has been untouched. The entrance is through a distyle-in-antis portico with Ionic columns. On either side is a niche and a plain pediment above. The gable is crowned by a cupola. It is well-proportioned, simple and effective with excellent detail.

Strickland designed another church in Nashville, the First Presbyterian Church. The old building had burned down in September, 1849. A committee to raise money was immediately organized, and another to select a suitable plan. Various plans were submitted, including two by Briscoe Vannoy, a young man whose father was a builder and who later became a moderately successful architect. Strickland's plan was chosen. He submitted not only ground plans and elevations but also a diagonal projection which seemed to appeal to the members of the congregation. He employed the Egyptian style which he had used before in 1824 in the synagogue of the Mikveh-Israel on Cherry Street in Philadelphia. That was built of brown stone with an interior dome. The Presbyerian church was built of brick, painted gray, with marble trim. In fundamental design, it is not different from that of the Gothic St. Stephen's which he designed in 1823. Both have rectangular auditoriums and towers on either side of the front façade. The details of the shape of windows and doors, the outside moldings and the inside papyrus columns, batter and cavetto moldings, the sun disc with the hawk wings and the serpent's head, were the recognized characteristics of the Egyptian Revival Style which Strickland employed on the exterior. The interior is plastered and painted to represent an Egyptian temple. The ceiling is coffered and the large stained-glass windows are decorated with palm trees. Since the church was built before the Civil War, it was necessary to include a gallery for the slaves. The lotus columns at the front of the church on either side of the chancel are hollow tin painted to represent marble. On the end wall columns and stone beams, sky and clouds are painted in perspective to give a sense of space.

While Strickland was in Nashville, he designed three monuments. Two are in the City Cemetery, the Walker monument and the Kane monument. The other was for the remains of President Polk and was first erected on the grounds of the Polk house, diagonally across from the Capitol. When the Polk house was torn down to make way for an apartment house, the monument was moved to the grounds of the Capitol. He made another design for a monument to be erected to the memory of the men who fell at Monterey, but money was not raised for it and no memorial to the men of the Mexican war was built in Nashville.

In 1848, Strickland made another ill-fated design, that for a new hotel which was to be built on the City Square.

The big question in the history of Strickland's

architectural career in Nashville is whether he designed the several handsome residences which are traditionally attributed to him and, if he did, how much he was helped by his son Francis. No papers have been found yet to substantiate any of the attributions. Stylistic evidence is never satisfactory because it can be so easily adapted to wishful thinking. The best and most handsome of these houses are the Acklen mansion "Belmont," now part of Ward-Belmont School, "Belle Meade," the Harding house on the Harding Road outside Nashville which is one of the most satisfactory of Greek Revival houses because it is completely Greek in feeling, design, and detail; "Burlington," the Elliston house which is now torn down and which was Italianate in style. "Lynnlawn," the Stratton house in East Nashville, is the least pretentious and least pleasing architecturally, but of all the houses it is the one which is stylistically most akin to the Governor's house on the grounds of the Naval Home, or the drawings for Hillhouse, or the sketches in the Strickland portfolio in the Tennessee State Library.

If all these houses which are attributed to Strickland are his, then it is evident that he developed immensely in his last years. It would be a logical development and one that parallels the growth of his civic designs. On the whole, Strickland's sense of proportion and feeling for restrained ornament increased as he grew older. The use of the Italianate at "Burlington" would be logical since Strickland had been in Italy in 1838 and had made sketches of both Renaissance and medieval buildings and thus was well prepared to accept and use the new style. It may have been, however, that it was his son Francis who was the Italianate innovator, for he also had been abroad and in Italy and it is likely that the new style would appeal more to the young man than to the older. Also, while the tradition says that William Strickland provided the plan for "Burlington," it also says that it was built after his death by his son.

The little that we know of Francis' work suggests that he was one of the mid-century architects who became bored with the severity of the Greek Revival and branched out into a hybrid Renaissance Revival which for convenience, since it is hard to define into its component parts, is called Italianate, and which led the way to the greater exuberance of the General Grant Baroque. Francis designed the Howard School in Nashville, which is a good example of the Italian villa style with a tower adapted from a medieval campanile. In his later years, after he served in the Civil War, he worked for a while in New Jersey building seaside hotels, and one of his last architectural employments was on the Library of Congress in Washington.

William Strickland was ill in 1851, and from then on he relied more and more on his son. In 1853, he was asked to do some work on the Union Bank, but both the negotiations and the work were carried on by Francis.

The work on the Capitol was also more and more entrusted to Francis and in 1854 Strickland tried to have him appointed assistant architect—he had been serving as such for several years. The legislature would not grant this and, indeed, tried to dismiss Strickland himself—or at least cut his salary—but the building committee was firm in its report that an architect was still needed and that the salary was not too high.

These were but a few of the difficulties and annoyances which beset Strickland during his tenure as state architect. He was criticized for the slowness of the work, but the legislature would not allot sufficient funds to continue it more rapidly. The acoustics in the Senate Hall were found to be poor when the hall was first used in 1853. However, the design of the building was always admired and Strickland's ability as an architect was never questioned.

On Thursday, April 6, at four o'clock in the morning, William Strickland died. The afternoon before, he had fallen on the steps of the post office. On Saturday, he was interred in a niche in the north portico of the Capitol since the legislature had passed a resolution that he should be so honored. The service took place at ten o'clock in the morning, with the Reverend Jesse B. Ferguson of the Church of Christ officiating. Later, a marble block was placed in front of the niche, upon which was carved the following inscription:

William Strickland Architect
died April 7, 1854. Aged 64 years.
By an act of the Legislature of Tennessee
his remains were deposited within this vault.

CHAPTER II

CHARACTER

WILLIAM STRICKLAND was one of the successful architects of the first half of the nineteenth century in the United States. His success may be measured by the number of important commissions which he received during his long career, the satisfactoriness of the buildings when they were new, and the pleasing quality of those which remain.

His success depended in almost equal measure upon his character and fortuitous circumstances. The most important of the latter was his acquaintance with Benjamin Henry Latrobe. If his father had not been employed as a carpenter on the Bank of Pennsylvania, Strickland would probably not have been apprenticed to Latrobe and, without the training he then received, it is most unlikely that Strickland would have been an architect. There are no anecdotes that relate that Strickland in his youth was fascinated by buildings, as was the case with his fellow-architect A. J. Davis. As a boy, he showed artistic aptitude and great facility in drawing and, as a young man, did scene painting, drawings for engravers, engraving, and landscape painting. Without the architectural training with Latrobe, his career would have probably been similar to that of his younger brother George.

On the other hand, if Strickland had not early showed marked ability, Latrobe would never have interested himself in him. As Strickland's talents developed, it is evident that he was better equipped to be an architect than a painter. He was more skillful than original with a pencil. His architectural drawings have more merit than his landscapes. He had a keener perception of good proportion in black and white than of color harmony. His engravings and wash drawings are superior to his paintings and colored aquatints. His eye, which was keen and quick, was observant rather than discerning. He was noted for his ability to accurately gauge dimensions, which is of great use to an architect but of little value to an artist. Lastly, he could make quick mental calculations as to the cost of a building, the number of bricks needed in a wall, or the amount of stone for a façade. This mathematical deftness aided him in his architectural work, but would have been of no value if he had continued as a landscape painter. To conclude, all Strickland's natural abilities were employed to the best advantage in his architectural and engineering career, but it is probable that without the early years spent with Latrobe, he would never have been an architect.

Another incident which furthered his career

was the pleasing impression which his personality and abilities produced when he was aiding as an engineer in directing the citizens of Philadelphia to erect fortifications during the War of 1812. He, himself, later said that the friends that he made then were influential in having his plan and design for the Second Bank of the United States awarded the first premium. In turn, his success with the Bank insured his position as one of the foremost architects in the United States.

Strickland's engineering career was also forwarded by fortuitous circumstances. The employment which brought his name to the notice of engineers both in this country and in Europe was that as agent for the Pennsylvania Society for the Promotion of Internal Improvement which commissioned him to make a study of engineering progress in Great Britain. The reason for his appointment may be traced to his early friendship with William Kneass, the engraver, with whom he worked after he left Latrobe. Kneass was one of the people interested in the formation of the Franklin Institute and, with him, Strickland was one of the first members of the Institute. Strickland became the first recording secretary of the Franklin Institute and in that office made a favorable impression upon the members, a number of whom grouped together to form the Pennsylvania Society for the Promotion of Internal Improvement.

In all these instances, Strickland showed himself to be worthy of the work offered him. His quick and interested mind, his sincere application to the task at hand, and his affable nature combined to make him profit by these opportunities. His talent and effort should not be underestimated, but neither can his character alone be credited with his success. He was not a dogged fanatic who could remove all obstacles by his belief in his principles. He had neither the blindness nor the conceit necessary to the artist who is to be an innovator. Instead, his work was usually done with the true humility of a good craftsman who understands his métier and respects it. His aim was to provide solid and convenient buildings, not to change methods of construction or forms of design. He was talented, able, and worked quickly, effortlessly and unself-consciously; he was more interested in materials and tools than in abstract questions of beauty and trends. He also had the greatest grace of the healthy mind, a sense of humor, which extended even to himself and his works.

Beside having an agreeable personality which attached his friends to him, he had a sense of loyalty which gave his employers confidence in him. The result of this confidence was that he was called upon again by former employers. For example, when the first building which he designed, the Masonic Hall, burned in 1818, Strickland was immediately called upon to make the necessary repairs and supervise the rebuilding. He made repairs for the Medical School of the University of Pennsylvania in 1817 and 1818, and when the trustees of the university determined to rebuild in 1828, Strickland was again called upon, first, for the medical school, and then for the college. When alterations were needed to convert the Bank of the United States to the United States Bank of Pennsylvania, Strickland was in charge. The Treasury Department was so well satisfied with his work on the Philadelphia Custom House that he was employed to make the design for the Custom House in New Orleans. Twelve years later, when the Department decided to build a mint in Philadelphia, Strickland was commissioned to make the design and supervise the construction of the building. Later, in 1835, when branch mints were to be erected in Charlotte, North Carolina and in New Orleans, Strickland was again requested to furnish the designs. Earlier, in 1826, after the Academy of Natural Sciences had purchased the Temple of the New Jerusalem, Strickland's second building, he was in charge of the alterations. The

Navy Department first employed Strickland on the Naval Asylum in 1826; when changes were to be made in 1842, and when new buildings were to be erected in 1844, Strickland continued to be the architect.

There are no records as to what sort of boyhood Strickland had. His father was never well-to-do, but appears to have been fairly regularly employed. Evidently the Stricklands moved from New Jersey soon after William was born since the census of 1790 records a John Strickland living on Cherry Street with two male children under age. Whether William went to school is not certain, but he must have had some education since his penmanship was excellent.

Latrobe thought that he was spoiled by his mother; at least they appear to have been very fond of each other and, after his father died in 1820, Strickland supported his mother until her death. Strickland took an interest in the education of his younger brother George and had him exhibit a drawing illustrating a verse of Scott's *Marmion* in the annual exhibition of the Pennsylvania Academy of Fine Arts in 1814, when George was only seventeen years old.

William was a good and faithful husband, and a devoted and generous father. He was happy with his parents and happy with his own family. They, in turn, all loved him.

An indication of the warmth of friendship that he inspired is the number of children who were named for him. His friend, William Kneass, named his fifth son Strickland and that has become a family name in the Kneass family. His friend, John Struthers, named a son William. A pupil, Gideon Shryock, named his first son for him. When he was in Nashville, James Birth, the foreman of the stonecutters named one of his sons William after Strickland.

Another indication of his amiable character, and also of his ability as a teacher, is the warm feelings that he inspired in his students, of whom he had three groups. One was the class of young men to whom he gave the lectures on architecture at the Franklin Institute during the winter of 1824-25. Another was the group who came to his office to be trained as architects. Among these were Gideon Shryock, who came from Kentucky to study with him during the winter of 1822-23, Thomas Ustick Walter, who was in his office during the winter of 1830-31, and two students named Andrew Binney and a Mr. Martin, who are known only through drawings which they made at that time. After Strickland was in Nashville, a man named A. C. Bruce came from Atlanta, Georgia to study with him. The other group were the men who were trained to be engineers. Three became successful railroad engineers which is not surprising since Strickland, because of his trip to England for the Pennsylvania Society for Internal Improvement, was one of the best informed people on the subject of railroads in the United States. The three who went from his office to build railroads in the West, the South, and Latin America were Samuel Honeyman Kneass, the son of his friend William Kneass; John Cresson Trautwine, and Edgar Thompson.

Strickland's relations with the men who worked under him on the buildings he supervised were always of the best. The master workmen often became his close friends, as did the master-mason, John Struthers, and the carpenter, John O'Neil. The foreman and clerks of works were loyal. The contractors who supplied lumber, bricks, and iron appeared eager to serve him. The samples of his business letters to Lewis Coryell, who supplied the timber for the Bank of the United States and Naval Asylum, might help to explain why. He was explicit and accurate in his orders and not unreasonable in his demands for delivery. His affable good nature and warm-hearted friendliness extended to all classes of workmen. During the building of the Naval Asylum, the Navy Department got far behind in the appropriations. Strickland wrote the Secretary of the Navy repeatedly to point out how necessary it was that the workmen be paid and what hardships the delay was causing. When the Philadelphia Exchange was completed, a banquet was held for all the men who worked on the building and Strickland proposed the toast to the artisans. In Nashville when John Kane, one of the stonecutters died suddenly, Strickland provided the design for his tomb.

His innate kindliness was apparent even to strangers. Manlow Hayes, a prominent Delawarian, in his memoirs remembered with pleasure his first meeting with Strickland when as a young man he had just gone to Philadelphia to study drawing. A friend invited him to dinner at a hotel with Strickland who was gracious, entertaining, and witty as though Hayes were not just a young man at the beginning of his career.

Another indication of how well he could get on with strangers was the reception accorded him by the British engineers in 1825. They aided him by giving detailed information, drawings, diagrams, and making it possible for him to inspect the various works in person. It must be remarked in passing that most of British engineers at that time were like himself, that is, in large measure self-educated and extremely interested in their undertakings.

With intelligent and sincere people of any class, Strickland could immediately be friendly, but he had no patience with people of mediocre endowments who, because of inherited money and position, thought themselves to be of great importance. Naturally, with such a temperament, Strickland enjoyed being with people and liked to go to dinners, receptions, banquets, and even dances. The Beefsteak Club was solely a dinner club. The Wistar Parties were Saturday night receptions for members of the American Philosophical Society. The newspapers record the toasts he proposed at Penn Society Banquets. In Nashville he went to a fancy dress ball, arrayed as Mr. Pickwick.

Strickland had a variety of religious experiences his first recorded connections being with the Episcopal church. He was married in Christ Church and his two sons who died in infancy were buried in the cemetery of Christ Church. His father was buried from Christ Church in 1820. In 1813, Strickland had become a Swedenborgian because of the example and influence of his friend William Kneass, the secretary of the Philadelphia group. It was his membership in the church that led to his selection as architect of the Temple of the New Jerusalem.

Strickland designed St. Stephen's Episcopal Church on Tenth Street, Philadelphia, in 1823. Twenty years later, on March 24, 1843, William Strickland and his four daughters were baptized there. His eldest daughter, Mary Trenchard, had married Thomas Large and their daughter Elizabeth, who had been born on May 6, 1839, was also baptized at that time. Her mother and grandfather were sponsors. The baptism of this first grandchild was probably the reason for the baptism of the rest of the Stricklands. Since Strickland had been a Swedenborgian at the time of the birth of most of his children, it was natural that they were not christened when they were babies. However, when Strickland died in Nashville, the funeral service was not conducted by an Episcopal clergyman but by Dr. Jesse B. Ferguson of the Church of Christ, which suggests that Strickland may have changed his religious affiliation again.

In his architectural practice, he was definitely nonsectarian; he designed eight religious edifices for as many different sects—Swedenborgian, Moravian, Jewish, Episcopal, Unitarian, Presbyterian, Catholic, and a nonsectarian Protestant chapel of the Mariners. He used almost as many architectural styles: Saracenic, post-Renaissance, Egyptian, Gothic, and Greek Revival.

He appears to have had a considerable religious curiosity and, also, a great religious tolerance. He witnessed the Good Friday and Easter celebrations in Rome in 1838 and wrote of them, "Perhaps there can be no more sublime and costly a show presented to the public than that belonging to an Easter festival at Rome." There is a tradition in the family that he was received by Pope Gregory and that he, thereafter, always wore a watch fob, blessed by the Pope.

Strickland's one known attempt at practical politics was to back the campaign of John Tyler for reëlection to the presidency in 1844. He went so far as to write Tyler about his projected visit to Pennsylvania and to inform him of his most eager adherents in Philadelphia. This was an unsuccessful attempt and probably Strickland's pressing need for architectural commissions and the hope of federal employment, rather than a strong political interest prompted his actions.

According to his good friend Judge Kane, Strickland could speak French, some Italian, a little Latin, and no Greek. His reading was largely devoted to books concerned with his profession. Otherwise, his favorite author was Shakespeare and his favorite poem, Butler's *Hudibras.*

His wit largely expressed itself in puns. For example, he wrote to Coryell to inquire about his "visit to the Poles" when he was ordering poles for the Naval Asylum roof. When he wrote Struthers about the forthcoming election in 1844, he said that the Tylerites would probably "become men of Clay." They were simple, unforced puns, enjoyed both by himself and his friends.

Strickland was an apt pupil and those subjects which he was taught—penmanship, architectural drafting, and diagrams for engineering projects—he mastered thoroughly. Architectural drawing was more of an art in the days before blueprints, and a code of colors was used to indicate the various materials: gray for stone, yellow for wood, red, pink or mulberry for brick, and black for iron. These were put in with water-color washes. Strickland's architectural drawings are as good as any of the period, with clear washes and firm, neat inking. The same is true of his engineering diagrams and designs, their clearness, accuracy, and neatness making them agreeable to the eye.

As a painter and engraver, he was largely self-taught and his technical skill was much less sure, although he was one of the first artists in this country to use aquatint and his work as a pioneer in the new method is considered excellent. The change in water-color technique is one of the reasons his paintings in that medium have less appeal today. Water color now relies largely on clear wash which was reserved for architectural drawings a century ago. Water color then was more like present-day gouache, opaque, using Chinese white.

In his early days, he was evidently considered a skillful water-colorist since he did the illustrations for a book on the art of water color. It is probable that he was also the author of the anonymous book which is a summary of other books on the subject with a few original remarks that sound very like Strickland—especially those which criticize the custom of teaching drawing by having the pupil copy paintings instead of observing nature, ". . . the lover of the art will improve far more by observing nature than by imitating the style of any drawing." (*The Art of Landscape Painting*, p. 2); and those which insist that the pupil should learn how to draw simple outlines before trying complicated and highly colored compositions.

> There can be nothing more preposterous than teachers giving their scholars high-finished coloured drawings to copy, before they are capable of drawing the simple outline. What is the consequence in such cases?—The indulgent teacher executes by far the greater part of them, which not only flatters the scholar, but also prompts the fond parents to encourage the very sycophant, who is busy all the while stemming the current of their children's genius.

The sketches in the Historical Society of Pennsylvania collection indicate that he drew from nature, but finished the paintings at home. The composition and outline were indicated only in the pencil sketches, and the main colors noted.

There is only one oil painting which is known to be Strickland's, but there are references to others which may yet come to light. The one, which is a large painting of Christ Church in Philadelphia, is well painted and of sufficient excellence to explain why, in the early Philadelphia directories, Strickland listed himself as a landscape painter. The painting was first exhibited in the annual show of the Pennsylvania Academy of Fine Arts in 1811, when it received favorable comments both by William Dunlap in his diary and by the critics for the newspapers and periodicals. According to Judge Kane, he sold it for ten dollars, a ham, and a box of cigars, and later Strickland bought it back for three hundred dollars, exhibiting it again in 1831. It eventually came into the possession of the Kneass family and, after the death of Strickland Kneass, was given to the Historical Society of Pennsylvania in 1891.

There are various engravings which Strickland made of famous men, but he does not seem to have had great ability in drawing the human figure or faces. He was most successful in rendering buildings, although his drawings of the naval battles of the War of 1812 also have a certain effectiveness.

There are several portraits of Strickland and one bronze bust to inform us of his appearance. He was a handsome man, of medium height, well-proportioned, with a good physique. His features were strong, large, not regular but harmonious. His hair was brown, his eyes dark, his coloring fresh, and in his youth and middle age his expression was alert and animated. The portraits done after he was in Nashville, when he was about sixty, make him appear less magnetic, but the caliber of the artists executing them as well as his age may account for the difference.

A summation of Strickland's character in a phrase would be "warm-hearted impetuousness." Both the good and the not-so-good traits stem from that fundamental characteristic. He was quick-tempered on occasion, but as quickly changed his mood. When with uncongenial people, he was apt to be uneasy and self-conscious; but with friendly people, he brimmed with good-nature and good spirits. He was imprudent both in personal relations and in business affairs. He had never been trained to budget his acounts and, while he tried to keep a record of his expenses at times, he was prone to spend money as soon as it came and did not try to save, either for his old age or for his children. In his late years, he became increasingly careless about money matters, and for several years in Nashville he did not receive his full salary because he kept no record of the amounts due or collected. When he first went to Nashville, he was to be paid quarterly, but he was soon needing money every month and later he was paid weekly. He did not have much strength of character for misfortune. He did, however, have a commendable perseverance, which was born of impetuous optimism more than of dogged tenacity. When commissions practically stopped after the panic of 1837, Strickland drew a number of plans for large buildings for societies and hotels which, in consequence of prevailing financial conditions, were never built. He turned to literary composition and prepared the small book on the new sarcophagi for the remains of George Washington and his wife at Mount Vernon. He also aided in the editing a volume on *Public Works in the United States.* When his employment on the Delaware Breakwater came to an end, he began bombarding the various departments of the federal government with letters suggesting possible commissions and positions for himself. He even went to Washington at the beginning of 1844 in the hope of obtaining some employment. As the agent for the United States Bank of Pennsylvania, he did negotiate the sale of the bank building to the United States, which, after alterations, was used for a customs house, replacing the smaller building which Strickland had designed and built in 1819. He kept hoping that something would turn up and small commissions such as that for surveying the land at the Depot of Charts in Washington, an estimate for improvement on the Marine barracks hospital in Philadelphia, and the more sizable commission to design and superintend the construction of the two residences on the grounds of the Naval Asylum at Philadelphia, kept him employed until the request to design the State Capitol of Tennessee came to justify his persistent optimism.

Judge Kane, who wrote the obituary of Strickland for the American Philosophical Society, was well fitted to do so since they had been friends for thirty-five years. He began his discourse by saying that Strickland had been an intimate friend since 1819 when he came a day after laying the cornerstone of the Bank of the United States to congratulate Mr. and Mrs. Kane upon their marriage. In summing up Strickland's character, Kane concluded that "the characteristics of Mr. Strickland's mind were directness and simplicity. There was nothing complicated or equivocal about him. A stranger could read him like a book." Kane did not remark upon Strickland's warmhearted friendliness, probably because he had been so closely associated with him that he could not recognize that fundamental characteristic.

A man's character is not necessarily responsible for his reputation. However, his reputed character is often a determinant of his success. Strickland was fortunate in having a good reputation throughout his life.

Latrobe began the establishment of Strickland's good reputation and continued to contribute thereto almost until his death, except for several periods when Latrobe considered himself to have been injured by Strickland. The first occasions were caused by Strickland's lack of obedience and unwarranted independence during his apprenticeship. The hard feelings then created were climaxed in 1810 when John Strickland tried to get some money for work that his son had done while he was in Latrobe's office. Latrobe replied that Strickland had left the office just at the end of his training period and before he could be of any use to Latrobe, but, as Latrobe himself said, he was incapable of harboring hard feelings for long and two years later when Strickland was married, Latrobe sent him warm felicitations. He also acted as an intermediary between Robert Fulton and Strickland when Fulton wanted to employ him as a draftsman in New York. The next year Latrobe asked Strickland if he would aid him on a canal survey. They exchanged letters about a number of matters pertinent to architecture. The final break came over the awarding of the premiums for the Second Bank of the United States. Latrobe was immensely eager to win the first prize for he had been connected with a number of unsuccessful engineering ventures and had had no good architectural commissions since he had resigned from his position as federal architect. However, even to the end of his life, Latrobe still claimed Strickland as a pupil, and wrote Rudolph Ackermann in London that "the Bank of the United States was being built by Mr. Strickland, a pupil of mine."

Strickland's reputation in Philadelphia was begun by his success as a volunteer engineer on the Committee of Public Safety at the end of the War of 1812 and was established by winning the first premium for the Second Bank of the United States. As early as 1820, Strickland was referred to as the "City Architect" and that appellation continued until he left for Tennessee where he became the "State Architect." He had a reputation for accuracy of estimates which followed him to Nashville and is cited as one of the reasons he was chosen the architect of the Capitol. It is difficult to see how or when he achieved this reputation since in the case of the Bank of the United States, the Naval Asylum, the Mint at Charlotte, the Capitol at Nashville, and the First Presbyterian Church there, final cost figures are available and can be compared with the initial estimates, showing the estimates decidedly the lesser figures.

As an architect, Strickland also had a reputation for completing buildings on time, a most commendable characteristic, but again it is difficult to ascertain how he came by such a reputation, since in the case of most of the largest commissions, money was delayed and the work was consequently delayed.

The third commendable practice for which Strickland was known was his insistence upon good materials and sound construction. All the buildings which still exist and which were built under his supervision give adequate testimony to this facet of his reputation.

Strickland was well-known and well-liked in Philadelphia and most of his architectural work was done there, but he was also known, to a certain extent, throughout the country. Buildings or monuments after his design are still in existence in eight states: Pennsylvania, New Jersey, Rhode Island, Virginia, North and South Carolina, Louisiana, and Tennessee. He received commissions in two other states, and in the District of Columbia. The extent of his American reputation is best shown by the recommendations which he received when the building commissioners for the Capitol of Tennessee were writing to inquire about Eastern architects. Another indication of the extent of his reputation, not only as an architect but also as an artist, is indicated by his election as an honorary professional member of the National Academy of Design in 1827.

His reputation as an engineer spread even farther, and he was elected a member of the Royal Institution of Engineers in London in 1842. In professional circles, he was also known in France, both through a number of French engineers who came to this country, and because the books which were written on engineering in the United States spoke highly of Strickland and his work, especially that on the Delaware Breakwater.

The greatest professional honor that Strickland received in this country was the presidency of the short-lived American Institution of Architects. It was founded in 1836 and the first meeting was held at the Astor House in New York on December 7, 1836. The second meeting was in November, 1837 in Philadelphia. There were twenty-one members and two associates who were from New York, Boston and Philadelphia, with the exception of Ammi B. Young, later known for his work with cast iron, who was at that time a member from Montpelier, Vermont, and James H. Dakin from New Orleans. Doubtless because of Strickland's suggestion, John C. Trautwine was also a member, although he had just gone to Athens, Tennessee to construct a railroad. It must have been an interesting gathering because these men counted Asher Benjamin, Alexander Parris, Isaiah Rogers, and Ithiel Town—the first generation of American architects—among their number. Architecture was then in the process of being recognized as a profession and these were the men responsible for its popular acceptance. Most of them were largely self-trained and more than half of them had not been out of the country, but they designed some important and pleasing buildings.

With great enthusiasm, these men formulated a constitution and by-laws which were printed by Lydia Bailey in Philadelphia in 1837. Article I stated the object of the Association to "be the general promotion of knowledge in architectural science in the United States of America." The next articles concerned membership of which there were to be three classes, professional, associate, and honorary. To be a professional member, it was necessary to have practiced architecture for five years and all candidates for admission were to take five examinations, the subjects being architectural history, principles of designing in architecture, principles of construction, professional etiquette, and properties of materials. Article V stated that honorary members must be persons "who have a taste for Architecture." The officers were to be a president, corresponding secretary, recording secretary, librarian, and treasurer. The annual meeting was to be held on the first Thursday of November.

There are two possible reasons for the Institution's short existence; one was the strict standard for membership, the other, the financial depression of 1837. Most of the members were dead before the present American Institute of Architects was started in 1856, except Thomas Ustick Walter who was recording secretary of the first society and was later president of the new organization.

Strickland therefore had all the earmarks of a successful man. He was talented and blessed with an agreeable personality. He was happy in his personal relationships with his family and with his friends. He was respected and admired in his profession. Towards the end of his life, when a series of unfortunate events occurred; the difficulty of finding employment, the death of his daughter Jane, and the criticism of the Legislature of Tennessee in the last years before the completion of the Capitol, his character tended to sour, but during the successful, busy, happy years of his middle life, all the best qualities of his character came to the fore.

CHAPTER III

ARCHITECTURAL STYLE

William Strickland was an architect for forty-six years, from 1808 until his death in 1854. During that time, there were a number of changes in architectural styles, in building materials, in methods of construction, and in the position of the architect in society. His career reflected most of these changes.

To begin with the position of the architect, the change which took place during these years was the establishment of the architect as a professional man. In general, before the nineteenth century, the man who designed a building was essentially a master builder. He was in charge of construction and acted as contractor, ordering the materials, hiring the carpenters, masons, and bricklayers, and supervising their daily work as a foreman. This procedure is still practiced, but as the architectural profession has become more clearly defined as that which is concerned with the design and plan of buildings, the architect has become the man responsible for the design and the contractor the man in charge of the construction. For a while, the emphasis was shifted from the building itself to the designs for the building. As the preconceived idea of the edifice became of more consequence than the actual physical constructions of the materials which make the edifice, the architect overshadowed the builder.

This was an understandable and inescapable development which mirrored the growth of the Industrial Revolution. As work was increasingly done by machines, work came to have less value. Before the invention of the steam engine, there was a harmony in plan, work and product, since men were responsible for all three phases. With the introduction of the machine, this harmony was disrupted and the plan, design, or idea which was still of human origin became most important.

Strickland's work, for the most part, belongs to the old tradition. He received his training as an apprentice, hence he learned from actual experience and observation and not from books and lectures alone. Strickland belonged to the first generation of men who formally called themselves architects. In his youth, he was eager and able to do a number of things to eke out his livelihood: surveying, designing for plasterers, scene painting, engraving, drawing, painting, illustrating, drawing maps, writing a book on the art of water-color painting, and the like. In his middle years, after he was established as an architect, he was also an engineer. Toward the end of his life, he wrote on a number of topics: engineering, architecture, history, and theory. By and large, Strickland maintained the Renaissance tradition of the versatile artist.

The indications which one can find in Strickland's career that the age of the specialized architect was approaching, the age where the architect is concerned directly with the plan and nothing else, are the number of buildings for which Strickland provided the designs, but of which he did not supervise the construction. These are not his most important buildings, for all those—the Second Bank of the United States, the Naval Asylum, the Philadelphia Exchange, and the Capitol at Nashville—were built under his direct and daily superintendence.

The buildings for which Strickland provided the plans only were mostly federal buildings. The first was the design for the custom house in New Orleans in 1819. The next was for the Court House in Meadville, Pennsylvania, finished in 1828, for which Strickland drew the plans in 1824. In 1835, he furnished plans to the Treasury Department for the mints at New Orleans and Charlotte, North Carolina. Two years later, he provided plans for the Athenaeum at Providence, Rhode Island. These buildings were constructed, but he was also commissioned to do a number of plans which were never used, the most important of which was that for the proposed War and Navy Building in Washington, drawn in 1843.

In his use of materials and in his methods of construction, Strickland was definitely conservative. He liked solid blocks of marble and thick brick walls. That some changes were being made, however, can be gathered from comparing the use of iron in the Second Bank of the United States, built between 1819 and 1824, and that in the Capitol in Nashville, built between 1845 and 1854. No structural iron is used in the former, although there is a surprising quantity of iron used, and the blacksmith's work for the period April 21, 1819 to December 29, 1820 cost $4,700. The iron in the bank was used as reinforcement, as, for instance, the iron chains encircling the brick piers in the basement. In the Capitol in Nashville, on the other hand, iron was used as a primary structural material, all the rafters being made of it.

Strickland's most extensive use of structural iron was in the United States Naval Asylum, where he used eighty-eight iron columns for the support of the piazzas on either side of both wings. Ffteen years later, when he designed and superintended the building of the residences for the Governor of the Naval Home and the Chief Medical Officer, Strickland again used iron for the columns of the piazzas.

Strickland's friend, John Haviland, who designed the Eastern Penitentiary, the Naval Home at Norfolk, and the Walnut Street Theatre in Philadelphia, was much more interested in the possibilities of iron and advocated its use for coping as a more lasting material than stone. Also, he used iron uprights in the construction of the Walnut Street Theatre. On the other hand, Strickland was impressed with the possibility of using iron for doors and windows as a help in fireproofing buildings. In his plan for the War and Navy Department Building in Washington, he specified the use of iron for window frames; again, in his first description of the Capitol at Nashville, he stated that the window frames and sashes were to be of cast iron. These specifications were changed and wood was used for the windows.

Another change resulting from the Industrial Revolution which affected architectural planning was in plumbing. Strickland's early designs all had privies in the courtyards. By the 1830's, indoor water closets were being introduced. In the Capitol at Nashville, provision was made to store the rain water which drained from the roof and which could then be used in the water closets.

Changes were also being made in heating methods. Fireplaces and stoves were used for heating in the first quarter of the nineteenth century. Those were the only means of heating the Second Bank of the United States where the small rooms each had a fireplace and the large banking room had two large stoves to warm the air. Strickland called the stoves "furnaces," had them constructed of cast iron lined with fire-brick, and said that they were to be "erected within an air chamber, through which the external atmosphere passes and becomes heated by the furnace, it then rises through the arch into a circular cast iron pedestal, perforated on the sides, out of which it is suffered to escape into the room."

The fireplaces in the bank were usually placed under windows, within the thickness of the wall, and covered with cast iron plates. This location made it necessary for the flues to be curved instead of straight. There is no record of the effect of this arrangement on the fires in grates, or whether the draft was hindered. There were two advantages in placing the fireplaces under the windows. The most important is that it saves space since the wall space under windows is too small to be of much use in placing furniture there, and inclement weather discourages the use of that part of a room. Also, a fireplace cuts into a wall so that by putting the two openings together, more wall space can be gained. The second advantage is that the heat of the fire can counteract the chill from the window and the whole room will be more temperate.

By 1845, in describing a proposed change to the Capitol in Washington, Strickland wrote, "Furnaces are to be constructed in the crypt to generate and diffuse warm air in the Halls and Chambers, as well as fireplaces in all the rooms, for the purpose of burning wood or coal and ventilating the building." It is interesting that fireplaces continued to be used and not only as a source of heat, but also of air.

During the first half of the nineteenth century, there were changes in architectural style. It was not a period of original creativeness but rather one of experimentation and variety which freed architectural thought from the Renaissance tradition and paved the way for the extended experimentation at the end of the century, and the styles, materials, and construction methods of the twentieth century. It must be noted, however, that the Renaissance tradition continued throughout the century and is an important element even today.

Strickland's architectural designs mirror, quite accurately, both the conservatism and the innovations of the first half of the nineteenth century. In all, he used nine distinguishable styles, most of which are derived from the Classic.

The most important and most widely used style in this period was Greek Revival, and it is in this tradition that Strickland designed his most important buildings. He seems to have genuinely felt that Greek architecture provided the best possible model. He is reported to have said repeatedly to the pupils in his office "that the student of architecture need go no further than the *Antiquities of Athens* as a basis for design." He practiced what he preached and his finest designs were inspired by the plates of James Stuart and Nicholas Revett, authors and illustrators of the book.

The Italian artists and architects of the first half of the fifteenth century were fired with an enthusiasm for antiquity, for the culture and art of Rome, and they wished to use Classic models. However, most of the statues and frescoes were still buried, and the temples and other buildings were ruined, half-buried, or incorporated into medieval structures. The fragmentary condition of the models which were available to the Renaissance artists explains, in large measure, why their buildings differ so greatly from the Classic ones. As the centuries passed, more Roman and Greek art objects were dug up, so that successive generations of artists always had new material to inspire them, which aided in the swift development of artistic styles in the Renaissance and post-Renaissance periods. The Revival styles of the nineteenth century do not offer any basic change in the approach to artistic inspiration. The idea was still paramount that the past offered superior examples of art which should be the inspiration and model for the young artist.

The reasons that the results were different were twofold. One was that a much larger body of material was available, and the other was that the approach was becoming increasingly archaeological. Pompeii and Herculaneum were excavated; Stuart and Revett went to Athens and, what is of prime importance, made restorations of the temples as they thought that they must have originally appeared instead of being content to make drawings of them as they appeared then, in the middle of the eighteenth century. Adams went to Palmyra, Napoleon took scientists and artists on his campaigns, the Roman Forum was dug up, and Egyptian art brought to public notice.

It is entertaining to consider the vagaries contained in the Greek Revival style. Take, for example, the Second Bank of the United States which is the first public building to be modeled upon the Parthenon in Athens. It was designed in 1818. At that time Greece was still ruled by the Turks. The Acropolis was a Turkish garrison and the Temple of Athena was a ruined shell which contained a Mohammedan mosque whose dome and minaret dominated the surrounding buildings. Strickland, like most of the Greek Revival architects, never visited Greece and was consequently undisturbed by any memories of the actual appearance or condition of the Greek temples and monuments which he used as the basis for his designs. Instead, his conception of Greek architecture, like that of most of his contemporaries, was entirely formed by the restoration drawings which Stuart and Revett added to their volumes and which, in large measure, explain the extraordinary influence of their work. Hence, the porticoes of the Bank were not copies of the contemporary Parthenon, but of the conception of the Parthenon in its original condition as illustrated in the *Antiquities of Athens.*

Another problem which presented itself for the Greek Revival architect, one of which Strickland was acutely aware, was the current increasingly scientific, or archaeological, approach to the art of the past which aimed at more accuracy in perceiving the original plan and decoration of an ancient building, posing a new question. Since the Greek Revival buildings were not temples but banks, customhouses, state houses, and churches, different interior plans were required, windows were needed for lighting, and chimneys for heating. Hence, in how many respects could a Greek Revival building copy a Greek temple?

Strickland began his description of the Second Bank of the United States which appeared in the *Analectic Magazine* in March, 1819 with a discussion of just this problem.

In the design and proportions of this edifice, we recognize the leading features of that celebrated work of antiquity, the Parthenon at Athens. In selecting this example as a model for a building such as a Bank, requiring a peculiar internal arrangement and distribution of space and light, it becomes a difficult task for an architect to preserve *all* the characteristics of a Grecian Temple, whose original design and appropriation was solely for the worship of the gods, and for the deposition of public treasure. The peripteros or flanking columns of a Grecian building produce a decidedly beautiful feature in architecture. But they cannot be applied with their proper effect to places of business, without a consequent sacrifice of those principles which have a constant application to internal uses and economy.

Twenty-five years later when Strickland was presenting a plan for a new building for the War and Navy Department, he discussed the problem again.

I have practiced architecture, *man* and *boy,* for thirty-five years. I know the theory in every *classical* point of view, but I am free to acknowledge that in all the buildings which I have built of marble in Philadelphia (and I have built nearly all of them), I have had more difficulty in reconciling the proportions of *ancient architecture* to modern purposes of utility, than any one thing else in my profession.

The solution was, as Strickland said in his description of the Second Bank of the United States, to use the leading features of the buildings of antiquity, such as the porticoes, and to omit those parts which interfered with the use of the building, such as the flanking columns. The only Greek features of the interior of a Greek Revival building should be in the details and decorations. The basic plan of the building remained the same as formerly, for the most part. On the exterior, the fundamental change was in the skyline—instead of the flat roofs of the Renaissance, with low-pitched hip roofs and balustrades, the gable roof became predominant.

There was also a change in the use of the Classic orders. The use of columns is, of course, a striking characteristic of Renaissance architecture in all its various phases. This is also the most obvious feature of Greek Revival designs. The differences are that in the Renaissance styles the columns are modeled on the Roman orders—the Corinthian, Composite, and Tuscan; pilasters and piers are used extensively; superimposed orders are employed; one-story colonnades and entrance porticoes are frequent; columns are less apt to be fluted; while in the Greek Revival style, the Greek orders of the Doric and Ionic are the ones most usually used, columns are apt to be fluted, to rise the whole height of the building, and to carry a full entablature. It is vain to be dogmatic in citing the differences between the Renaissance and Greek Revival use of orders, for exceptions can always be found, but it is possible to draw general conclusions.

Strickland, at one time or another, used all the orders, but in the principal buildings which make him preëminent as a Greek Revival architect, he chose either the Doric or Ionic. There are two forms of Greek Ionic, both of which he used. One is the elaborate form which was used on the Erechtheum in Athens. It has a wide necking under the volutes, a wide band of the anthemion motif, and moldings on the volute. The simpler form of the Ionic was illustrated in the plates of Stuart and Revett by the temple on the Ilyssus, just outside of Athens. It has a simple egg and dart necking and plainer, smaller volutes. Strickland used the elaborate Erechtheum form for the twenty-eight capitals of the four porticoes of the State Capitol of Tennessee. He used it also for the distyle-in-antis portico of St. Mary's Church in Nashville. A variant of that form, with the anthemion design omitted and a plain wide band substituted, he used for the columns of the main banking room of the United States Bank and for the porticoes of the United States Mint in Philadelphia. The simpler Ionic order, Strickland used for the impressive eight-column portico of the United States Naval Home. These columns are fluted. The four columns of the Ionic portico of the United States Mint in New Orleans, where he also used the simple form of the Ionic, are unfluted.

There are sixteen buildings designed by Strickland which are still in use, in good repair, and comparatively unchanged on the exterior. Of these, seven are Greek Revival and the others exhibit a variety of styles. That proportion explains why the first half of the nineteenth century is considered the period of the Greek Revival and why Strickland is called a Greek Revival architect. There were many styles used during the period, by Strickland and others, but the majority of the most important buildings were inspired by Greek architecture.

There was no monotony in Strickland's use of the Greek Revival style. Each building was different, depending on the type of capital used, or the relation of the portico to the whole building. The most original and unique of his designs was that for the Philadelphia Exchange, where he employed the Corinthian order on a curved façade on the main floor, and repeated the form in the tower which was copied from the Choragic monument of Lysicrates.

The first building which Strickland designed, the Masonic Hall on Chestnut Street, was not Greek in inspiration, but Gothic. As was the case with all Revival architecture, the stylistic derivatives were confined to ornamentation, for the most part, and to the shape of the openings. There are records of three buildings in which Strickland used medieval decoration. Two of them are still in excellent condition, the church of St. Stephen's on Tenth Street in Philadelphia, and the "Parsonage" in Burlington, New Jersey.

Strickland designed two buildings in the Egyptian Revival style and both were religious edifices. The synagogue for the congregation of the Mikveh-Israel has long ago disappeared, but the First Presbyterian Church of Nashville is in daily use.

There is only one building which seems to have been Saracenic Revival in form, the Temple of the New Jerusalem or Swedenborgian church which was later the Academy of Natural Sciences. It has sometimes been called Gothic Revival, but the dome gives it an un-Gothic character and pointed arches were used in both styles.

The steeple of Independence Hall is more than Colonial Revival in style; it was a conscious attempt to restore the tower to its original form. It is probably the first example of Colonial restoration and an early example of archaeological repair. Strickland also did work of the same kind at "Wyck" in Germantown, which is an early Colonial farmhouse that has been altered from time to time, and which received extensive alterations in 1824 when Strickland made a plan for his friend, Reuben Haines. This was not restoration but Colonial alteration and addition so excellently and harmoniously done that one is not conscious of any discrepancy between the earlier and later work.

Despite the fact that the *avant garde* style was Greek Revival, and slurs were cast upon Roman architecture as lacking the chaste purity of the Greek—Strickland indulged in a few himself—the bulk of the work in this period was still derived from the Roman in one manner or another. There was little work that was purely Roman Revival, such as the early work of Thomas Jefferson, but there was some, and much of it was in the style which Kenneth Conant of Harvard calls Stripped Classic. This term describes those buildings which are almost bare of ornament, but which have gable roofs and where the general plans and proportions show a consciousness of Classic forms. These buildings might be called Rational, as are their counterparts in Europe. Then there is a great variety of design which might, for convenience, be gathered under the heading of Renaissance. These are buildings which derive from not only the three main periods of the Italian Renaissance, such as Hoban's White House in Washington; but also from the various periods of the French Renaissance, such as McComb's City Hall in New York, and from the English and Colonial forms of Renaissance architecture. Some of the features of these buildings are pediments, pilasters, and round-headed windows. In the 1840's, another variant of Italian architecture began to be popular, the Italian villa type, characterized by a tower, derived from a campanile, strongly projecting eaves, sometimes heavily bracketed, and, often, round-headed windows derived from the early Florentine Renaissance style. Soon after, the Italianate style, which might best be described as a Renaissance mélange, began to be used.

The most consciously Roman Revival design which Strickland made was the Triumphal Arch which was erected opposite to the State House in honor of Lafayette's visit to Philadelphia in 1824. In his description of it, he stated that he intended to copy the Triumphal Arch of Septimus Severus. Fourteen years later, when Strickland went to Rome and examined the original arch, he found little to comend it, but since his arch had long since disappeared (it had been of canvas painted to simulate stone on a wood frame), his early copying probably did not haunt him.

The main entrance of the Philadelphia Almshouse at Blockley, with its portico of six Doric columns, may be called Greek Revival, but the bulk of the buildings were completely utilitarian and unornamented and should more properly be called Stripped Classic.

A building which was definitely Stripped Classic was the Friends' Asylum in Frankfort, undecorated except for a one-story porch over the main entrance.

A large group of Strickland's designs can be called Renaissance, although there is a great variety among them. One of his early buildings, the church of the Moravians, built in 1820, and which is known only from an early print, is among these. It is simple, with a prominent gable and three round-headed windows in the façade. It is on the basis of these windows that it would be assigned to the Renaissance tradition. All nine of the designs which show Renaissance features date from the 1820's. Of these, three are distinctly Georgian in proportion and roof. They are the Philadelphia Orphan Asylum, the Indigent Women's Home and the Court House in Meadville. The last has a Doric portico and a Doric frieze about the building, but the general form, the cupola, and the use of red brick make it more Georgian than Greek Revival.

The buildings for the University of Pennsylvania were unique and unlike his other work. They were Federal in character and gave no indication of the Greek Revival. Perhaps Strickland was unconsciously influenced by the old University building which was torn down to make way for his—the mansion intended to be the Presidential residence. The Strickland buildings were squarish rectangles with low gable roofs, decorated with pilasters and lunettes. The two theatres which Strickland designed were also handsome examples of this style. The Chestnut Street Theatre had an upper-story colonnade of Corinthian columns which were carved in Italy and imported especially for the building. The Arch Street Theatre had paired Tuscan columns on the lower story.

The last style which Strickland employed in the 1850's was the Italianate. Unfortunately, Strickland's authorship of the two fine examples of that style which were built in Nashville is traditional and no proof has been forthcoming as yet as to who was the architect of "Belmont" and "Burlington." On internal evidence, the stairs and details of decoration, it would seem that Strickland was certainly the architect of Belmont which is now part of the buildings of Ward-Belmont School. Since Strickland visited Italy in 1838 and spent several weeks in Rome, he would have had every opportunity to become familiar with Italian styles of architecture. It is true, however, that he found little to commend it, if we are to judge by his essays on "Roman Architecture."

To summarize Strickland's use of architectural styles, he began with Gothic Revival and ended with Italianate. His innovations were those current in his period; the use of Revival styles and conservatism in relying on Renaissance styles and building methods.

There are indications that he had in him leavenings of the spirit which produced twentieth-century architecture with its emphasis on plan, materials, and simplicity of forms. In his letter to the Building Committee of Congress describing his plan for the War and Navy Building, dated February 12, 1844, he wrote, "Look around you—in your Hall of Representatives—Look at the show. Where is utility? You cannot hear yourself nor your colleagues speak—No, sir, usefulness first, and ornament made to bend to the propriety of the purposes of the building."

Strickland wrote one essay which was a conscious attempt to present his aesthetic credo. It was published in the Nashville *Port Folio* in May, 1848. As is often the case with practicing architects, he seems to have had difficulty in expressing his ideas, and the organization of the essay is free. However, there are stimulating comments in it which seem to bear out the thesis that Strickland would have been an even more brilliant architect if he had lived a century later when the current aesthetic would have been more congenial to him. He would have been free of the problem of "reconciling the proportions of *ancient architecture* to modern purposes of utility," and he could have given freer rein to his engineering bent which led him to search always for the most practical method of planning a building.

One instance of this preoccupation with practicality was the arrangement of the fireplaces in the Second Bank of the United States. Another instance of it is found in the letter which he wrote to James A. Hillhouse of New Haven on September 15, 1828, in which he described and explained the plans which he had made, on order, of a residence for Hillhouse. He wrote that the fireplaces in the drawing room and the dining room had best be placed in the inner wall, for then they could be recessed and so placed flush with the wall and the cornice of the room could then be straight. The fireplaces could be backed by heaters which would warm the hall, and the flues could be brought out in the center of the roof which was the best place for the appearance of a chimney.

Despite Strickland's interest in utility, he did not produce many innovations in ground plan. Without deviation, he used a central entrance with a symmetrical façade and an almost symmetrical plan. Every building except the Philadelphia Exchange was based on some proportion of the rectangle which varied from an almost perfect square, as in the Temple of the New Jerusalem, to the long and narrow Providence Athenaeum. In houses, his preference was for the square; in civic buildings, for the long rectangle.

In almost every building the ceiling was high, about seventeen feet for the average height in a residence and up to forty-three feet in a civic building. The whole nineteenth century as an era of extremely high ceilings. A possible explanation for this is as follows: Peasants' huts and workmen's cottages had low ceilings because they were cheaper to build and easier and cheaper to keep warm. Kings' palaces and noblemen's mansions had high ceilings and large rooms because the owners had wealth sufficient to build large edifices, to decorate them, to heat them in winter, and to keep them clean. The height of ceiling had implied class distinctions. The nineteenth century was the century of so-called growth of democracy which is best expressed by the often quoted statement of the American in Europe, "In our country, we are all Kings and Queens." The benefits of democracy were extended to the upper middle class and they showed their appreciation by having higher ceilings.

A contribution of the early nineteenth century to architectural thought was the ideal of a fireproof building which could be achieved by eliminating wood, and using stone and brick construction entirely. Latrobe emphasized the importance of fireproof construction, especially in public buildings. Robert Mills has been credited with constructing the first such edifice in 1826. Strickland, in his description of the Second Bank of the United States in 1818, stated that he would try to make it fireproof. All through his career, Strickland tried to cut out fire hazards. In consequence, he used heavy masonry walls and vaulted ceilings whenever possible. A great majority of his buildings were faced with marble, so many that he seems to have felt superior to the Emperor Augustus when he was in Rome because he wrote that Augustus must have made a vain boast if he ever said that he found Rome a city of brick and left it of marble, since there was less brick and more marble in Philadelphia. In Strickland's obituary, Judge Kane spoke of his having given Philadelphia her marble era. Probably one reason that Strickland did so little experimenting in construction methods was that the majority of his commissions provided for marble walls and even a marble interior in the case of the Capitol in Nashville.

Some of Strickland's buildings were built of brick. Two are still standing in Nashville, the First Presbyterian Church and the residence "Lynnlawn." Both have been painted gray. The explanation is to be found in the second of the "Sketches of Roman Architecture" where he bluntly condemns red brick by saying that nothing "can be in worse taste than a *red* brick house contrasted, as an artist would say, with a clear blue sky." He continues that no matter how well planned or proportioned a building may be, if the color is so vivid as to affect the play of light and shadow, the virtues of the building are lost and concludes, "*Red* is the last colour that an Architect would choose in the composition of any of his designs." This dislike of red brick was part of the contemporary aesthetic and Alexander Downing in his *Rural Architecture* warns against it and recommends roughcasting the brick and then offers a table of the appropriate hues to paint the stucco.

It is worth noting that there is no record that Strickland ever designed or built an edifice that was constructed entirely of wood. One reason for this was that the majority of his buildings were for civic uses. Another was that wood had never been used as extensively in eastern Pennsylvania as it had been in New England, and was later to be used in the Middle West. Lastly, wood as a building material was inimicable to his profound belief in fireproof construction.

Strickland showed great variety, if not originality, in his treatment of openings, especially windows. He used five main types of windows, short rectangle, long rectangle, square, round-headed, and pointed. The pointed windows appear only in those buildings which were designed to be Gothic or Saracenic. The round-headed windows are used on the ground floor, usually with the same type of door. Also, occasionally, he used lunettes as in the Bank of the United States and the University of Pennsylvania buildings. On the Chestnut Street Theatre, he used an arched colonnade for the entrance. Round windows and doors appear more often than might be expected, and testify to the continuing Georgian or late Renaissance tradition. Square windows appear almost exclusively in the second or top story. They are used generally with long rectangular windows on the ground story and are in buildings which belong to the Greek Revival style. This fenestration may be a conscious attempt to produce the design of a Greek temple; the long windows representing the longitudinal line of the portico, or encircling colonnade, and the square openings repeating the motif of the metope. Windows of the short rectangular type, Strickland reserved for the utilitarian buildings, such as the Friends' Asylum and the Philadelphia Almshouse. A sixth type of window occurs in important civic buildings, such as the Philadelphia Exchange. This is the tripartite window, a wide light, flanked by narrow lights and separated by marble piers. Both Robert Mills and John Haviland, upon occasion, used the tripartite window, with variations, the former in the Record Office in Charleston, South Carolina, and the latter in the Moody House in Haverhill, Massachusetts. This tripartite opening may be a Greek Revival adaptation of the Palladian window.

While it is a fundamental architectural tenet that the plan and design of a building must be adapted to the site, it is equally true that an architect rarely has an opportunity to select the site for his design. Despite this curtailment of choice, the architect has his individual preferences in all these matters. Strickland, for instance, had a definite preference for high ground and a good vista. He was fortunate in the site provided for the Capitol at Nashville which is just such a one as he would have chosen himself. It is only natural that an architect likes to have his building show to the best advantage. However, in Strickland's case there seems to have been another reason for this preference and that was the character of the terrain of the Acropolis in Athens which provided such a site. Since the Greek temples of Athens provided the best models for the Greek Revival architect, so, ideally, did the Acropolis provide the best model for a site. On the other hand, in Rome a number of the ancient buildings around the Fora were on low ground, and of the Coliseum site, Strickland wrote that it is "in a low *pond like* place," and added that it "is difficult to discover why the Emperor Flavius should have chosen such a site for the construction of this enormous Theatre." He was not impressed by the Capitoline hill and remarked that it "is a very inconsiderable eminence," and it "is impossible to conceive how it ever could have sustained the number of Temples that historians and antiquarians have, from time to time, placed upon this small compass of a hill."

Strickland's approach to architecture was practical; his first concern was for the plan to be as useful as possible, and his second, for the construction to be lasting and fireproof. He extended this utilitarian attitude to architectural elements. Among his writings there are several paragraphs which deal with columns and they are sufficient to show that he was not beguiled by novelty, but looked on columns as an element of support which should proclaim their function.

He was especially critical of the twisted columns which support the baldachino over the altar of St. Peter's in Rome. He said that it was executed and designed in the worst possible taste, that it was like a mammoth in a museum and spoiled the vista of the nave, that it was out of keeping with the surrounding architecture. The canopy, supported by twisted columns, fifty feet high he likened to "our grandmothers bed posts" and added, "when a column is *twisted* all idea of support is lost." Again he referred to the baldachino as "this *brazen monstrosity* of *twisted columns!*"

In his essay on "The Three Orders of Architecture," Strickland discusses columns further. One paragraph states that it is not sufficient for a column to furnish support; it must also satisfy the eye that it supports in a rational proportion to the weight that it bears. He criticizes the Caryatides of the Porch of the Maidens of the Erechtheum for the same reason and inquires who can look at them with a sensation of pain and a feeling of incongruity that a statue of a woman should bear such a load and concludes, "If the Grecian Artist had not been fully imbued with the idea that women were made for slaves, he would perhaps, have had more reasons to make columns in the form of his own sex."

For the same reason, he criticizes the cornstalk columns which Latrobe invented for the Capitol in Washington. Strickland admits that the proportions are good and the carving excellent and in general they

> have a very pretty effect. The Architect flattered himself that he had made a hit and established a new order of Columns. In this instance the eye was satisfied with the novelty, but not so with the mind; somebody said, it was Timothy Pickering, at that time Secretary of State—"what idea of strength or support can we have from a bundle of corn stalks set on end?"

Strickland seems to have sincerely felt that the Greek temples offered the best models of architectural beauty and in his essay quite derided the architects who were experimenting with the elements of Greek architecture and trying to produce something new. Nevertheless, in his design for the War and Navy Department building in Washington, he pursued what he called "the *American plan* of putting windows in the blank space of the frieze." He defended this design by saying that it had been used in some of the best buildings in New York and Philadelphia and cited the Custom House in New York, "that classical building" where "windows have been introduced in every one of the spaces of the triglyphs." He further defended the practice as "purely an American improvement in the art of building"; he said that it saved height and did away with the "blank space which has always given a heavy appearance to the attic story," and concluded, "besides, it is useful to do so, notwithstanding the rigid rules of ancient architecture." Since this building was never built, Strickland was not guilty of such a deviation from the classic rules. It is interesting that he mentions it with such approbation, for the custom of putting small windows in the frieze under the eaves became a widespread and characteristic feature of the simpler Greek Revival farmhouses which were built in the 1830's and later in northwestern New York state and on westward to the Mississippi. These frieze windows were filled with decorative iron grills.

Strickland used a variety of roofs and skylines in his designs. The most famous are the two towers based on the Choragic Monument of Lysicrates. Three times he used cupolas: on the steeple of Independence Hall, the Indigent Women's Home and the Courthouse at Meadville. Only once did he use a dome and that was for his early plan for the Swedenborgian church, where he designed a low dome with a circular cupola. His visit to Rome in 1838 included a prolonged and attentive inspection of St. Peter's. He did not admire it and wrote rather sarcastically of it. "Nine hundred and ninety-nine persons out of a thousand are *wrapt* with St. Peter's! 'Size is part of the sublime.' St. Peter's is the largest building in the world, therefore St. Peter's is sublime." He was not impressed by the dome and wrote that it is "decidedly ugly, being too high for its diameter. It is too much of a conoid to be graceful." He likened it to dome of the State House in Boston and "unlike that of the kettle bottom *renversé* of the Capitol at Washington [the Latrobe dome]." However, he conceded that nothing in city architecture could be more strikingly beautiful and grand than a well-shaped dome, although there were few either in Europe or the United States which he considered to be well-proportioned. He said that the true shape for a dome should be between the hemisphere and the parabola, and cited St. Paul's in London as an example.

Strickland made severe remarks about Roman architecture, although there were some features that he enjoyed, but the triumphal arches brought forth some of his most caustic comments. For instance, of the fourth century sculpture on the Arch of Constantine he wrote, it "is the most miserable trash that ever was chiselled out of the surface of a block of marble." He concludes his description of the triumphal arches with the following words:

> The plinths, pedestals and imposts have confused and disorderly positions between the columns. All the decorative sculpture is diffused, colossal and overloaded; in short these relics of the ancient triumphal arches mark an age of luxury, riches and extravagance, and afford examples of architecture extremely prejudicial to beauty and good taste, which the young architect had better not copy. What a contrast do these ruins present when compared with the simplicity and purity of the Grecian model!

His allegiance to Greece and condemnation of Rome almost slipped when he discussed arches.

> It is a singular fact, not generally known, that the Romans were the inventors or discoverers of the Arch and the principles of the circular form of construction. . . . The beauty and utility of the arched form in domes, bridges, &c. is everywhere apparent, and notwithstanding this prevalence in all the structures of ancient and modern Rome, the mind as well

as the eye becomes more and more converted to the curved line, as the most graceful.

He draws himself up short by concluding, "but in a classic point of view certainly not the most tasteful."

When one carefully goes through the illustrations of Strickland's architectural work, one finds that in almost every building of which there is any record, the arched form has been used either in windows, doors, archways, or niches. Even in the most consciously Greek of his buildings, the Second Bank of the United States, there are lunette windows in the middle of the side walls which light the main banking hall which is roofed by a barrel vault, and the entrance vestibule is oval.

Strickland may have been influenced by his visit to Rome in his attitude towards stairways. In his early work, the stairways are small and out of the way. They are not on the main axis. In his letter to Hillhouse, he wrote that he had changed the position of the stairway to furnish more privacy and convenience to the dining room and kitchen and gave as an additional reason, "I have never thought of beauty in a Stairway; indeed it is difficult to produce this effect in small buildings without too great a sacrifice of room and comfort." Even in the United States Naval Home where the stairs have always been remarked upon as having been constructed upon the principle of the arch instead of the post and lintel, they are discreetly placed at either side of the central building and have only construction and utility to recommend them.

On the other hand, in the Nashville period, he designed some handsome and effective stairways. In the Capitol, Strickland placed the stairway on the cross axis on the west side, therefore there is not an effective vista leading up to it from the basement story, but there is a handsome view of it from the main story. It is composed of two parts, a free-standing, central stairway, eleven feet in width, rising to a wide landing from which two stairways rise on either side to the main story. The balustrade is of unfluted Doric columns with a broad marble hand-rail. These stairs are constructed on the principle of the arch.

In the private houses which are attributed to Strickland in and about Nashville, all have handsome stairways on the main axis. The most ingenious are the stairways at "Belmont" which rise unsupported by walls; a central stairway rises to a landing, then divides into two stairways from the landing to the second story, and from the second story, two stairways again lead to a central landing, and from there a single stairway leads to the lookout tower on the roof. At "Belle Meade" and "Lynnlawn," the stairs are in the back of the central hall, rising against the left wall to a landing of generous proportions where there is a niche in the wall. The stairway then turns in the reverse direction and extends to the front part of the upper hall.

There are two experimentations which Strickland made in designing interior doors. Both were based on utilitarian considerations. In 1824 when Reuben Haines asked him to come to "Wyck" to make a plan for the alterations, he suggested an arrangement of doors which may be cited as a forerunner of the current architectural emphasis on movable walls. At "Wyck," he designed two pairs of doors of equal size which he had hung on swivel pins placed in the floor and lintels. The door jambs and the inner edges of the doors were rounded. In this way the doors fitted snugly in any position, which is not possible with doors on hinges. These doors are placed directly opposite each other on either side of the entrance hall. The door on the right leads into the drawing room, the one on the left into a wide hall. When the doors are shut in their usual position, the rooms and the hall are separated. When the doors are opened at right angles, they form partitions across the hall, dividing it into an entrance vestibule and a small square hall by the stairs, and also form a wide hall joining the rooms on the right and left which make them like one large hall for entertaining.

The other experiment with interior doors was one that became a familiar expedient in the nineteenth-century houses with long narrow drawing rooms which were often divided by doors into a front and back parlor. Strickland used such doors in the houses which he designed for the Governor and Medical Officer of the United States Naval Home in 1844. When he wrote the Secretary of the Navy that the houses were almost complete on February 12, 1845, he said that the drawing room parlors were long saloons with two columns, one on either side of the middle of the room and he recommended using a curtain there, but on the other side of the house he used large double doors on hinges to divide the office from the dining room.

One of the favorite trims of the period for both doors and windows was the Erechtheum type with crosettes. That is, the upper lintel extended beyond the upright jambs. Strickland used this form extensively throughout his whole career, as early as the Bank and as late as "Belle Meade," outside Nashville.

Some of Strickland's art criticism has been quoted already. It is usually stimulating; it appears to be sincere and based upon unprejudiced observation. It is also interesting to note how much the engineering problems attracted him. For instance, he responded to the suggestion found in his guidebook that the course of the Tiber could be changed by selecting the best route, and then concluded that the expense would be too great. When he went to St. Peter's, the feature of the building which really aroused his interest and admiration was the spiral ramp leading to the roof, and the draining system of the roof. At the Coliseum, his most interested inquiry was how the awning which shaded the arena was supported. The Baths, which he condemned as "courts of rendezvous for the most licentious indulgence," aroused his respect for their complicated water systems, and the knowledge of hydraulics which they displayed.

In discussing the architecture of Rome—ancient, Renaissance, and modern—Strickland felt completely uninhibited by any compulsive respect, which later generations, as well as his German contemporaries, felt. Greek art was the good art which could present no flaw. Roman art was full of flaws and he did not hesitate to say so. Of Michelangelo's Capitoline buildings, he commented that they were "constructed with little judgment or taste; although they were built from the designs of Michel Angelo, they only prove this great artist to be a much better sculptor than architect."

By and large, Strickland appears to have had a democratic and pragmatic standard for beauty. His insistence upon the superiority of Greek art was in some measure a deviation from his natural standards. His training under Latrobe, as well as the prevailing fashion of the period, largely explains his admiration for Greek architecture. He was sincere intellectually, but probably not completely sincere emotionally. Judge Kane thought that his natural inclination was toward a more ornate style and that he willfully made his style severe. The following sentence does not quite ring clear, there is more than a hint of verbiage.

> All the civilized world acknowledges the existence of permanent principles established by the wisdom, strength and beauty of the proportions and the symmetry of the Grecian Temples; and the homage that is paid to these forms, is not at all conventional or accidental, but is produced by the innate sense of the propriety of these laws of order.

His aesthetic criteria were fitness, utility, and simplicity. He thought that everyone, even the most uneducated, could perceive beauty in nature and in art, and that the influence of well-designed works of art "upon the most ignorant and uncultivated is greater than is generally supposed. To be surrounded by objects constructed in simplicity and good taste opens a never failing school for the cultivation and elevation of the mind."

When asked to define beauty and taste, he said, they existed "in the very essentials of proportion and symmetry; in the adaptation of all the parts to the whole." For an example, he cited the Venus de' Medici and pointed out that "if it were carved out of a diamond it would not be more beautiful than it is in Parian marble, for its beauty is in its proportions and if it lacked those, no matter of how expensive a material it was made, it would cease to be admired," even by the rude and uninformed. He thought that anyone and everyone could understand and enjoy a work of art, if he paid a little attention to the subject, for the basic principles of proportion, fitness and simplicity could be evident to all.

He hoped that every artist and artisan, although they might be working by principle or rule, had

> an irresistible impulse to that perfection which it should be their desire at all times to attain. It may be asked, how are Artisans and Mechanics to become acquainted with the rules of proportion applied to their particular branches or trades? Why simply, by becoming acquainted with the materials which they use and the purposes to which they are to be put.

Strickland considered simplicity to be of prime importance, and in his following discussion of the subject he antedates Cézanne by simplifying architectural design to basic geometric forms.

> Simplicity in any work of art consists in the fewness of its principal parts. . . . Suppose any, or all of the geometrical superficies and solids constructed by their forms into dwelling houses, churches, Palaces, &c. The dwelling house, in outline, a Cube; the church, a Cone; and the Palace, a Pyramid. Now these outlines are very simple and symmetrical, rigidly so; and understood by almost every body, but again suppose, that they are all combined in one edifice, as its general outline; it would not be difficult to prove a want of harmony and judgment in the design—strength might be one of the component parts, in the formation of the mass, but beauty could not exist under such combined forms in one simple structure.

In his long architectural career, Strickland exemplified the best in American architecture, since he observed the three basic principles of good architectural practice: the fitness of the plan, the solidity of the construction, and the proportion of the design.

APPENDIX A

A CHRONOLOGIC, BIBLIOGRAPHIC AND DESCRIPTIVE CATALOGUE OF THE ARCHITECTURAL AND ENGINEERING WORK OF WILLIAM STRICKLAND

Notes:

An asterisk (*) denotes that a building is standing (January, 1950). All buildings are in Philadelphia unless otherwise indicated. The following abbreviations are observed throughout:

A.P.S., for American Philosophical Society, Philadelphia.
H.A.B.S., for Historic American Buildings Survey, the files of which are now in the Fine Arts Division of the Library of Congress, Washington, D. C.
H.S.P., for Historical Society of Pennsylvania, Philadelphia.

1804

Copy of the designs made by Benjamin H. Latrobe for the United States Capitol in Washington, D. C.

Reference: Latrobe Letters, 1803-17, Manuscript Division, Library of Congress (p. 69). Letter to John Lenthall, Clerk of the Works, Washington, dated "Newcastle April 10, 1804." "Mr. Strickland is now employed in making you a copy of the designs which I have sent to the President." Letter to the same (p. 75), "April 26, 1804," "William Strickland is quite careless enough to give me infinite plague— But as the calculations were made by me I must settle that matter with you." To the same on August 19, 1804 (p. 117), "You will herewith receive the Section of the Ground story . . . the lines were drawn by William Strickland— I have corrected some of his omissions with the pen."

1805

Survey of Newcastle, Delaware, made with Robert Mills and Peter Lenox, while apprenticed to Benjamin H. Latrobe.

Reference: Letter from Benjamin H. Latrobe to Strickland, now in the Library of Congress, dated "Ironhill, August 10, 1805," stating that Strickland should call for a "draft for $25 . . . paid by the Commissioners of the town of Newcastle for the regulation of the streets."

H. M. Pierce Gallagher, *Robert Mills, architect of the Washington Monument* (New York: Columbia University Press, 1935), p. 126.

1808-11

Masonic Hall, north side of Chestnut Street, between Seventh and Eighth streets (Plates 5 and 11).

Design dated: November 21, 1808.

Cornerstone laid: April 17, 1809.

Building dedicated: May 27, 1811.

Grand celebration: St. John the Baptist's Day, June 24, 1811.

Interior and tower burned: March 9, 1819.

Reference: Norris S. Barratt and Julius F. Sachse, *Freemasonry in Pennsylvania, 1727-1907* (Philadelphia 1908), II, 398-400.

Print in the collection of the Historical Society of Pennsylvania, "to James Milnor, Grand Master of the Lodge, this Plate inscribed by his brother

W. Strickland." Engraving by William Kneass after drawing by "Wm. Strickland arch. 28th Oct. 1813."

Port Folio, V (1811). Pamphlet at the end gives an account of the dedication of the Masonic Hall in which are the words, "Brother Darrah, the architect." No primary source has been found to authenticate the statement that Strickland was the architect.

James Mease, M.D., *Picture of Philadelphia in 1811* (Philadelphia), p. 151. Excellent detailed description.

The Hermit in America on a Visit to Philadelphia (1819), p. 151.

The decoration of the saloon, independent of certain dark-looking figures, (apparently in bronze,) which are placed at certain intervals around, are plain, but neat and ornamental. The figures alluded to have the most comical effect imaginable, and are, no doubt, placed there for the purpose; seeing that no place is better adapted to the free and admissible use of the risible muscles, than a ball-room. The ingenious managers deserve credit for their invention, for I believe that it is indisputably original.

The figures referred to are probably the statues of Faith, Hope, and Charity which were carved in wood, especially for the Hall, by William Rush. They are now painted white and in the Philadelphia Museum of Art.

Port Folio, August, 1812. "Review of the Second Annual Exhibition of the Society of Artists and the Pennsylvania Academy," p. 148. "No. 14, is a perspective view of the new masonic hall in Chesnut-street by William Strickland, the architect. The subject is faithfully represented, and has a very picturesque appearance; it is now in the hands of the engraver for the purpose of publication."

Catalogue of the Second Annual Exhibition (1812). "Subscriptions for the print will be received by J. Vallance, at the Academy."

Hazard's Register of Pennsylvania, X. The Masonic Hall was one of the first buildings in Philadelphia to be lit by gas. A small private plant used for making the gas caused complaints as late as 1832 because it leaked gas and water.

Copies of the prints and old photographs are in the collection of the H.S.P.

Style: Gothic; pointed windows and doors, cusping, battlements, pinnacles, and steeple.

Plan: Two-story, rectangular.

Materials: Brick, wood, and plaster.

Outstanding feature: Wood steeple, 180 feet high.

1810-18

General surveying.

Reference: *Proceedings of the American Philosophical Society, 1854-58,* VI, 29. "He levelled a houseplot, computed a water power, surveyed a field or a farm where the lines were too complex for the everyday workers in mensuration."

1812

Strickland made ten drawings which were engraved by William Kneass and used for the illustrations of the volume, *The Constitution of the incorporated Practical House Carpenters' Society, of the City and County of Philadelphia: together with Rules and Regulations for measuring and valuing House Carpenters' Work.*

The drawings were: elevation of a building, plan of the basement story, three roofs, door frame, fan lights, Palladian window, staircase, geometrical stairs, Gothic door with canopy-like balcony, and a Gothic window.

Strickland's father, John Strickland, was a member of the Practical House Carpenters' Society and in this year is listed as a member of the Committee of Regulation.

1813

Design for a Washington Monument in Washington, D. C., exhibited in Philadelphia in May, 1813.

Reference: *Catalogue of the Third Annual Exhibition of the Columbian Society of Artists and the Pennsylvania Academy,* p. 19.

No. 96. Design of a Grand National Monument, Commemorative of the Illustrious Washington, W. Strickland, A.C.S.A.

This superb edifice to be erected in the city of Washington, commanding a view of the public buildings. It should be composed of granite, freestone or Pennsylvania marble.
It stands on a basis sixty feet square, and its entire elevation is ninety feet. On each of its four fronts it

exhibits a semicircular arch of forty feet span. These arches spring from a grand basement one hundred feet square, having its surface richly tesselated in the Mosaic style, with a flight of steps on each of its four sides, corresponding to the four semicircular entrances. In the center of the basement, elevated on a massy pedestal of granite, stands in civil costume, a colossal statue of Washington. In each of the four surrounding corners are niches, in which appear statues of Hamilton, Green, Knox and Wayne, who constituted his council both in the cabinet and the field. Over the whole springs a groin arched ceiling enriched with allegorical figures and ornaments, in basso-relievo, emblematical of his virtues and character as a statesman.

On each of the four fronts of the basement, without the edifice, stand four lofty columns of the Doric order. These columns support a trussed cornice and pediments, extending over the whole fronts, in the Tympanum of which are represented, in bold basso-relievo, the *surrender* of lord Cornwallis, the battle of *Princeton*, the battle of *Trenton* and the still more august and affecting spectacle of Washington, after he had achieved the Independence of his country, surrendering up his commission to the grand council of the nation from which he had received it. On the four corners over the Doric columns stand, in well executed statuary, Victory, Fame, the Genius of America, History, and other appropriate allegorical figures.

The basement is surmounted by a rotunda thirty feet diameter, composed of thirteen lofty columns, with insulated pilaster. Upon the entablature over each column is represented, on an escutcheon, the armorial bearings of the particular state of which the column is intended to be emblematical. Behind these, and forming, as it were, a canopy of the whole, springs a dome, supporting on its crown the frustum (fragment) of a column. Upon this fragment a passing Eagle is in the act of perching—an event intended as emblematical of the dismembered colonies of Great Britain receiving a new and more exalted character. In the centre of the rotunda is the figure of Liberty in a sitting posture, having her attributes portrayed in the panels of the dome.

The whole edifice is to be regarded as a grand allegorical figure. The characteristic strength of the Doric order represents the firmness of Washington as a statesman and warrior, setting forth that he laid the foundation-stone of our Independence in strength, upon which was erected the Temple of Liberty, supported by the Wisdom and Beauty of the confederation.

1813

Possible survey of a canal for Benjamin H. Latrobe.

Reference: Letter from Latrobe to Strickland, dated Washington, D. C., February 10, 1813. In the possession of Mrs. Ferdinand C. Latrobe (1950).

Dear Sir,

There never was a moment since I knew your father and family that I would not have done all in my power to serve you and there was a time when I could promote the interest of my friends, but that time is passed nearly. As to the situation your father wishes it is occupied by a very excellent Ship-joiner, Hadrach Davis, who is a great favorite with the Navy Department. The subordinate departments are not worth his acceptance. I have resigned all my positions under the government after the 1st of May next and shall return to Pennsylvania. Every dog has his day! Do you think you could undertake to explore 50 miles of Country under my general direction for a Canal this Spring? by yourself with assistants.

Yrs. truly

B. H. Latrobe

I will not forget your father's wishes.

1814

(September) Member of Sub-committee of Defense, Corps of Topographical Engineers, in charge of a survey of the country for nine miles west of Philadelphia.

Reference: *Pennsylvania Magazine of History and Biography*, XXIV (1900), 374-75. Letter from William Strickland to Jonathan Jones:

Philada. Septr. 7, 1814

Sir, The Topographical Corps of Engineers under the direction of Gen'l Jonathan Williams are requested to call upon the information of Mr. Jonathan Jones relative to the grounds suitable for military positions near the city. They will be at the falls of Schuylkill this afternoon at 4 o'clock, when you will be pleased to attend if possible.

Original map and report were given to the library of the American Philosophical Society by General Jonathan Williams (size: 220 x 185 cm.). *Early*

Proceedings, American Philosophical Society, 1744-1838, p. 452. "Feb. 3, 1815. Large and elegant map deposited by Col. Williams." The map is an excellent example of Strickland's draftsmanship. The report which was written on the map is as follows:

Map of the Country Nine Miles west of the City of Philadelphia and between Darby Creek and Young's Ford on the River Schuylkill. Surveyed by order of Genl Jonathan Williams Chairman of the Sub-Committee of Defence. Philadelphia 28th September 1814.
To General Jonathan Williams Chairman of the Sub-Committee of Defence of the City of Philadelphia:
We have agreably to your order surveyed and examined the Country nine miles west of the City of Philadelphia & between Darby Creek and Youngs Ford about 17 miles distant through a tolerably level country crossing in its course Darby creek near Worrells mill, the West Chester road at Bittles Tavern—Cobbs' Creek at Humphrey's Mill—there by Dutch Church, crossing the Lancaster roads—and Mill Creek at McClenachans' Mill—then to said Ford— There are however some parts of it which are bad and where an enemy could be much annoyed— Passing the Darby Creek near Worrells mill the ground is high and rugged—the banks of the Creek at this place offer some difficulties to the march of an Army—positions might be chosen at this spot from which an enemy might be considerably harrassed—there is another position on this road at Cobbs' Creek near Humphrey's mill which should not be lost sight of, as a redoubt might be placed here which would command this road for at least half a mile and also another road which intersects at this point—after leaving the old Lancaster Road near the nine milestone there occurs a very deep ravine where nature has done so much that with a little labour an enemy could be completely checked—the passage through this ravine being not more than ten or twelve feet wide—very rough—and continues nearly a mile—from the place to Young's Ford the road is tolerably good—from the nine milestone on the old Lancaster Road as well as from the Dutch Church there is a direct rout and good roads to Robin Hood Ford, Falls and Riters Ferry— The Fords on the Schuylkill are easy of access—good crossage—water shoal—River narrow and Bottom good— The roads approaching end near the Western bank are good— The Eastern Bank is steep, rugged and for defensive Military Position commanding—at any of the Fords oppositions could be posted which would so decidedly give us the advantage that an enemy must be cut to pieces should a passage be attempted—
We have no Idea however that a crossing on the river Schuylkill would be attempted at any other place than the Fords—the general character of both Banks at all other places we think would forbid such a movement as the Hills rise suddenly from sixty to 160 feet above the level of the River. The Hills at Darby and the high grounds near the Bell Tavern on the Baltimore road offer such advantageous positions for Defence that we must warmly recommend them to your immediate attention. In concluding this report we are proud to acknowledge the important services rendered by Jona[n] Jones Esq. of Lower Merion.

William Strickland
Topographical Engineers Rob. Brooke
Wm. Kneass

Scale 8 inches to a mile.

1814

Engineer, Philadelphia Committee of Safety, War of 1812 (one of the citizens in charge of fortifications of Philadelphia).

Reference: Obituary of William Strickland by John K. Kane. Manuscript in the A.P.S. library. *Proceedings of the American Philosophical Society, 1854-58*, VI, 29-30.

He was trying on his uniform jacket as a volunteer, the night before he was to set out for camp: it was in the fall of 1814, and all who had nothing else to do, and a good many besides, were marching off to keep away the British; when an accident brought him into more public view.
The older part of the town had turned out to make fortifications, those strange looking earth-works that many of us remember at all the roadcrossings, and some of which promise to remain there like Indian mounds to puzzle the coming generation of antiquarians. Dr. Patterson had been elected one of our virtuoso engineers, and he bethought him of Strickland as another. Of course there was no difficulty in getting his commission from the Committee of safety: old general Bloomfield added a furlough to relieve him from camp duty; and before six o'clock the next morning Strickland had mounted the blue cockade, and was teaching all

sorts of patriotic people to toss sods to the music of a fife.
I have heard him refer much of his professional success to this trivial incident. It happened that some of our influential citizens were struck by the efficiency he manifested in his extempore office. He thought they over-valued it; though he complained for a while that like some heroes of more sanguinary fields, he had harvested more from fame than abiding emolument.

1815-17

Friends' Asylum for the Insane, Frankfort, outside Philadelphia (Plate 9A).

Organized and funds collected in 1814, and site bought for $10,000. Building started in 1815 and opened for patients in May, 1817. Total cost, $45,000.

Reference: J. Thomas Scharf and Thompson Westcott, *History of Philadelphia, 1609-1884.* II, 1069. Strickland is credited with this building, but no primary source has been found to authenticate his authorship. *Philadelphia in 1830* (*Philadelphia: Carey and Hart,* 1830), p. 64:

The building for the reception of patients is of stone, and consists of a center edifice, three stories high, and about 60 feet square, and two wings, each about 100 feet long, 24 feet wide and two stories high. The wings are divided into rooms, about 9½ each by 10 feet, with a passage or hall 10 feet in width. Each room has a window and a transom over the door. The sashes are of cast iron, but resemble wood work so much, that the difference is not easily perceived. Several of the rooms are so constructed as to admit rarefied air from stoves in the basement story, and having a ventilator in the ceiling opening into the garret, can be made perfectly dark, and have the advantage of heat, when necessary to keep patients continually in them.

1815(?)

Mechanics Bank.

Reference: *Proceedings of the American Philosophical Society,* VI (1854), 30. Obituary of William Strickland by John K. Kane.

No reference has been found to substantiate this statement by Kane. There are a number of inaccuracies in the obituary which are minor details, but it seems strange that Kane could attribute a building as important as a bank incorrectly. A Mechanics Bank was chartered in 1814 and a Mechanics and Farmers Bank in the thirties. So far, no clue connecting Strickland with either of these buildings, now demolished, has been found.

1816

Temple of the New Jerusalem, Swedenborgian Church, George and Twelfth Streets (Plate 18A).

Cornerstone laid: June 6, 1816.

Consecrated: January 1, 1817.

Sold to the Philadelphia Academy of Natural Sciences: 1826.

Reference: Thomas Wilson, *Picture of Philadelphia in 1824.* The size of the lot was 90 feet on Twelfth Street and 99 feet on George.

Style: Saracenic-Gothic Revival. Wilson calls it Gothic, but the engravings make it appear Saracenic, with the squat dome and four-point arches. It was a square building with a dome, and with Early American Gothic decoration.

Plan: Square auditorium with galleries.

Area: 44 by 50 feet.

Materials: Brick, stone trim and wood.

Outstanding features: Dome—as far as is known at present, it is the only one which Strickland designed.

1816-17

Plans submitted in the competition for the Pennsylvania State Capitol, Harrisburg, Pennsylvania.

Reference: *Analectic Magazine* (n. s.), II:1 (July, 1820), p. 46, Art. V. Copy of a letter among the notes on Strickland, collected by Fiske Kimball, Director of the Philadelphia Museum of Art. (The original of this letter was advertised for sale at $18.50 by the American Autograph Shop, Merion, Pennsylvania, in their catalogue, *American Clipper,* XII, No. 5 (November, 1941), p. 314, Item 204.)

In 1816, the State of Pennsylvania passed a resolution and an appropriation for a new Capitol building. It was determined to obtain the plan by a competition with a first premium of four hundred dollars, and a second premium of two hundred dollars. An invitation to the artists of Philadelphia, New York, Boston, Baltimore, and Washington to furnish plans was published in the newspapers of those cities. Stephen Hills, of Harrisburg, won the first premium, and Robert Mills of Baltimore, the second.

Strickland made every effort to win the competition as the letter to Nicholas Biddle indicates.

Philadelphia, February 24th, 1817.

Dear Sir,

I have just this moment received information from one of my friends in Harrisburg that Mr. Mills has qualified his last proposals to the Legislature in such a manner as will perhaps be calculated to influence the vote of the house in his favor. Thus he proposes to superintend the erection of the building for *Three dollars* per day provided an *assistant* be appointed to make the necessary contracts for materials etc. Your good sense will discover at once that this is a mere *trick*, for the assistant must be paid for his services, so that the State will gain nothing by the scheme—his proposals are 200,000 dollars for the whole cost. I will thank you to state to the gentlemen explicitly the following proposals on my part.

I will agree to erect the State Capitol according to my last plan in a substantial and durable manner for the sum of $180,000., for the compensation of $5 per day for professional services, which always includes the *making of contracts, procuring materials etc., etc.* That I require no more than 30,000 dollars as an appropriation for the first year, and I will agree to accomodate the session of 1818-19 in the State Capitol for a further appropriation of 60,000 for the year 1818.— Your dissemination of these terms among the gentlemen of the two houses will be duly appreciated by

Yours with the greatest respect and esteem
William Strickland

Nicholas Biddle Esq.

P.S. I wish you would be so good as to confer with Mr. John Read as to the best plan of making these sentiments known to the house.

1817

Engraved a plate entitled "Ancient View of Baltimore" for Messrs. Coale and Maxwell of Baltimore, Maryland.

An example of this engraving is in the New York Public Library Print Collection, Mark -1752-B-70.

American Historical Prints, Early Views of American Cities etc., I. N. Stokes and Daniel C. Haskell (New York, 1933), p. 17 (description).

The inscription, engraved by H. S. Tanner is as follows: "Baltimore in 1752. From a Sketch then made by John Moale Esqr. decesd, corrected by the late Daniel Bowley Esqr. from his certain recollection, & that of other aged persons, well acquainted with it; with whom he compared notes."

Two letters in the H.S.P. and one in the Manuscript Collection of the New York Library indicate that Strickland made the plate and the prints were colored by Strickland's younger brother George and C. R. Leslie's sister, Eliza Leslie, who later became well-known as a novelist and writer of cookbooks.

1817

Improvements on the Medical Hall, University of Pennsylvania, Ninth Street, November, 1817, at a cost of $10,000.

Reference: University Papers, MSS Letters, University of Pennsylvania Library, IX (#47, 53, 58, 65, 77, 83, 90, 94, 97).

1818

Anatomical Museum, Medical Hall, Ninth Street, University of Pennsylvania.

Reference: University Papers, MSS Letters, University of Pennsylvania Library, X (#40, 40a, 64, 65).

In the summer of 1818, it was decided that more work on the Medical Hall was needed, especially the Museum. On June 23, W. E. Horner wrote to James Gibson reporting on the condition of the Museum and recommending that it be enlarged so that the exhibits could be properly shown, especially, "I allude to models in wax, they are very useful and at the same time very captivating to the Eye, but so expensive that an individual cannot conveniently purchase them."

This report was evidently promptly acted upon because the next letter was addressed to John Sergeant.

Dear Sir,

I have seen Mr. Strickland and he has no difficulty in judging of the expense of erecting the museum. He will execute it completely for $900. The real value of such a room will be very great if connected, as is contemplated with the anatomical theatre.

Very respectfully and sincerely yrs
H. H. Dorsey
Sat. 4 July 1818

As the work on the Museum progressed, more repairs were needed, and Coxe addressed a letter to the Trustees.

Gentlemen,

As Dean, I am directed to lay before you the inclosed statement of Mr. Strickland in relation to the present state of the *back* or north rooms of the Medical Building. The necessity of something being done for the absolute safety of the interior part, is too apparent to admit a doubt. It is indeed but a few days past, since a considerable portion of the ceiling in the chemical room fell down—& more will speedily follow—the latheing being rotten—and the joists having sunk considerably, so as to require temporary support. Such being the case, the Medical Faculty have no doubt the Board will see the propriety of its being immediately attended to; & under this impression, have desired me *to* ask a loan to the amount mentioned by Mr. Strickland to accomplish it. The Faculty agreeing to pay the interest for the same.

I am also directed to state the necessity the anatomical Department labours under of having a new Sink—for certain purposes necessarily connected with it. The old one being so nearly filled up, as to have become a nuisance to the premises. As far as I can learn, the expenses attending this, will not exceed one hundred dollars* and if this can also be advanced to us as a loan, the Interest will be added to the Annual payment.

As so very short a period remains before the ensuing course of Lectures, in which to accomplish the above repairs, the Medical Faculty earnestly request your Board to take some immediate steps on the occasion—or to authorize the Building committee to do what may appear requisite upon investigating the subject.

I am
Gentlemen
With greatest respect
Yr. very Obdt. Svt.
John Redman Coxe

Aug. 31, 1818

* I have just learned that Mr. Strickland estimates the expense of this at from 100 to 110 dollars.

Strickland's estimate is preserved with Coxe's letter.

Philada. Aug 31st 1818

The Medical faculty of the University of Pennsylvania

Gentlemen—

I have examined the state of the floors and Joists in the Rooms attached to the different Lecture rooms, and as far as I am able to judge of their present condition, from external appearances I think a new set of floors and Joists ought to be introduced in the first and second stories and a new floor in Dr. Dorsey's dissecting room with a gutter, lined with lead in the center. I estimate the whole cost of these repairs at 425$ including all materials.

Yours very respectfully
William Strickland

The Board of Trustees acted promptly, for on Coxe's letter is the notation "read Sept 1, 1818 request granted am. adv. $500."

1818-19

Philadelphia Custom House, west side of Second Street, below Dock Street (Plate 9B).

Reference: The National Archives, Washington, D. C. Office of the Secretary of the Treasury. Collector Small Ports, April 1, 1818—December 31, 1826, #4, 10, 22, 27, 32, 78, 83, 112, 116, 122, 128, 132, 141, 226, 241, 329, 330, 354, 356, 372. Treasury Department, Letters from the Collector at the Port of Philadelphia, June 27, 1803—December 20, 1826, III, #236-38, 242, 248, 250-52, 256, 258, 262, 268-69, 293, 296, 299. This is the correspondence of the Secretary of the Treasury, William H. Crawford, and John Steele, Collector of the Port of Philadelphia.

The correspondence concerning the proposed customhouse began in June, 1816, and concluded on June 19, 1818, when Huckles lot on Second Street was purchased.

In May, 1818, Secretary Crawford wrote Steele that Congress had allotted a sum for customhouses and asked that a plan be sent him, adding that it must include stores because "In the erection of the buildings, utility must predominate over ornament and show."

By the middle of June, Steele replied that he

had had two interviews with Strickland, but that Strickland did not give so minute a report as was wanted and that he wished to supervise the construction of the building for 5 per cent of the cost.

Had he mentioned a definite sum, I should think better of the proposition, for however fair and honorable a character Mr. S. sustains, a commission on the cost would furnish no motive for economy in the general expense of the building.

Crawford answered,

If Mr. Strickland will not agree to erect the main building for the sum estimated by him and stipulate that the materials shall be of good quality and the work executed in the best manner, it will be advisable to invite proposals without delay in the manner suggested by you. If the undertakers are masters of their business, there will be very little necessity for a superintendent—at all events the compensation demanded by Mr. Strickland is inadmissable. . . . As very extravagant prices have been asked for drawing plans of Custom Houses in other Districts, I wish to be informed what sum was paid to Mr. Strickland for the one he furnished.

By August the matter was settled. Strickland agreed to do the work under contract for the original estimate of sixteen thousand dollars. His charge for the plan of the Custom House was thirty dollars.

Work on the building went ahead during the winter of 1818-19, so that Steele could write on February 24, 1819, that the carpenters were doing so well, that the plasterers would be in by April,

and I think it due to Mr. Strickland the Architect to say that I think the whole will be finished in a manner, that will be honorable to himself and satisfying to the Government.

During the spring of 1819, there was considerable correspondence concerning a change in plan which was finally agreed upon on July 12. In August, the Secretary of the Treasury sanctioned that arches might be built over the gates in front of the customhouse provided that the expense would not exceed four hundred dollars.

The building was opened for use on December 11, 1819.

By the spring of 1823, the slate roof was leaking and a side wall was in danger of falling down. The Secretary of the Treasury directed that repairs should be made. By July 10, 1823, Strickland had been informed of the condition of the building and repaired the leak. He informed Steele that the slate roof needed to be redone and the job would cost four hundred dollars. Steele felt that the leak was due to faulty construction and that the cost of the repairs should be borne by Strickland. On the other hand, Strickland wished to be paid for the repairs.

On July 16, 1823, Crawford wrote to Steele, "the cheapest mode of determining the matter in dispute with Mr. Strickland, will be to submit it to the decision of impartial men, you are hereby authorized to pursue that course."

The roof was repaired, but the settlement of the bill was not adjusted. Crawford wrote on April 16, 1824, to inquire why the dispute with William Strickland had not been settled as directed in the letter of July 16, 1823. He directed that the matter should be settled immediately, either by paying Strickland half the expenses of repairing the defective roof of the Custom House or by referring the dispute to impartial referees. He concluded, "The adopting the new mode of slating on a public building by way of experiment is deemed to have been injudicious. P.S. Tell W.S."

Steele replied that Strickland had been out of town the past July, but on his return, they had had a conversation in which Strickland said he was not eager to take on more expense and did not want the matter brought before the public as it might injure his career.

For the reasons above stated and conceiving Mr. S. might be rather straitened than easy in his circumstances having an aged Mother to support in addition to his own family, I have felt disposed to allow him the opportunity of obtaining any indulgence or remission you might be pleased to grant him in the case.

The matter was adjusted in October, 1824. The total cost of repairing the roof was $457.34. Strickland and Steele each paid half.

Thomas Wilson, *The Picture of Philadelphia in 1824*, p. 92. The edifice is neat and in good taste.

The front of the basement story is of marble, the remainder of the exterior is of brick. In a niche in front of the attic story is a statue representing Commerce, by Rush. The design of the building was furnished by Strickland, under whose superintendence it was erected.

Plan: Rectangular building set back from the street with stores on two sides.

Materials: Marble, brick, plaster, and a slate roof.

Outstanding features: Arched gateways leading to paved area about the building. The niche in the middle of the front of the top story for the statue of Commerce by William Rush. The slate roof, with the slates applied in a new manner.

*1818-24

The Second Bank of the United States, Chestnut Street, between Fourth and Fifth streets, extending south to Library Street (Plates 6-8, 49B).

Architectural competition held: 1818.

Cornerstone laid: April 19, 1819.

Building completed: August, 1824.

Charter not renewed: April, 1836.

Assets of bank rechartered by State of Pennsylvania as United States Bank of Pennsylvania.

Building sold to the federal government: September, 1844.

Philadelphia Custom House: 1844-1932.

Restored and repaired by the Works Project Administration 1939-41.

Leased by the National Park Service to the Carl Schurz Foundation: 1941.

Reference: Manuscript material, H.S.P. (letters, canceled salary check); Tennessee State Library (page of accounts, drawings).

Contemporary accounts: *Analectic Magazine*, March, 1819; *Port Folio*, September, 1821; Philadelphia newspapers, all notices concerning the bank appeared in *The Philadelphia Gazette; Ackermann's Repository*, January, 1821; C. G. Childs, *Views in Philadelphia* (1830).

Secondary material: *Architectural Record*, LVIII (1925), 588 ff.; Fiske Kimball, "The Bank of the United States in Philadelphia." *The Pennsylvania Magazine of History and Biography*, LXVII, pp. 272-79; Agnes Addison, "William Strickland." Pp. 290-95; Agnes Addison, editor, "A Latrobe Letter in the William Jones Collection." *Journal of the American Society of Architectural Historians*, II:3, July, 1942, Agnes Addison "Latrobe vs. Strickland."

The Second Bank of the United States was chartered by the federal government for twenty years on April 10, 1816. "On March 13, 1818, Resolved that a Committee be appointed and Authorized to Purchase a Site for a Banking House." (Etting Papers, H.S.P.)

In the Philadelphia Gazette and Daily Advertiser, May 13, 1818, the following notice appeared for the first time:

Bank of the United States

May 12, 1818

Architects of science and experience, are invited to exhibit to the Board of Directors, on or before the 1st day of August next, Appropriate designs and elevations for a Banking House, to be erected on the site purchased for that purpose, bounded on the north by Chesnut and on the south by Library street, containing one hundred and fifty-one feet in width east and west, and two hundred twenty-five in depth north and south.

The ground plan will include an area of about ten or eleven thousand square feet in a rectangular figure of equal or unequal sides, as may be best adapted to the interior arrangement. The building will be faced with marble, and have a portico on each front, resting upon a basement or platform of such altitude as will combine convenience of ascent with due proportion and effect.

In this edifice, the Directors are desirous of exhibiting a chase imitation of Grecian Architecture, in its simplest and least expensive form.

Five hundred dollars will be paid for that design, which shall be approved, and two hundred dollars for the next best specimen.

By order of the Board of Directors,

Jona. Smith, Cashier.

On Wednesday, July 29, 1818, a new notice was added in the *Philadelphia Gazette* and other newspapers.

Bank of the United States,

July 28th, 1818.

Notice is Hereby Given, that the time prescribed for exhibiting to the Board of Directors "appropriate designs and elevations for a Banking House," has been extended to the 31st day of August next, ensuing, and that such as have been or may be deposited at the Bank, will remain sealed up until that day, unless called for by the artists to whom they respectively belong.

By order of the Board,
Jona. Smith, Cashier.

On Saturday, September 12, 1818, the following notice appeared in the *Philadelphia Gazette,* page 3.

The Directors of the United States Bank, have selected the plan, drawn by Mr. Strickland, of this city, to whom they have awarded the first premium —and that Mr. Latrobe's plan has been approved as the next best, to whom they have awarded the second premium.

This notice was copied in the other papers on Monday, September 14, 1818.

Five architects are known to have entered the competition, including the winners, William Strickland and Benjamin H. Latrobe. The other competitors were: Robert Mills, Hugh Bridport, and George Hadfield. There are two letters from Mills to the building committee, dated July 31 and August 31, copies of which are among the notes of Fiske Kimball. Latrobe, in a letter to Captain John Meany, mentions Bridport and Hadfield (*Pennsylvania Magazine of History and Biography,* July, 1943, pp. 290-95).

Probably John Haviland, who had recently come from England and Maxmilian Godefroy, the Frenchman who had been working in Philadelphia and Baltimore for the past decade and who designed the Baltimore Exchange with Latrobe, also entered designs.

The decision of the Board of Directors was accepted by all the contestants except Latrobe, who, when writing to Rudolph Ackermann in London two years later, stated that the bank was his design, except for the principal room, and that it was being built by one of his pupils, Mr. Strickland.

This statement, which was published in *Ackermann's Repository* (January, 1821), and copied in *The Literary Gazette* (I:16, April 21, 1821), was refuted by Strickland in the May 12 issue of the same magazine (p. 304), with the statement, ". . . the one adopted was exclusively Mr. Strickland's."

The reason for Latrobe's assertion can be learned from the letter that he wrote to Captain Meany. In it, he stated that he had seen Strickland's design which was for a Doric basement, with an entablature all the way around, and an Ionic temple above. When Latrobe wrote Meany on September 23, 1818, Strickland had been awarded the first premium and Latrobe had accepted the second one of $200. When he came to Philadelphia, Latrobe was told that Strickland had been permitted to change his design after the close of the competition and that his new—and winning—design was very like the one submitted by Latrobe.

Fiske Kimball, in his article on "The Bank of the United States 1818-1824" (*Architectural Record,* 58:2, 1925), states the reasons which at that time convinced him that the design was Latrobe's. He is still of that opinion and the National Historic Site marker on the Bank states that the "building follows in many regards Latrobe's design of 1818."

For various reasons Latrobe seems to have been mistaken in thinking that Strickland used his design, and he would have probably not have thought so if he had seen Strickland's final drawings. The similarity was that both used Doric porticoes. There were a number of differences: Strickland's plans were copied directly from the plates of Stuart and Revett's illustrations of the Parthenon in Athens (*Antiquities of Athens,* II), while Latrobe's were not. Latrobe carried the Doric frieze about the building and Strickland did not. Latrobe used a dome over the main banking room, the roof of which rose above the gable roof, while Strickland used a barrel vault which was covered by the gable roof. The arrangement of the side windows differs; Latrobe used only rectangular windows and Strickland used a semicircular window to crown the group of windows on each side of the banking room. The differences in the ground plan, Latrobe himself acknowledged.

Latrobe was justified in objecting to the fact that Strickland was given the opportunity of changing his design after the conclusion of the contest, but he was unable to complain for he had tried to do the same thing, as a drawing in the Manuscript Collection of the Historical Society of Pennsylvania shows. The notice of the competition asked for a banking house of an area of ten to eleven thousand square feet. The plans which Latrobe drew in July had an area of over 15,000 square feet. Later in September he drew a reduced plan which brought the area to 11,289.6 square feet. The exact date of Latrobe's plan is difficult to decipher. It appears to have been September 5 originally, and then to have been changed. Fiske Kimball reads the date as September 19. The matter of importance is not the exact date, but that Latrobe also tried to change his design after the first of September.

Since Latrobe did not take his complaint to William Jones, the president of the Bank, no changes were made in the award and Strickland began work immediately. On October 29, 1818, he signed a draft for twenty dollars to Samuel Haines for surveying the lot on Chestnut Street (Etting Papers, H.S.P.).

Nicholas Biddle was made a director of the Bank on January 31, 1819, and was a member of the building committee with John Connelly, James C. Fisher, and Joshua Lippincott when the cornerstone was laid on April 19, 1819. Sometimes Biddle has been credited for the choice of the Parthenon design of the Bank, but he was not a director in May, 1818, when the notice of the competition was held and which included the paragraph, "In this edifice, the Directors are desirous of exhibiting a chase imitation of Grecian Architecture, in its simplest and least expensive form." Nor was he a director when Strickland's plan was changed and selected.

In the Historical Society of Pennsylvania, there are three letters from Strickland to Lewis Coryell who supplied the lumber for the building. They are dated April 11, 1819, May 7, 1819, and May 8, 1820.

Among the Strickland papers in the Tennessee State Library is a report to the building committee giving the expenditure from April 21, 1819, to December 29, 1820, at $174,798.18, to which amount he added the estimate of $31,000 for the Library Street portico, making a total of $205,798.18. By that time the work was almost complete except for the Library Street portico and the finishing of the Chestnut Street one, which was completed in 1821 and engraved on the inner architrave of the portico in Roman letters,

A.D. 1821
W. Strickland arch^{t}
I. Struthers Mason.

When the Library Street portico was finally finished in 1824, a similar inscription was cut on the corresponding architrave. However, these letters have been recut in Victorian Gothic lettering.

The cost of the completed building is given as half a million dollars in contemporary accounts.

Description: Strickland wrote two descriptions of the Bank, the first of which was published in the *Analectic Magazine*, XIII, 3, March, 1819, accompanied by an illustration of the front elevation. The second account appeared in the *Port Folio*, September, 1821. The first paragraphs are identical, but the second description is longer and more detailed and is as follows:

Art. XIX. New Bank of the United States, in Philadelphia.
[We are indebted to the publisher of that valuable manual, "The Builder's Assistant," for the annexed representation of the interior and exterior of the splendid edifice which is described in the following article. The description is from the pen of the ingenious architect, Mr. William Strickland, by whom the plan was designed.]
In the design and proportions of this edifice, we recognize the leading features of that celebrated work of antiquity, the Parthenon at Athens. In selecting this example as a model for a building such as a bank, requiring a peculiar internal arrangement and distribution of space and light, it becomes a difficult task for an architect to preserve *all* the characteristics of a Grecian temple, whose original design and appropriation was solely for the worship of the Gods, and for the depositories of public treasure. The peripteros or flanking columns of a Grecian building produces a decidedly beautiful feature in architecture. But they cannot be applied with their proper effect to places of business, without a sacrifice of those principles which have a constant application to internal uses and economy

The design before us is of the Grecian Doric, characterised as Hypaetheros, having eight fluted columns 4 ft. 6 inches in diameter, embracing the whole front, taken from the Parthenon, or Temple of Minerva, Hecatompedon at Athens, being divested of the columns of the peripteros and pronaus, of the sculptured metopes of the frieze, and the basso-relievo figures in the Tympanum of the pediment.

The columns rise from a basement six feet in elevation supporting a plain entablature, extending along the sides of a parallelogram 86 by 160 feet including the body of the building and porticos that project ten feet six inches from each of the fronts. The vertical angle of the pediment is 152° forming an uninterrupted line from end to end of the ridge or apex of the roof.

The ascent to the porticos from the street is by a flight of six steps, to a terrace or platform, extending sixteen feet on each flank, and in front of the edifice. It is on this terrace that the building is reared, and from it derives a great portion of its effect. The gateways on the right and left, open into paved avenues, which extend from Chesnut to Library streets, along each of the flanks serving to insulate the building from the surrounding objects, it being inclosed along these avenues by a return of the iron railing exhibited in the front elevation.

This edifice is situated in a north and south direction fronting on Chesnut and Library streets.

Its length including the portico, is 161 feet, and breadth in front 87 feet. The floor of the principal or ground story is elevated nine feet, surrounded on all sides by a terrace 14 feet wide, rising three feet, and paved with large flag stones joined together. The main entrance is from Chesnut street, by a flight of marble steps extending along the whole front of the portico.

The door in the centre opens into a large vestibule with circular ends embracing the Transfer and Loan offices on the right and left, together with a commodious lobby leading to the banking room.

The vestibule ceiling is a prolonged panneled dome divided into three compartments, by bands enriched with Guilloches springing from a projecting impost containing a sunken frette.— The pavement is tessilated with American and Italian marble throughout.

The Banking room occupies the centre of the building, being 48 feet wide, having its length 81 feet, in an east and west direction, and lighted exclusively from these aspects. Its leading features present a double range of six fluted marble columns 22 inches diameter, at a distance of ten feet from the side walls, forming a screen or gallery for the clerks' desks which are placed within the intercolumniations.

The columns are of the Greek Ionic Order, with a full entablature, and blocking course on which the great central and lateral arches are supported; the central arch being semi-cylindrical is 28 feet in diameter, 81 feet in length, and subdivided into seven compartments with projecting concentric platbands over and of equal diameter with each column, the intervals being enriched with square sunken moulded pannels; this ceiling is 35 feet from the floor to the crown of the arch, executed with great precision and effect.

An Isthmian wreath, carved in one entire block of Pennsylvania white marble, surrounds the clock-face, which occupies the space of the first pannel over the entablature in the centre, the design of which is copied from the reverse of an antique gem, found at Corinth, and described by Stuart in his valuable work on the Antiquities of Athens.

The tellers' counters are composed of marble, forming panneled pedestals across each end of the banking room commencing at the first column from each of the end walls.

The stockholders' room is a parallelogram of 28 feet by 50 feet, being lighted from the south front, having a groin arched ceiling, with projecting platbands, enriched with the Guilloches springing near the base of the groin angle, across the semi-circular intrados of the arch. Each end of the room is ornamented with niches eight feet wide, the heads of which form an architrave concentric with the semi-circular pannels in the tympanum of the shortest diameter.

The committee rooms from the stockholders', open right and left, flanked by two flights of marble stairs, leading to the clock chamber, and the other apartments in the second story. The private stairway from the banking room leads to the directors', engravers', and copper-plate printers' rooms being lighted from the roof by a plain convex glass light, 20 inches in diameter, and six inches thick, manufactured in Boston by Messrs. Jarvis & Co., the light being inserted in a marble curb, is placed on the apex of a cone which perforates the arch above the stairway.

All the internal door jambs, sills, and imposts are

of marble. The fireplaces are principally under the windows, and formed within the thickness of the external walls, and covered with thick cast-iron plates.
The banking room is amply warmed by two cast-iron furnaces, lined with fire-brick, being simply erected within an airchamber, through which the external atmosphere passes and becomes heated by the furnace, it then rises through the arch into a circular cast-iron pedestal, perforated on the sides, out of which it is suffered to escape into the room.
The whole body of the building is arched in a bomb-proof manner from the cellar to the roof, which is covered with copper. All the groin arches are girdled at the springing line with iron straps, passing round within the body of the division walls.
It may be here practically useful to observe, that all buildings of a public nature, should be thus constructed, as the only safe-guard against the ravages of the incendiary, and the no less fatal but inevitable attacks of time.

Alterations were made, under Strickland's supervision, when the Bank was rechartered as the United States Bank of Pennsylvania in 1837. Many more extensive changes were made during the years that the building was a Custom House. Gas, water, and stairs were introduced and additional doors cut in the upper story. Few changes were made in the walls since the basement walls are six feet thick, and those of the upper stories, two feet.

During the most recent alterations completed in 1940 by the federal government under the Works Project Administration, an attempt was made to restore the interior to its original design as described in the foregoing article and accompanying illustrations.

Style:

Greek Revival: The features which were taken from Greek architecture are the two porticoes, the moldings about the doors, windows of the façades, the Ionic colonnades in the banking room, the decoration of the ceiling of the vestibule and the banking room, and the ornamentation around the clock. The window arrangement on the side walls is late Georgian. Most of the windows are plain, long rectangular sash-windows. On the interior, the introduction of the oval vestibule is Georgian. The other rooms, square or rectangular, are utilitarian in design.

Plan:

A cross axis was used. The north and south axis divides the building symmetrically, with only one exception which is the flight of stairs on the right between the lobby and the president's room. The transverse axis is from east to west across the center of the banking room and defined by the crown of the barrel vault which roofs it. This does not make a symmetrical division since a different arrangement of rooms was needed at the two ends.

Materials:

The building is constructed primarily of a pleasing Pennsylvania marble, white with blue veins, which weathers well. It is called Chestnut Hill marble and came from the Marble Hall quarry near Flourtown. Stone was used in the foundation. Brick was used for the inside walls, barrel, and groin vaults of the ceilings. Wood was used for the rafters of the roof, and copper for the roofing. Iron was used to reinforce the arches. The inside walls were plastered. The floors of the vestibule, lobby, and banking room were of marble; the other floors, of wood.

Outstanding features:

On the exterior, the exceptional features are the Doric porticoes with eight fluted columns. That they were consciously copied, even in small detail from the porticoes of the Parthenon, as illustrated in the plates of Stuart and Revett, make them an important landmark in the development of the Greek Revival style in this country. Equally important, is the plain gable roof which gives the building the Greek temple silhouette. On the interior, the chief remarkable feature is the large transverse banking room which is roofed by a barrel vault, supported by a colonnade of six Ionic columns on either side. Other noteworthy features are the placing of the fireplaces under the windows and the use of sash weights in the windows.

1819

Estimate of belfry for the University of Pennsylvania.

Reference:

MSS University Papers, XI:25. Library of the University.

Philadelphia, May 3rd 1819.

Nicholas Biddle Esqr.
Sir,
I have considered the subject of a bellfrey for the University Building. The situation of the present skylight would perhaps be the best place for it as to the appearance & utility—but this plan would be attended with very considerable expense & alteration of the Roof in the centre— I suggest to your consideration the propriety of converting the large window over the door of entrance on Ninth Street into a niche and to hang the bell in the head so as to be rung from the passage inside— The bell itself will be hid by a blind on the front, affording a proper escape for the sound and may be heard a very considerable distance. This will be unquestionably the cheapest plan, and will not cost more than 200$.

Yours very respectfully,
William Strickland Archt

1819

Plan of the Custom House at New Orleans.
Reference:

Office of the Secretary of the Treasury, Collectors of Small Ports, April 1, 1818–December 31, 1826. The National Archives, Washington, D. C. (#152, 160, 161, 170, 176, 177, 208, 214).

On December 10, 1819, the Secretary of the Treasury, William H. Crawford, wrote to John Steele, the Collector at Philadelphia, to acknowledge a letter of November 23, which was

accompanied by Mr. Strickland's plan of a Custom House to be erected at New Orleans, which upon inspection meets my entire approbation.
Being desirous of availing myself of the knowledge which Mr. Strickland and yourself have acquired in such matters, I will thank you in conjunction with that Gentleman to frame an advertisement inviting proposals until the first of Feb'y ensuing for the constructing of a building in the course of the ensuing spring and summer in conformity with the plan lately received from you, and which is returned by this conveyance.

He said that the advertisement should appear "twice a week in newspapers in which laws of the U.S. are published and in one Gazette of most extensive circulation until 1st of Feb'y ensuing," also that it should appear in Boston and Baltimore. He wished a copy of the advertisement and of all proposals received to be sent to his office. All expenses, "Mr. Strickland's service, the Printer's bills, postage, etc." were to be paid by Steele. He recommended adding three feet to the basement story and noted that "Mr. Strickland said nothing about a firm foundation." (#152)

On January 6, 1820, Crawford wrote that "people have said that the foundation should not be dug more than two feet owing to softness of ground and that rough casting will not last more than a year." He wished Steele to ask Strickland what the deduction should be for only two feet of digging and omitting the roughcast and also "if in estimate he intends that all exterior walls be of what is called *Front Brick*?" (#160)

On January 8, Crawford again wrote, requesting the return of Strickland's plans and description, stating, "people say that the basement is too low and not enough support for fireproofs." (#161)

On April 1, 1820, Crawford sent to Beverly Chew, the Collector at New Orleans, a copy of the contract with Major Joseph Jenkins for the Custom House at New Orleans which was to be erected on the site chosen by Chew who was to act as agent. The contract was carefully worded with "ample bond for good performance," and the new building was to "combine every convenience with durability." (#170)

Crawford notified Chew on May 25 that by an Act of Congress of May 15, "an addition to the Custom house is to be used as the district court of the United States." Mr. Jenkins was to make the addition and there was to be no communication between the two. (#176, 177)

On December 15, 1820, fifty thousand dollars was sent. (#208)

By March 3, 1821, the building was completed and the two thousand dollars which had not been spent, Secretary of the Treasury William H. Crawford, recommended should be applied toward the cost of the lot.

1819-20

Rebuilding of Masonic Hall, north side of Chestnut Street, between Seventh and Eighth streets. (Plate 11)

Damaged by fire: March 9, 1819.

Dedicated: November 20, 1820.

Used as a Masonic Hall until 1835; then bought by the Franklin Institute and used for an exhibition hall.

Demolished: 1855.

Reference: Norris S. Barratt and Julius F. Sachse, *Freemasonry in Pennsylvania,* III (1835-55).

Color print published by S. Kennedy in June, 1819, showing "The conflagration of the Masonic Hall—9 March 1819, painted by S. Jones, figures by I. L. Krummell, engraved by J. Hill and dedicated to the Fire Engine Hose Companies." Print Collection, H.S.P.

Woodcut showing the building without the steeple, H.S.P.

Photograph taken about 1851, H.S.P.

The wooden steeple, 180 feet high, and all the interior fittings burned; the brick walls remained intact. The building was rebuilt, following the original plans.

1819-20

Indigent Widows' and Single Women's Home, north side of Cherry Street, lot 54 feet 8 inches by 134 feet. (Plate 13)

Reference: Reports and minutes of the Indigent Widows' and Single Women's Society of Philadelphia. The residents moved into the brick building in the spring of 1820. The minutes state that Strickland's first plans were on too large a scale and had to be reduced. It was constructed at a cost of about ten thousand dollars.

The National Archives, Washington, D. C., Naval Records.

PN—Philadelphia Naval Asylum. Letter from Robert Ralston to the Secretary of the Navy, Philadelphia, November 1, 1826. Ralston wrote to recommend Strickland for his "skill, good judgment, punctuality and fidelity." Ralston had been in charge of all the payments for the Asylum which had been "constructed and erected" under Strickland's direction. A view of it is in C. G. Childs *Views in Philadelphia* (1830).

Style: Late Georgian with arches, windows, and doors on the ground floor, and a cupola on top; three-story, square building.

Materials: Brick and wood.

1820

Church of the Moravians, or United Brethren. Broad Street or Moravian Alley, between Second and Third streets, near Race Street. (Plate 9C)

Demolished: 1856.

Reference: Thomas Wilson, *Picture of Philadelphia in 1824,* p. 54. ". . . a very neat edifice erected from a design by Strickland."

Brinton Coxe, "Views in Philadelphia," #34, a collection of prints, H.S.P.

1820

Estimate for a block of stores in connection with Paul Beck's proposal for renovating the Delaware water front.

Reference: *Hazard's Register of Pennsylvania,* XI, 15-16. January, 1833.

"A Proposal for Altering the Eastern Front of the City of Philadelphia with a view to prevent the recurrence of Malignant Disorders, on a Plan conformable to the Original Design of William Penn, by Paul Beck, Jr., 1820." His arguments in favor of this proposal were that yellow fever could be stopped only by changing the east end of the city; that he knew the feasibility of the plan, having transacted business in Water Street for nearly forty years; that it was a good time to do it as prices were down and money plentiful; that it would furnish employment; that "it would remove many dram-shops and other immoral nuisances; it would materially lessen the risk from fire; and in fine, it would make Philadelphia the handsomest of cities." The cost of the purchase of the land between Vine and Spruce streets, including the east side of Front Street to the Delaware, he estimated at three million dollars. To incite his fellow-citizens, he noted that about fifty gentlemen in Boston had subscribed half a million dollars for a wharf. To pay the interest on the investment, he suggested having stores built and using the rents. For that part of the plan,

he called upon Strickland who provided a statement which was also printed.

The following is an estimate of the cost of one block of stores, size 40 by 100 feet, 2½ stories high.

Logs for foundations	$200
Laying 200,000 bricks including lime and sand	800
Slate 4 squares	820
Carpenter's work	1,500
Plank for floors	400
Blacksmith's work including fireproofs	2,000
Ironmongery and nails	400
Painting and glazing	500
Roughcast the fronts on the river and on New Front street	230
Stone-cutter's work at heads and sills	300
Digging out foundations	300
Total cost of a block 40 by 100 feet	$7,450
One half of a store 20 by 100 feet	3,750
number of stores	132
Net cost of 132 stores	$495,000
The following is an estimate of the total cost of pulling down old buildings and cleaning 50 millions of bricks, allowing ten millions to be broken and unfit for use	$65,000
Removing and hauling rubbish, filling up old cellars, etc.	8,000
Building stone wall along the bank on east line of Front Street from Dock to Vine	18,000
Iron railing along the east line of Front Street	15,000
Brick and stone paving and regulating wharves and street	50,000
	$156,000
Total cost	$651,000

(Signed) William Strickland, Architect.

1820-22

Chesnut Street Theatre, or New Theatre, Chestnut Street between Sixth and Seventh streets. (Plate 12A, B)

Demolished: 1856.

References: Three drawings, H.S.P. (The old theatre burned down on Easter Sunday, April 2, 1820. New shares for six hundred dollars were issued and sold.) The first drawing is inscribed, "Proposed Design for the rebuilding of the front of the Philada Theatre. Scale ½ of an inch to the foot. William Strickland Archt. Philada. May 2nd, 1820." In the central section this design differs from the one built which has a small entrance with four Tuscan columns and three round-headed windows in the second story with rectangular depressions above, crowned by a pediment. The second drawing is inscribed "Ground plan of the Theatre Chesnut Street and adjoining buildings." It shows a recessed portico with five columns, with the lobby, pit, and stage behind. To the right, the Green Room and to the left, along Sixth Street, a store, an auction room, an engine house, and a tavern.

The third drawing is signed "William Strickland Archt. Scale ¼ of an inch to the foot." It is a drawing of the façade as it was built with a loggia of five arched openings in the central part, a colonnade of four Corinthian columns, two pilasters above and a horizontal roof line, with niches in the upper part of the flanks for the statues by William Rush of Tragedy and Comedy.

One drawing, Ridgway Library, in the scrapbooks of Philadelphia, VII, 93. Inscribed as follows: "Plan of the foundation walls of the New Theatre. Scale ⅛ of an inch to the foot. William Strickland Archt. Philada. March 25th, 1822."

Thomas Wilson, *Picture of Philadelphia in 1824,* p. 195. The theatre opened on December 2, 1822. Size 92 by 150 feet. Seating Capacity: 2,000. It was possible to discharge the most crowded audience in less than three minutes.

This theatre, which combines beauty and convenience with great security, was designed and executed in 1822 by William Strickland, to whose taste and skill Philadelphia is indebted by the Bank of the United States, the church of St. Stephen's and many other of its most classical architectural ornaments.

Scharf and Wescott, *History of Philadelphia,* III (1793).

Its columns Corinthian, in Italy sculptured,
Attest how the arts mongst ourselves have been cultured;
Fluted off and got up without flaw or disaster,

What a shame they omitted to flute the pilaster;
Their arrangement is neat, and supporting—but, rot it,
A pediment, only the builder forgot it!
—Microsmus Philadelphicus

Philadelphia in 1830 (Carey and Hart), pp. 140-42.

The principle front . . . is of marble, in the Italian style. Its leading features are an arcade, supporting a screen of composite columns and a plain entablature, and flanked by two wings. These are decorated with niches, containing statues of Tragedy and Comedy, which are justly considered the best productions from the chisel of Rush; and immediately below them are semi-circular recesses, with basso relievos representing the tragic and comic Muses. The approach to the boxes is from Chesnut Street, through an arcade of five entrances, opening into a vestibule 58 feet long by 8 feet wide, communicating at each end with the box-office and a withdrawing room. Screen doors, immediately opposite and corresponding to the entrances of the arcade, lead from the vestibule into spacious lobbies, warmed by fireproof furnaces, and capable of containing a thousand persons: from these, two flights of large staircases conduct to the lobbies of the second and third floors, and to a splendid saloon and coffee-rooms on the second floor.
The audience part of the house is described on a semi-circle of 46 feet in diameter, containing three rows of boxes, resting on cast-iron columns, and secured with iron sockets, from the foundation to the dome; the whole being combined laterally with a strong wall, bounding the lobbies and supporting the roof. The dress-circle of the boxes is formed by a seat on a line with the columns, covered with a canopy, in the style of the Covent Garden theatre, London. The peculiar form of this part of the house places the mass of the audience within 35 feet of the stage, securing to them the important objects of distinct sound and perfect scenic view.
The dome is 46 feet in diameter, rising 6 feet to the crown, which is perforated and formed into a ventilator.

1821

Plans for the Eastern Penitentiary.

Reference: Richard Vaux, *Brief Sketch of the Origin and History of the State Penitentiary for the Eastern District of Pennsylvania at Philadelphia* (1872). Extracts of minutes of Commissioners to build Penitentiary at Philadelphia (pp. 53-55). At the meeting on July 3, 1821, the

Board opened plans for Pennitentiary in pursuance of the resolution of the Board of May 11, 1821. The architects who submitted plans were as follows: Charles Loss, Jr., of New York; William Strickland, John Haviland and Samuel Webb of Philadelphia. The plan submitted by John Haviland was selected.

1821-23

Survey of a route for the Chesapeake and Delaware Canal.

Reference: *Early Proceedings of the American Philosophical Society* (Philadelphia, 1884).

Communication from the Chesapeake and Delaware Canal Company; and a Report and Estimate of William Strickland, to the President and Directors (Philadelphia: Joseph R. A. Skerrett, 1823).

Plan and longitudinal section of a canal from Christiana Creek to Ogle Road, surveyed for the Chesapeake and Delaware Canal Company, August, September, October, 1823. (In the manuscript collection of the Tennessee Historical Society.)

Hazard's Register of Pennsylvania, I, 415.

Proceedings of the American Philosophical Society, VI, 28.

On September 10, 1821, the American Philosophical Society appointed William Strickland, Dr. Patterson, J. G. Biddle, Reuben Haines, Dr. James Mease, E. J. Du Pont, of Delaware, John Adlum and Dr. De Butts, of Maryland, "to examine and explore the shortest and most practicable route for a Canal connecting the waters of the Chesapeake and the Delaware, view being had to the possibility of sloop navigation." One hundred dollars was appropriated for the use of the committee.

A new canal company was formed in 1822 and various engineers were consulted before the plan by John Randel, Jr. was adopted. Strickland presented a report to the president and directors of the company, dated July 22, 1822, on his survey of the route from Newbold's landing opposite Pea Patch Fort, to Back Creek, a distance of fourteen miles and the shortest distance possible. He suggested a canal 8 feet deep and 60 feet wide, with 16 locks, each 80 feet long and 20 feet wide, with lifts not exceeding 8 feet. On the following day (July 23, 1822) Strickland completed an estimate of the cost, exclusive of feeders or reservoirs.

Digging canal, embankments, side drains
and puddling at $20,000
per mile, say 14 miles 280,000
Building 16 locks at $10,000 160,000
and many other items bringing total to ...$702,000

In the manuscript collection of the Tennessee Historical Society, there is a handsome working drawing of a proposed route for the canal. It is entitled "Surveyed for the Chesapeake and Delaware Canal Company August–September–October 1823 By William Strickland Esqr. Joseph H. Siddall, Surveyor. Scale 2 chains to the Inch."

The drawing gives both the topographical plan of the canal and the longitudinal section. The medium is water color and ink on several sheets of lightweight water-color paper, backed on a continuous strip of muslin, 32 feet long. Each sheet is 21¾ inches in height.

This survey gives more than half of the proposed route, for it shows a little more than eight miles of the canal from its beginning where Mill Creek goes into Christiana Creek, past Newport and past the road to Prince's Mill, which is the eight-mile point to Ogletown Road.

(Note: The surveyor's chain is 66 feet, or 80 chains to a mile.)

Strickland's survey was not used. Judge John K. Kane mentioned it in his obituary of Strickland for the American Philosophical Society. "He made in 1824 a reconnaissance for the Chesapeake and Delaware Canal; and projected one of the routes across the Peninsula: I was a director of the Canal Company at the time; and I never doubted, and there are few who doubt now, that it was the best route proposed."

(Note: Kane in this instance, as in many others, was inaccurate in the date.)

*1822-23

St. Stephen's Episcopal Church, Tenth Street, between Market and Chestnut streets. (Plate 10)

Cornerstone laid: May 30, 1822, by Bishop White.
Consecrated: February 27, 1823.

Enlarged on the north side in 1878, and in 1918, the gallery on the south side was taken down to conform to the north side.

Reference: Box of papers in the Parish House, relating to the history of the church. The first meeting of the building committee was on April 17, 1822, when it was decided to employ William Strickland, architect; Daniel Groves, master-mason; John Struthers, marble-mason; J. O'Neill, master-carpenter.

C. G. Childs, *Views in Philadelphia* (1830). Description and plate.

An oil painting showing the original arrangement of the interior in the chapel of the Burd School, Forty-third Street and Baltimore Avenue.

Style: Early American Gothic. There is an attempt to use all the characteristic features of medieval architecture without any understanding of Gothic construction. The Gothic forms used are the towers, pointed windows and doors, clustered piers, and the effect of vaulting on the ceiling.

Plan: Georgian meeting house with galleries on three sides.

Area: 102 by 55 feet, with an elevation of 60 feet. The two towers increase the frontage to 61 feet. The towers are 86 feet high.

Materials: Stained glass from England. Front and towers of gray stone; walls, roughcast brick; interior, plastered; roof, wood gable high over ceiling of auditorium.

Outstanding feature: Stone and brick foundation in excellent condition; many of the rafters still intact.

1822-25

Mikveh-Israel (Hope of Israel) Synagogue, north side of Cherry Street above Third Street. (Plate 18B)

Cornerstone laid: September 26, 1822.
Building dedicated: January 21, 1825.
Demolished: 1860.

Reference: Archives of the Mikveh-Israel Synagogue. A small notebook, entitled "Hebrew Congregation," contains copies of the minutes of the building committee.

Thomas Wilson, *Picture of Philadelphia for 1824* (Philadelphia: T. Town, 1823), p. 55. "... principal entrance through an elevated door-way formed with inclined jambs, supporting a large coved cornice, in which is sculptured the globe and wings . . ."

Philadelphia in 1830 (Philadelphia: Carey and Hart, 1830), pp. 47-48. The interior embraces two semicircular blocks of seats, displaying to the north and south of the *ark and altar.* The dome is supported by Egyptian columns copied from the temple at Tentyra, and is formed by semicircular archivolts, joining a richly paneled segment, extending over the ark and altar.

In the centre of the dome is a lantern, which gives light to the altar.

The ark is situated in the east side, immediately opposite the altar, and is neatly decorated with pilasters, supporting a coved cornice, enriched with the globe and wings, together with a marble tablet, containing the Ten Commandments in Hebrew. It is approached by a flight of three steps between check-blocks which support two handsome tripods, crowned with lamps.

The galleries are semicircular, extending around the north and south sides of the building, and are supported by columns which extend to the dome.

History: The members of the building committee were Simon Gratz, John Moss, Hyman Marks, and Joseph Gratz. On August 30, 1822, Solomon Moses was added. At the meeting on September 6, 1822, it was "Resolved to engage the services of William Strickland" and he was ordered to begin work. It was agreed that the architect should receive 5 per cent of the cost with the understanding that the building should not cost more than eight thousand dollars.

On September 26, 1822, instead of laying one cornerstone, four were laid: southwest, John Moss; southeast, Hyman Gratz; northeast, Jacob I. Cohen; northwest, Isaac Moses. A copperplate was deposited, engraved by William Kneass, on which were the following names: "William Strickland, Architect; Daniel Groves, Master Mason; Samuel Baker, Master Carpenter."

At the dedication of the building in 1825, many prominent people attended including Bishop White and judges of the Supreme Court.

Style: Egyptian Revival. That is, the basic form is Georgian, but Egyptian details are added.

Plan: Rectangular, 40 by 70 feet. The auditorium, with galleries on three sides, is lighted by a lantern over the center of the dome.

Materials: Falls of Schuylkill stone.

Cost: In the minutes of the building committee on January 7, 1825, it is recorded that $8,884.35 had been collected for the building fund and that $8,693.33 had been spent. On January 21, it is added that there are outstanding bills amounting to $3,000. The cost in secondary works is given as $16,000.

Outstanding features: The use of Egyptian ornament, and the semicircular arrangement of the interior.

1823(?)

Ink sketches of chairs, now in the possession of Philip Strickland Harper, Chicago.

The inscription on the paper is "Design for the Gothic Chair—St. Stephens Church." It is not signed or dated. The handwriting and drawing may be Strickland's, if it were done in a great hurry.

There are two front elevations and one side elevation of the chairs. The backs are pointed with crockets, surmounted by a cross. All are armchairs with cusping on the underside of the support of the seat. The seat and back were to be upholstered in purple velvet. One design has a central light on the back, the other has two lights.

1823

Building for the Orphans' Society of Philadelphia, Eighteenth and Race streets. (Plate 13)

Reference: Records of the Department of the Navy, Office of Naval Records and Library, PN—Naval Asylum, Philadelphia; construction. Letter of Robert Ralston to the Secretary of the Navy, November 1, 1826.

Childs, *Views in Philadelphia,* description and plate.

Note: The Society was founded in 1814, incorporated in 1816, and the first building was completed in 1818. It was destroyed by fire on January 24, 1822. A description and view of the asylum are to be found in *Port Folio* (5th series), IX (1820), 147. There is no mention of Strickland in connection with this first building, but since he rebuilt the asylum after the fire, it is likely that he designed the first building also.

*1824

Alterations at "Wyck," Germantown, Pennsylvania.

Present address: 6026 Germantown Avenue, Philadelphia 44. Now the home of Mr. and Mrs. Robert B. Haines 3rd, who have furnished the following material.

Reference: Five ground plans in the possession of Mr. and Mrs. Haines.

1. Ground floor plan before 1824.
2. Ground floor plan of proposed alterations in 1821.
3. Proposed alterations upstairs, 1821.
4. West end of ground floor, as altered in 1824.
5. West end of upper story, as altered in 1824.

None of these drawings are by Strickland. It is possible that the last four were done by Samuel Honeyman Kneass, who was a pupil in Strickland's office at that time.

Letter from Reuben Haines to his wife Jane B. Haines, dated Germantown, 5 mo. 23rd, 1824, in the possession of Mr. and Mrs. Haines.

When thee ran away and left me to get through with the repairs as well as I could without thee I determined not to let thee know how we were getting along [but] I have concluded to make the repairs more extensive than I first contemplated. . . . I am encouraged to go on, and can find no satisfactory stopping place short of laying a new lower floor from one end of the house to the other. The dining room floor was so bad that Wm. Lehman wonders we did not get into the cellar. The Hall was so bad that *not one single foot of sound joice remained and the whole could have easily passed through a sieve* ! ! ! . . . The joice under the front parlour were rotten in my father's time . . . and I feel little inclination to "patch the patches." Whenever the front parlour floor comes up I have always contemplated pulling down the chimney, putting it up where the front middle window is and removing that to where the closet is. I had thought to have left this part of the plan to be executed next year but many things conspire to render the present time more desirable. . . . Wm. Lehman who is almost unexceptionable will remain by me until it is done, and he is carpenter, mason and stone cutter as occasion requires. . . . We have concluded to put up *no partition* in the dining room but *two windows* on the garden similar to those in front making the dining room 16 feet by 26. *Thy closets* will be those of the front parlour removed into the kitchen against the partition of the dining room. A door could be made into it through the partition, but it would spoil the symmetry to dining room. We have a folding door cut through the wall of the hall opposite the niche, another is to be cut into the entry and another into the front parlour, the two latter so arranged as to meet together across the entry, cut the stairs off on one side and a vestibule on the other, and throw the parlour, Hall and dining room into one complete suite of rooms. This plan is due to Strickland who was up to see us last week. Everything will be done as cheap as possible and as plain as consistency will require.

These alterations are still to be seen at Wyck. Further alterations have been made, and the former kitchen is the present dining room. The arrangement of the folding doors is of great ingenuity and is a nineteenth-century forerunner of the present *plan libre*, the adaptability of interior space.

All these alterations are in perfect harmony with the building which dates to the end of the seventeenth and middle of the eighteenth century.

Note: William Lehman's name appears as one of the subscribers to the *Reports on Canals, Railways, Roads, etc.*, where he is designated as a Civil Engineer. He was in charge of the Raritan Canal.

1824

Design for a Masonic Hall, Germantown (not constructed).

Reference: Front elevation and ground plan, signed "William Strickland Archt," not dated, in the possession of Mr. and Mrs. Robert B. Haines 3rd, "Wyck," Germantown, Pennsylvania. In 1824, Reuben Haines, owner of "Wyck," purchased a lot south of his property with a one-hundred-foot frontage on Main Street, Germantown, opposite Haines Street, from Christopher Mason, to be transferred to the Masons of Hiram Lodge as a site for a hall. Two hundred dollars was raised towards the new building and the basement was built and used for parties until it became evident in 1833 that no more money was to be contributed. Reuben Haines died in 1831, and he appears to have been an influential backer of the project. This is strange since he was a Quaker, but he may have been influenced by Strickland who was always closely affiliated with the Masons.

Description: The drawing is an excellent example of Strickland's work. The scale is 3/16 of an inch to the foot. The façade is a Greek temple type with four Doric columns raised on a base with central steps, a Doric frieze, and a 14 degree pediment ornamented by a rayed, rising sun. The front wall behind the portico has a central door and recessed areas of the same side on either side to break the monotony and to insure symmetry. The upper wall is ornamented by three square plaques, carved with open laurel wreaths, tied with bows at the bottom and enclosing the emblems of the Masons, a plumb bob on the left, the calipers and square in the center, and the plane on the right. The height of the base is 3 feet, the columns 21 feet, and the entablature 7 feet, making a total elevation of 31 feet from the ground to the cornice.

The ground plan shows a rectangular building 37 feet wide by 78 feet long, or 87 feet 6 inches with the portico. The diameter of the columns is 3 feet 6 inches at the base. The depth of the portico is 6 feet. The walls are all 2 feet thick. There are six windows on either side and one large one at the back. The front door leads into a hall 8 feet wide, with a flight of stairs and a committee room, 12 feet by 11 feet, on the right. On the left is a room with a large fireplace, labeled the "Withdrawing Room," 12 feet by 21 feet. At the back is the room for public meetings, 34 feet wide by 52 feet long. (It would appear that the side walls must be 1½ feet in width.)

*1824

Musical Fund Society Hall, south side of Locust Street, between Eighth and Ninth streets. (Plate 14A)

Cornerstone laid: May 25, 1824.

Building completed: December 24, 1824.

First concert given in Hall: December 29, 1824.

Enlarged and remodeled by N. LeBrun in 1847 at a cost of $5,000.

The Musical Fund Society sold the Hall to Yahn and McDonnell in 1942. The firm altered the building in 1945 to serve as a warehouse, display room, and offices.

Reference: The archives of the Musical Fund Society are now kept in the Society's office in the Public Ledger Building.

The Musical Fund Society of Philadelphia (1930). "1824, May 1. The site of the Musical Fund Hall was the Fifth Presbyterian Church purchased for $7,500. and the alterations necessary to transform the church into a Hall were done under the superintendence and plan of Wm. Strickland, one of the members of the Society."

Annals of Music in Philadelphia and History of the Musical Fund Society, compiled by Louis C. Madeira, edited by Philip H. Goepp (1896). Strickland was a member of the building committee, as well as architect for the Hall. The Society recorded that "he executed his important trust with the greatest faithfulness and ability." A newspaper account of the building (p. 99) stated that it "does honor to the taste of Mr. Strickland, an architect of whom Philadelphia may be justly proud."

The National Gazette and Literary Register, Philadelphia, Saturday, August 21, 1824. "A Communication of the Musical Fund Society's Hall," signed "S," gives a description of the building and states that the "raising of the rafters for the roof was accomplished on Thursday the 12th inst.," and concludes with this paragraph, "Great care has been taken to have the best materials and workmanship, and from the acknowledged skill and talents of the architect, the public may feel every security in the stability of the building."

Style: Stripped Classic.

Plan: Area: 140 by 60 feet, set back 15 feet from the street. Two stories and basement. First floor: 13 feet high with four rooms; back one 57 by 30 feet, for rehearsals and practice; west room 63 by 23 feet; entry 9 feet. In front, a vestibule from which two great stairways ascended to the saloon that occupied the entire second floor. It was 26 feet high.

Materials: Roughcast brick and wood.

Outstanding feature: The roof of the main hall which is covered with a flattened segmental vault which insures excellent audibility. It is covered with a wooden, gable roof.

1824

Mariners Church, 332 South Front Street.

Reference: Records of the Department of the Navy, Office of Naval Records and Library, PN—Naval Asylum, Philadelphia; construction. The National Archives, Washington, D. C. A letter to the Secretary of the Navy from Robert Ralston, dated Philadelphia, November 1, 1826.

Three large buildings, the Orphan Asylum, the Indigent Widows' and Single Women's Asylum, and the Mariners Church have been constructed and erected under his direction, in each of which, I have had to make all the payments, and consequently have derived information which enables me to bear testimony to the skill, good judgments, punctuality, and fidelity of Mr. Strickland.

Letter of Thos. G. MacInnes to Roberts Vaux, dated April 30, 1824, in which he expresses gratification over the laying of the cornerstone of the Mariners Church. (Reference given by Miss Catharine H. Miller of the Manuscript Department of the H.S.P.)

1824

Triumphal Arches erected for Lafayette's visit to Philadelphia, September, 1824. (Plate 50)

Note: Thirteen arches were erected in Philadelphia in honor of Lafayette, all designed and constructed by Strickland, aided by his pupil Samuel Honeyman Kneass. The most important arch was on Chestnut Street opposite the old State House.

Reference: *Port Folio* (Series 5, October, 1824), XVIII, 335-36.

Grand Civic Arch. This arch displayed great taste and judgment in the design, and skill in the execution. It was constructed of frame work covered with canvas, admirably painted in imitation of stone. The plan was derived from the triumphal arch of Septimus Severus at Rome. Its dimensions were forty-five feet front by twelve in depth—embracing a basement story of the Doric order, from which the principal arch springs to the height of twenty-four feet above the pavement. The spandrels, or abutments on each front were decorated with figures of Fame, painted in basso relievo, having their arms extended, and mutually holding a civic wreath over the key-stone of the arch. The wings on each side of the centre, were of the Ionic order, being decorated with niches and statues representing liberty, victory, independence and plenty—each having appropriate mottos, inscribed in corresponding pannels. The whole of the building was surmounted by an entablature, thirty-eight feet from the pavement and supporting a flight of steps in the centre, upon which were placed the arms of the city, executed in a masterly manner by Sully. On each side of the arms were placed the statues of Justice and Wisdom, with their appropriate emblems, sculptured by Mr. Rush, in a very superior style. They had all the beauty and lightness of drapery, of the Grecian school; and so excellent was the workmanship, that it was not until after positive assurances, that a spectator would give up the belief that they were executed in marble. The arch was designed by Mr. Strickland, and executed under the direction of Messrs. Warren, Darley, and Jefferson, scene painters of the new Theatre. The superficial surface of painted canvas amounted to upwards of three thousand square feet.

1824

Decoration of Room in State House for the Reception of General Lafayette.

Reference: *National Gazette,* Philadelphia, August 21, 1824. Names of the twelve members of the committee on arrangements is given, including Strickland. "We understand that a committee of the City Councils have directed the Room in the State House, in which the Declaration of Independence was signed, to be fitted up, under the direction of Mr. S., as a Levee Room for General Lafayette."

1824

Decorations for the Grand Ball in honor of General Lafayette, held September 28, 1824, in the New Theatre (The Chesnut Street Theatre, designed by Strickland in 1820 and completed in 1822).

Reference: *Port Folio* (Series 5, October, 1824), XVIII, 336. "Those who came to the house early were at once struck with the floor, which was brilliantly painted for the occasion, from designs furnished by Mr. Strickland."

1824-28

Crawford County Court House, Meadville, Pennsylvania, erected on the Diamond, or Public Square. (Plate 14B)

Demolished: 1868.

Reference: John E. Reynolds of Meadville, author of *In French Creek Valley* (1938) and an authority on the history of that region, furnished the above information and the illustration of the courthouse; a newspaper reproduction of the woodcut made from a drawing by Sherman Day in 1840 which was printed in the *History of Pennsylvania* (1840). That the Doric building with a cupola is of the Court House is verified by a pencil sketch drawn by Mr. Reynolds' father. Mr. Reynolds added that the Strickland building was the third courthouse in Crawford County and the first one to be built of brick.

National Gazette, Philadelphia, July 10, 1824. A letter from Meadville dated January 5, 1824, gives an account of Mr. Strickland's plans and the difficulties in the way of starting construction and concludes by saying, "We feel truly indebted to the liberality and kindness of Mr. Strickland in this distinguished mark of attention."

Hazard's Register of Pennsylvania, III (January, 1829), 10.

Meadville, Crawford Co., Pa.
Immediately fronting the square, on the east, is the Courthouse, which, in point of beauty, convenience and workmanship, is not surpassed by any in the state. The *plan* was gratuitously furnished by our distinguished Architect, Mr. Strickland of Philadelphia. Its walls are of brick and cut stone and it is adorned by a handsome cupola.

1825

Map for the Committee on Inland Navigation, Canal Documents, 1825.

Reference: *Hazard's Register of Pennsylvania,* I, 164.

1825

Consultant engineer for the Delaware and Raritan Canal.

Reference: *Hazard's Register of Pennsylvania,* II (December, 1828), 323.

Report from the Commission on Inland Navigation in the Delaware and Raritan Canal. Letter from Strickland, giving his opinion, dated Philadelphia, January 27, 1825.

1825

Note: A pamphlet of 28 pages entitled *Internal Improvement, Railroads, Canals, Bridges, Etc.,* dated Philadelphia, March 15, 1825 (which formerly belonged to H. D. Gilpin, and is now in the New York Public Library), has been tentatively ascribed to William Strickland, but internal evidence proves that it cannot have been written by him. It is a noteworthy pamphlet as it contains the first printed suggestion for a transcontinental railway, seven years before Carver's similar suggestion which appeared in an article in the *New York Courier and Inquirer.* However, the author of the pamphlet says that it contains "remarks, several of which are the result of personal observation, during a tour in Europe." The author, therefore, cannot be Strickland as he did not sail to England until March 20, 1825, and this is dated March 15. Also, the author favors railways rather than canals or roads, but is not in favor of steam engines for use in this country. Strickland immediately realized that the advantage of a railway was in the use of locomotives and hence would have never suggested a transcontinental railway using horse-drawn vehicles.

1825

Agent in Great Britain for the Pennsylvania Society for the Promotion of Internal Improvement.

Reference: Pamphlets published by the Pennsylvania Society for the Promotion of Internal Improvement:

a. An Address, Philadelphia, October 27, 1824.

b. Railways, First Edition, February 22, 1825.
Second Edition, March 22, 1825.

c. Appeal to the Citizens of the Commonwealth of Pennsylvania, March 4, 1825.

d. Extracts from correspondence between the Society and William Strickland, Philadelphia, December 21, 1825.

e. First Annual Report of the Acting Committee of the Society, 1826, *The Franklin Journal, and American Mechanics' Magazine; Devoted to the useful arts, internal improvements, and general science* (under the patronage of the Franklin Institute of the State of Pennsylvania, edited by Dr. Thomas P. Jones, Professor of Mechanics at the Institute); I (Philadelpiha, 1826).

William Strickland, *Reports on Canals, Railways, Roads and Other Subjects* (Philadelphia, 1826).

History of the Pennsylvania Society for the Promotion of Internal Improvements: A group of men, most of whom were members of the newly-formed Franklin Institute, realized that trade was leaving Philadelphia for New York and Baltimore. Therefore, in an effort to arouse both public interest and the state legislature, they formed this Society late in 1824. On January 19, 1825, the Society determined to send an agent to Europe to gather at first-hand the latest information on recent developments in transportation facilities and manufacture. On February 3, 1825, William Strickland "in whose competency everyone had the fullest belief and who enjoyed the confidence and respect of the community," was appointed. The Society raised three thousand dollars for this project to pay the salary and expenses of Strickland and his assistant and pupil, Samuel Honeyman Kneass. The Society also allotted £100 to be spent in procuring information on the smelting of iron, and a like sum for pamphlets, models, machines, etc.

On March 18, two days before he sailed, Strickland was given full instructions as to what he should try to learn on the trip. These instructions were published and distributed widely. An abstract of them was printed in the *Franklin Journal.* He was instructed to go to England, Scotland, Wales, and Ireland and afterwards to France, Holland, and Germany. He was requested not to be technical in his reports, but to procure working plans of roads, railways, canals, bridges, etc., that could be erected in Pennsylvania without a skilled engineer. Twenty questions were asked: one was "Are steamboats permitted on canals?" which he answered on page two of the *Reports* by saying that steamboats were absolutely prohibited as wash destroys the banks, hence speed was restricted. The chief query concerned railways, "Of the utility of railways and their importance as means of transporting *large burdens,* we have full knowledge. Of the *mode* of constructing them, and of their cost, nothing is known with certainty."

Summary of trip:

Sailed March 20, 1825, from Philadelphia to Liverpool.

April—Liverpool, Manchester, North of England.

May—Leeds, Sunderland, Newcastle on Tyne, Scotland.

June—Glasgow.

July—Glasgow, Dublin.

August—Bristol, London.

September—London.

October—London, Liverpool.

November—Liverpool.

December—Sailed back to Philadelphia.

The principal canals which Strickland visited were the Thames and Medway, Grand Trunk, Rochdale, Birmingham and Liverpool, and Mersey and Irwell Canals.

The railways upon which he reported were: Mr. Brandling's Railway from Middleton Collieries to Leeds, Yorkshire; Hetton Road Railway, and the Duke of Portland's Tram Railway.

Importance of trip: The trip had far-reaching results because of the publication of the *Reports* which he had sent back to the Society during his sojourn abroad and the publication of the drawings, sketches, and plans which illustrated the *Reports,* of which there are seventy-two in all. As early as February, 1826, proposals for publishing the *Reports* appeared in the *Franklin Journal.* On the cover of the March issue, there was a list of the copperplate engravings which were to accompany the reports. The price was ten dollars and the reports were to go to press as soon as two hundred and fifty copies had been subscribed.

Three hundred and thirty-four copies were subscribed for before publication. The list of subscribers gives us an idea of the widespread interest in the work. The largest subscriber was the federal government, with twenty-five copies ordered for the House of Representatives. The State of Maryland and two booksellers were next with ten each. Strickland, the Governor of Louisiana, and the United States Military Academy at West Point each ordered four copies. The War Department and the Delaware and Hudson Canal Company each requested three, while

P. Obregon, Thomas Astley, and the Chesapeake and Delaware Canal Company, ordered two each; The Navy and Post Office Departments and the United States Engineers also subscribed. Most interesting is the list of architects and engineers who subscribed: Colonel de Witt Clinton, Jr., Robert Mills, Alexander Parris, Alexander Telfair, William Lehman, S. V. Merrick, and Benjamin Wright. Some Europeans, including Duke Bernard of Saxe-Weimar, also subscribed.

Canals, breakwaters, turnpike roads, railways and locomotive engines, bridges, iron, coke, blistered and cast steel, rollers for bar and hoop iron, gas lighting, copper rollers for printing calico and docks were all discussed in the *Reports* as were accounts of the more advanced practices in Great Britain. The *Reports* encouraged the industrial progress of the United States as much as any other publication. The clearness and intelligibility, both of the text and the plates, contributed to its usefulness.

1826

Report on canal from Swartara for the Canal Commissioners, dated March 10, 1826.

Reference: *Hazard's Register of Pennsylvania,* IV, 243.

1826

Design for a Washington Monument.

The only record of this design which has been found so far is in a newspaper account of the Fifteenth Annual Exhibition of the Pennsylvania Academy of Fine Arts, May, 1826. A clipping of this account of the exhibition is to be found in the Catalogue for 1826 in the Library Company of Philadelphia.

Returning through the saloon, we remarked with pleasure an interior of Christ's Church, one of the very few old buildings in Philadelphia that have been suffered to retain any thing of the reverend aspect of antiquity, amidst universal *renovation.* It is drawn in water colours by George Strickland, an ingenious draughtsman, kinsman to the celebrated architect of that name: by whom there is a design for the intended Washington Monument which has been, it seems, approved by a vote of the committee of superintendence: but this unadvised selection, will, probably, never be acted upon, since this massy monument of national gratitude is unperforated by a single loophole, to relieve the eye, though its altitude is nearly equal to that of the Western Shot-tower as if our regard for Washington were to be measured by the square foot; and as though the place it is to occupy had not been bequeathed to the city, on the express condition, that it should be *left open forever,* for the benefit of air.

Subscriptions were slow in coming in and it was not until February 22, 1833, that the cornerstone —a marble block—was laid with an appropriate Masonic ceremony and handsome procession. The monument was not erected.

1826

Examination of Hall of Representatives, Washington, D. C., and Report on a method for improving the acoustics.

Reference: Memorial of Charles Bulfinch to House of Representatives, referred to the Committee on Public Buildings, January 25, 1830.

Reprinted in *The National Capitol* by George C. Hazelton, Jr. (New York, 1902).

On May 19, 1826, there was a resolution passed by the House to employ William Strickland as a consultant on the acoustics of the Hall of Representatives. Strickland examined the Hall on July 1, 1826, and again, with Bulfinch, on October 21, 1826. His opinion was incorporated in a report presented to the House on February 8, 1827. He was in favor of flat walls, as was Bulfinch, but both thought they would "disturb the effect."

Appended to the Memorial were four letters:

1. Washington, August 28, 1826; Matthew St. Clair Clarke to William Strickland.
2. Philadelphia, September 12, 1826; William Strickland to Clarke.
3. Washington, October 31, 1826; William Strickland to Henry Clay.
4. Washington, November 1, 1826; Charles Bulfinch to the Secretary of State, Secretary of War, and the Attorney-General.

1826-27

(March-June) Engineer for the State of Pennsylvania, in charge of the Eastern Division of the Mixed

System, including the railroad from Columbia to Philadelphia, at a salary of $3,000 a year and expenses.

Reference: *Report and Correspondence of the Commissioners for Promoting the Internal Improvement of the State* (Harrisburg, 1825).

Report of the Canal Commissioners of the Commonwealth of Pennsylvania, For the promoting of the Internal Improvement of the State, I (Harrisburg, 1828).

Documents accompanying the Report, II. December 28, 1827.

Report of the Canal Commissioners of Pennsylvania Relative to the Pennsylvania Canals and Railroads (Harrisburg, 1830).

Hazard's Register of Pennsylvania, I, 20.

Proceedings of the American Society of Civil Engineers, I, 237.

All the canal papers and reports are deposited in the Department of Internal Affairs of the Commonwealth of Pennsylvania. They are available, but not filed or catalogued, according to Warren Daniel, custodian.

History: By an act of March 27, 1824, a Board of Commissioners was appointed for the internal improvement of the state. Their chief object was to supervise the building of a new system of transportation connecting the eastern and western parts of the state which were divided by the Allegheny Mountains. Surveys were made by the state and by the United States Engineers. A four-mile tunnel was proposed as the most efficient and least expensive way of circumventing the ridge of the mountains, but the proposal was greeted with laughter and sarcasm. "Even good men, who love to see the improvement of their country, have been startled at the idea of burrowing in the ground for a few miles, to let large boats pass through the bowels of the Allegheny."

The first appropriation of $300,000 was granted by the state on February 25, 1826, for the plan known as the Pennsylvania Mixed System which was made up of 81¾ miles of railroad from Philadelphia to Columbia, a canal from there to the divide and 37 miles of portage railway over the Alleghenies and a canal again to Pittsburgh, which, with six minor divisions, made a total of 426 miles of canal. The Mixed System was not an efficient method of transportation since it required three shifts of freight.

Strickland was appointed engineer for the project in March, 1826, and was in charge of the Eastern Division. Moncure Roberts, appointed in April, supervised the Western Division. The first contracts were signed in June and work started so promptly that the ceremony of the breaking of ground was celebrated on July 4.

Strickland, in his estimate for the Eastern Division, gave the figure of $405,511 to which he added $39,700 for increasing the width from Peters Mountain to Harrisburg. In the report of December 28, 1827, Strickland's estimate was commended and it was thought that the actual cost would be $8,505 below that figure.

In the accounts of the Eastern Division, two of Strickland's assistants are listed as Samuel H. Kneass and William Rodrigue, at wages of $1.50 a day to the former, and $1.00 a day to the latter. William Groves was to be the superintendent of stonework at a salary of $1,200 a year, or $3.00 a day. Target-bearers were to receive $1.50 a day and chain-bearers, axmen and cooks, $1.00 a day.

Section II of an act of April 16, 1827, provided that no engineer should receive more than $2,000 a year and that he should devote all his time to the work. On May 2, at 9 a.m., the canal commissioners wrote the engineers to acquaint them with the new ruling. By 3 p.m., they had received answers. Guilford accepted. Strickland, Roberts, Geddes, and Major Douglas, who was professor of engineering at West Point, all declined. Their services and salary continued until June 1, 1827, when their work was taken over by another group of engineers.

Strickland's reply was as follows:

Harrisburg, May 2, 1827.

Sir,—The engagements of my business, which the claims of an increasing and dependent family do not permit me to renounce, are such as make it impossible for me to devote myself exclusively to the duties of engineer under the board; and as I understand by the law recently passed, the terms of which are communicated in your letter of to-day, the engineers in the service of the state, are required to be in constant attendance on the line of canal, I am compelled to tender my resignation of the situation which I have so far had the honour to hold.

I am sure that it is unnecessary, though I trust it will not be deemed improper for me to say, that I yield to the necessity of this step, with painful reluctance. Feeling as a native and a citizen of Pennsylvania, a proper degree of pride in the stupendous work which is now begun under the auspices of the board, it was for me an object of peculiar interest, as an engineer, to assist, with however humble capacity, in its progress to completion. I withdraw myself, therefore, from this employment, with the strongest and most unaffected regret.

I beg leave to add, that if by occasional visits of inspection and advice to the division heretofore under my more immediate charge, I can in the opinion of the board at all promote its rapid and proper execution, I shall hold myself pledged to obey their wishes. Of course, all such services on my part, will be without further charge to the state, than the amount of my absolute expenditure while so engaged.

I have the honour to be,
Most respectfully, Sir,
Your very obedient servant,
William Strickland.

To Joseph M'Ilvain, Esq. Sec'y of the board of canal commissioners.

Strickland's main contribution as a state engineer was in advocating the superiority of railroads to canals. The commissioners and the legislature were both inclined to prefer canals and hence would not try the experiment of such a mileage of railway. Strickland's insistence was responsible for the railroad between Philadelphia and Columbia, the first state-built railroad in the nation. While the Mixed System was not a financial success, nevertheless, its route, for which Strickland was largely responsible, was followed by the Pennsylvania Railroad in the 1850's.

1826-27

Brandywine Shoal Lighthouse, Delaware River.

Reference: National Archives, Washington, D. C., Treasury Department Archives, Coast Guard Records: (Record Group 26) Lighthouse Records, Deeds and Contracts, Vol. D (1822-27), 214-15.

Brandywine-Shoal Light-house .... Contract
Articles of agreement made and concluded on this 27th day of July in the year of our Lord one thousand eight hundred and twenty six between Allen McLane Esq. Superintendent of Light-houses, Beacons, Buoys, and Piers on the Bay and River of Delaware of the one part & William Strickland of the city of Philadelphia, Architect and Engineer of the other part. . . .

Witnesseth,
That the said William Strickland for the consideration hereinafter mentioned doth hereby for himself, his Executors and administrators, covenant promise and agree to and with Allen McLane Superintendent of Light-houses &c. and his successor in Office by these presents that he the said William Strickland shall and will at his own proper cost and charge furnish the best and most durable materials for and in a substantial and workmanlike manner construct, erect and build on the southeast end oft the Brandywine Shoal in the Bay of Delaware a Light-House of the following description and dimensions ..... that is to say

The *foundation* to be eighty feet in diameter formed of rubble-stone sloping regularly on every side up to the base of the Light-House at low water-mark each stone to weigh at least one half of a ton. At low-water mark the *base* of the *light-house* to be thirty feet in diameter and built up in a curved line with regular courses of blue-marble to the height of thirteen feet above the high water, each course of ashlar to be at least two feet on the bed and to be clamped with iron across each of the joints.

The *thickness* of the *walls* to be four feet six inches resting upon an inverted arch fourteen feet in diameter which arch will form the *bottom* of the *oil-room.*

The *superstructure* above the first story to be built with circular brick work in walls of three feet six inches in thickness to the height of sixteen feet above the first-story and coped with a stone curb three feet in width to which the wrought-iron *lanthorn* is to be secured.

The *Lanthorn* to be six feet in diameter and eight feet in height covered with copper and surrounded by an iron-railing on top of the curb-stone.

A circular wooden stairway to be formed from the first story to the Lanthorn with suitable *closets* and *provision-rooms* under it for the accommodation of the Keeper.

The *Entrance* to the Light-House to be formed to the South by means of a causeway commencing at

low water mark into which ring-bolt are to be inserted to moor the Keeper's boats &c.
The whole of the above work agreeably in all respects to the above description and to the Plan & Elevation furnished by the said William Strickland to the said Superintendent of Light-Houses &c. to be finished by him the said William Strickland in a complete and substantial and workmanlike manner on or before the first day of November in the year one thousand eight hundred and twenty seven. . . .
In consideration whereof the said Allen McLane Superintendent of Light-Houses &c. promises, engages and agrees to with the said William Strickland his Executors and Administrators when the whole of the aforesaid work shall have passed the inspection and been approved of by two Inspectors for such purpose to be appointed by the said Superintendent of Light-Houses &c. and the possession thereof delivered up to him to pay or cause to be paid unto the said William Strickland his Executors or administrators the entire sum of . . . . .
Twenty nine thousand two hundred dollars, money of the United States, of which conditions agreements and payments the said parties respectively bind and oblige themselves and their legal representatives firmly by *these presents* in the penal sum of fifty eight thousand four hundred dollars to be paid by the party defective to the party complying herewith . . . . .
In Witness whereof the said parties to this agreement have hereunto set their hands and seals the day and year first written above.

Sealed and delivered by Allen McLane in the presence of us (signed)	[Signed]	Allen McLane seal Superintendent of Light-Houses &c. &c. William Strickland seal

James S. Farmer
J. K. Kane

Sealed and delivered by
William Strickland
in the presence of us,
[The word *July* in the eight line from the bottom of the first page having been first erased and the word "*November*" substituted in its place]
[Signed]
Joseph McIlvaine
Wm Darlington.

1826-28

Hall of the Academy of Natural Sciences, Twelfth and George (Sansom) streets. (Plate 18A)

Reference: W. S. W. Ruschenberger, M.D., *A notice of the Origin, Progress and Present condition of the Academy of Natural Sciences of Phila.* (2nd ed., 1860).

American Philosophical Society, Early Proceedings, 1744-1838.

The first meeting of the Philadelphia Academy of Natural Sciences was held on January 25, 1812. Strickland was elected a member of the Academy on June 19, 1813, and resigned on January 29, 1828. From 1815, the Academy used a hall owned by J. Gilliams. On November 7, 1823, the American Philosophical Society received an inquiry from the Academy of Natural Sciences of Philadelphia as to whether the former could accommodate the Academy by "raising an additional story to its building." This was referred to a committee, composed of Vaughn, Strickland, and Du Ponceau, which made a report on December 5, 1823, opposed to an additional story.

More than a year later, on January 25, 1825, the Academy appointed a committee to find suitable quarters. The members of the committee were: Isaac Hays, M.D., William Mason Walmsley, William Strickland, William S. Warder, Samuel George Morton, M.D., and Roberts Vaux.

On January 3, 1826, after a year's deliberation, the committee reported that it had decided upon the purchase and remodeling of the Temple of the New Jerusalem, the Swedenborgian church at the corner of Twelfth and George (Sansom) streets. It had been built in 1816 by Strickland, after his design. The academy bought it for $4,300, and the estimate for remodeling was $1,700. This site was criticized by the members as remote and inaccessible, but the work was begun on May 9, 1826, under the supervision of Strickland, and the building was opened to the public in 1828.

The galleries were used for the exhibition of the collections of the Academy, the ground floor for a library and reading room, lectures and meetings, and additional exhibition cases.

The lot was 99 by 45 feet, and the building 44 by 50 feet, surmounted by a dome.

There are various prints of the building, including an illustration in the *Journal*, VI, of the Academy of Natural Sciences.

On May 25, 1839, the cornerstone of a new hall for the Academy was laid at the northwest corner of Broad and George streets. This building was completed on February 7, 1840, and cost $13,333. No record of the architect for this building has been found, either among the papers of the Academy, or in guidebooks.

1826-29

Naval Asylum (United States Naval Home, after 1879). (Plates 15-17)

Grays Ferry Road at Twenty-fourth Street.

Cornerstone laid: April 3, 1827.

Dedicated: December 3, 1833.

Attic rooms added in 1848, roof raised and dormer windows added in the 1870's. In good repair and in use (1950).

Reference: Records of the Department of the Navy, Office of Naval Records and Library, housed in the National Archives Building, Washington, D. C.

PN—Naval Asylum, Philadelphia; construction. 1826-1935. A collection of 113 items concerning the building of the Philadelphia Asylum and seven letters dealing with the work of John Haviland, architect of the Norfolk Asylum. These items are, for the most part, letters, requests for money, and acknowledgments. A good record of the work done by Strickland during his tenure as architect and of the difficulties which he had in getting appropriations, as well as a history of the construction of the building are included.

A letter dated July 6, 1826 (#2), is from George Strickland at 14 Library Street to Secretary of the Navy Southard requesting information as to the lot, appropriation, and number of men to be housed in the Naval Asylum. This indicated that there must have been some notice in the papers, although whether or not there was a competition has not been learned. It is certain that George, as well as his brother, sent in plans because #7, dated September 21, from George Strickland to Captain Charles Morris stated that he sent his plans and estimate to the wrong board and requested that they be transferred to the Board of Commissioners of Hospitals.

It seems likely that no decision was made by the first of November, for on that date Robert Ralston wrote to the Secretary of the Navy recommending William Strickland highly (#4).

A folded sheet of paper (#1) with a drawing on one side, entitled "Sketch of the Principal Story of the Naval Asylum," shows the main features which are the same as in the extant building, except for changes in details, as in the axis of the stairs. This is a quick pen sketch with notations in Strickland's handwriting. On the other side is the following letter:

Philadelphia, December 25, 1826.

Honorable
Saml S. Southard
Secy of the Navy
Sir,

I have the honor to transmit for your consideration the following Estimate of the cost of constructing the Naval Asylum at Philadelphia: The plan will embrace a front including the wings of 385 ft and the centre Building of 90 ft with Eight marble columns of the Ionic order.—

The Basement story will be formed of Granite. The principal, and attic stories of marble:—These stories will contain about 250 dormitories and will be arched throughout making the whole building fireproof to the roof.—

I will suggest for your sanction the propriety of authorizing me to conclude all the contracts for the materials during this winter, as they can be had upon much more advantageous terms than at any other season.—

Granite Basement story	6,000.
Building stone in Cellar walls including work	2,740.
3,000,000 Bricks including laying lime & sand	30,000.
13,580 cu. ft. of marble ashler	25,334.
8 Ionic marble columns	11,520.
Entablature and Pediment	5,000.
Marble stairways	2,500.
Carpenter work	9,000.
Lumber	9,000.

Painting and Glazing	3,000.
Plastering including materials	5,500.
Blacksmiths work and Iron mongery	3,500.
Covering of the roof	5,666.

Total =	$118,760.

Respectfully submitted
William Strickland Archt.

On January 1, 1827, Strickland again wrote to Southard (#12). His plan and esitmate had been accepted and he was writing about copying the plans and depositing the original with the Board of Commissioners of Naval Hospitals. (All the working drawings for the project seem to have been destroyed or lost.)

In 1827, the work on the Asylum went ahead smoothly and money was remitted promptly when requested. Strickland received a total of $71,000 during the year. In 1828, work continued but at a slower rate and money was more difficult to obtain—only $35,594.06—was received. Strickland, in his report of December 30, 1828 (#50), estimated that $75,000 more would be needed to complete the building.

In 1829, no money was remitted until March 31, despite repeated requests. Strickland's letter (#70) of March 30, 1829, to John Branch, Secretary of the Navy stated: "It is now four months since the workmen engaged at the building of the Naval Asylum have received their wages:—The importunities of 100 men induces me again to request that you may be pleased to direct me a remittance of 20,000 dollars for the purposes thereof, and for the further progress of the building."

This request was granted and half of the sum was sent on March 31; the other half on June 13. The difficulties which Strickland experienced the winter of 1828-29 were doubtless due to the presidential election and the change of cabinet.

On April 16, 1829 (#77), Strickland wrote to John Branch, John H. Eaton, and S. D. Ingham, Commissioners, Naval Hospitals, in response to an inquiry as to the increased cost. He explained that the back of the building and the wings of the principal part of the front in the rear of the piazzas were to have been roughcast, but instead it was decided, with the approbation of the President and the Secretary of Navy, to complete the building with marble and granite. He added:

"It very rarely happens in the construction of public works of this kind that some excess beyond the estimated cost does not take place; in this case it is owing eventually to a strong desire to produce not only durability, but a suitable and defined architectural finish." He concluded by stating that the utmost economy was pursued in the purchase of materials and asked that they refer to the accounts in Mr. Fillebrown's office.

To add further proof, Strickland again wrote on April 18, 1829 (#78), to show that all contracts were concluded at rates lower than current prices.

In June and August, there were further requests for money because neither the mechanics nor the creditors were being paid.

On August 21, 1829 (#58), Strickland wrote to Secretary of Naval Hospital Fund Bradford, giving a report of the state of the building at that time. The exterior was roofed and the doors and windows ready for hanging. A small expense would make the structure "beyond the risk of injury from the weather." In the interior, the plastering was complete in one story and considerably advanced in the others. Most of the floors were laid, and the "entire upper story containing about 87 rooms . . . ready to receive its furniture and inmates." Above the debts, $8,000 or $10,000 was needed to complete the interior; $9,000 or $10,000, needed for the exterior. The portico was unfinished, seven shafts and two capitals were needed; the remainder of the blocks were ready to be put in place. "The marble is on the ground and stone cutters of approved skill and industry are engaged in working it." To suspend work would increase the cost. If necessary, work could be stopped on the exterior and the interior finished. About three months would be needed to entirely complete the building. Congress appropriated $125,000 for the Naval Hospitals at the last session, of which $75,000 was for the Philadelphia Asylum and as yet Strickland had received only $20,000. "P.S. $25,000. just arrived."

On September 1, 1829 (#57), Strickland again wrote to Bradford sending accounts, payroll, bills, receipts, lists of bills due, requisitions, survey of grounds, and a list of extravagant charges.

Strickland's last communication, before resigning as superintendent in charge of the construction of the Asylum on December 31, 1829, was sent to John Branch, John H. Eaton, and Samuel D. Ingham, Commissioners of the Naval Hospital Fund, Washington. It was dated Philadelphia, December 1, 1829, and was later reprinted in reports to Congress. It contains an excellent description of the building which was used in all subsequent accounts of the Asylum. It concludes with an estimate of the probable total cost.

Amount expended to date	198,000.
Amount due. salaries 1,500.	17,500.
Amount required to finish work	
Introduction of Schuylkill water & annual rent, 500.	27,300.
	―――――
Total	242,000.

Strickland resigned at the end of December, and George Harrison, the Navy agent for Philadelphia, took over the supervision of the buildings and the accounts. During the year 1830, he continued to call upon Strickland occasionally to check bills, as in the case of Ewing's account for plumbing and lead work (#90), Sept. 27, 1830.

"Debts due on Naval Asylum, January 1, 1830," appear in #99. The amount exclusive of furniture, $13,024.65. Some of the items were:

George Strickland for 1 quarter & 10 days salary as clerk	138.70
William Strickland architect 1 quarter ..	500.00
J. & W. Ewing for water closets, 40 Bath tubs, shower baths, cisterns, Copper Boilers, Sheet lead at	$5,500.53

Coryell Papers, Manuscript Collection, H.S.P., II, 18.

1. The printed notice dated Philadelphia, January 4, 1827, and signed William Strickland, Architect, Thomas Harris, M.D., stated:

"Sealed Proposals will be received until the first of February next at No. 117, South Ninth street, for the supply and delivery by contract, at the lot of ground on the river Schuylkill below South street, of the following described material, viz." Then follows a list of the wood, poles, scantlings, boards, planks, needed for the Asylum, with the concluding paragraph,

"The pine to be stated by the thousand foot and for each pole the whole to be of the best quality, and to be delivered at the site in such quantities as may be required for the contemplated building between the first day of march and the first day of May next."

2. The letter which follows:

Philadelphia, January 3, 1828.

Lewis Coryell Esqr.
New Hope, Bucks Co.
Dear Sir,
I will thank you to inform me by return of mail the lowest terms upon which you will contract to cut and deliver the enclosed bill of scantling for the Roof of the United States Marine Asylum.
I wish the whole to be of good sound white pine free from sap and wind shakes.

Yours very truly,
William Strickland.

3. Another letter from Strickland to Coryell, accepting the terms offered by Coryell for the wood for the roof of the Asylum, states that it should be delivered the following May at the wharf on the Schuylkill (dated January 15, 1828).

Hazard's Register of Pennsylvania, X, 284-85, November, 1832. Strickland's final report of the progress and completion of the Naval Asylum, noted above (#74) in Naval Archives, is reprinted here from the *Reports to Congress—1830.*

Pennsylvania Magazine of History and Biography, VII, No. 2 (1883), 117ff.

"Some Account of the Origin of the Naval Asylum at Philadelphia, by Edward Shippen, M.D., U.S.N."

On May 26, 1826, Surgeon Harris, U.S.N., was appointed by Secretary of Navy Southard to purchase the Pewhaton Estate on the Schuylkill. In January, 1827, Harris and Strickland were appointed commissioners to build the Asylum at a salary of $1,000 a year each.

Plan: Front—385 feet in length with a central building, 142 feet wide by 135 feet deep. Marble portico with eight Ionic columns in center. Three stories with piazzas, or verandas, on each story, front and rear.

Basement: Dining room, 113 feet in length; kitchen, wash-house, laundry, pantries, storeroom, office, and warming apparatus.

Principal story: In the front, eight parlors, officers' quarters, chapel—56 feet square lighted by a lantern in the dome—connecting passages, piazzas, surgeon's apartment, infirmaries, apothecary's room; bathrooms, closets between chapel and hall.

Attic (third story): In main building—rooms for officers, governor—or manager of the institution; apartments for the insane, bathrooms, closets, etc.

Wings: Dormitories; 180 rooms, well-lighted and ventilated, for 400 men. In the extremities, social halls warmed by fireplaces, workshops, operating room, and offices. Communicating piazzas and interior passage.

Construction and materials: Fireproof construction, vaulted throughout to roof. Arched vaulting in cellar, barrel vaulting in corridors, groin vaulting in rooms, ovoid dome over chapel with spandrels springing from the floor and arches and bull's-eyes in upper part with circular glassed-in lantern over oculus at top. Masonry construction throughout with granite used for the basement and Pennsylvania marble for the upper stories and portico. The piazzas are supported by eighty-eight iron columns with granite piers in basement. The Ionic columns are three feet in diameter. There are nineteen steps leading to the portico with buttresses at the ends. The roof of the central building was covered with copper and the roofs of the wings were originally covered with slate. The interior was finished with brick, lath and plaster, and painted. Sashes and frames and doors were of wood. The windows were two-sash with twelve panes each. There were double stairs from the hall, which were so-called hanging stairs, that is, constructed on the arch principle. They are, as is usually the case with such stairs, the object of admiration. The building was originally heated by a hot air furnace and fireplaces.

Cost: $250,000, including building, fence, and grounds. The addition of the cost of the land and the wharf on the Schuylkill brings the total to $276,332.45.

Style: Greek Revival. Columns of the portico were copied from the Stuart and Revett plates of the Ionic temple on the Illyssus near Athens. The building was excellently proportioned when the roof was lower and without dormer windows. A central open portico is flanked by two solid sections, relieved by a tripartite window on each floor, then wings with open piazzas and veranda, terminated by solid ends, again relieved by tripartite windows. It is a long façade, but admirably varied and unified. The portico dominates the structure, with its plain but well-proportioned pediment and handsome columns and is set off by the flanking solid walls. The wings are subordinated by the piazzas, which make them appear less heavy and also repeat in triplicate the shadows of the main portico. The whole is completed by the masonry walls at the ends which repeat the walls and windows on either side of the portico. In the rear, there is a pediment on the main building and piazzas on the wings; it is otherwise without ornament.

Outstanding features: The excellence with which a portico of pure Greek Revival design is incorporated in an utilitarian building, beautifying the façade and dignifying the main entrance without detracting from the usefulness of the building.

The use of iron columns for the support of the piazzas which is one of the early examples of constructional use of iron supports.

The ground plan, which was well-adapted to the function of the building; and the innovation of piazzas leading off the dormitories, providing the inmates with the maximum amount of air and sun with the minimum effort on their part.

1828

Draft of a plan for the Naval Hospital at Pensacola, Florida.

Reference: Records of the Department of the Navy. PN—Naval Hospital, Pensacola. A letter to Secretary of the Navy Southard from Dr. T. B. Salter, dated Philadelphia, March 22, 1828.

I send by this day's mail a plan for a Hospital at Pensacola, which I think is best suited for that place. The design is my own; the draft was by Mr. Strickland, and is executed in a way sufficient plain, to render further explanations unnecessary. The main building, as is shewn, is intended for 180 patients.

A building at one end with apartments for 20 officers, will constitute the number of 200. On the other end, a corresponding building will be necessary for a Medical officer. A kitchen in the rear.

1828

Designs for a house for James A. Hillhouse, New Haven, Connecticut.

Reference: Two letters, three elevations, and one ground plan in the manuscript collection of Sterling Library, Yale University, New Haven, Connecticut.

Two drawings, signed and dated January 14, 1828, one of the south front elevation, the other of the east flank. The building shown has a three-story, gable-roofed, long, narrow, central section 29 by 45 feet, with two-story side wings 18½ by 35 feet, and one-story Doric porticoes, front and back, on the central section. With the drawings is a note of the same date from Strickland to James Lloyd, stating "that the expense of the drawings for Mr. Hillhouse is Twenty doll[s]"

A long letter, dated September 15, 1828, from Strickland to James A. Hillhouse, enclosing a view of the south front and a ground plan, signed and of the same date. The house in the second design is a compact, squarish, two-story building with a gable roof, ending as a pediment with an attic story as high as the ridgepole and central chimneys and a half-basement story. A small central, four-column portico, raised on steps with a balcony above, is the only decoration of the plain façade.

The ground plan shows a circular vestibule with a 13-foot hall behind. To the right, a drawing room 18 by 20 feet, with a library 18 by 21 feet behind, and a dining room 18 by 25 feet to the left, with a small flight of stairs, closets, pantry, and passages behind.

1828

College of Charleston at Charleston, South Carolina. Expanded and remodeled.

Reference: Beatrice St. Julien Ravenal, *Architects of Charleston* (Charleston: Carolina Art Association, 1945), pp. 170-71. Plans for the building were provided by Strickland. The construction was in the charge of Messrs. Bell and Schierle. Money for the college was obtained from voluntary subscriptions of Charleston citizens. The cornerstone was laid on July 7, 1828, and the work completed in March, 1829. In 1840, the building was roughcast and painted pink. In 1850, the portico and wings were added by Edward B. White. Following the earthquake of 1886, the east wing was rebuilt after plans by E. R. Rutledge, modified by Gabriel E. Manigault.

Description: The college seal bears an impression of the original Strickland façade, a two-story brick structure on a basement with a pediment in the center of the south front and gable ends on the east and west.

1828

First Congregational Unitarian Church, Tenth and Locust streets. (Plate 23A)

Cornerstone laid: March 25, 1828.

Building dedicated: November 5, 1828.

Demolished: 1885.

Reference: C. G. Childs, *Views in Philadelphia* (1830). Description and plate drawn by Hugh Reinagle, engraved by C. G. Childs.

Joseph May, *A Farewell to an Old Home.* Sermon preached on February 1, 1885. A pamphlet in the collection of papers and photographs in the Parish House of the Unitarian Church, Chestnut and Van Pelt streets.

History: In 1796, the first Unitarian congregation was formed in Philadelphia under the leadership of Joseph Priestly. By 1812, there was a need for a church building. The Octagon Church, designed by Robert Mills, was dedicated February 14, 1813; a drawing of it is in the present parish house. In 1825, W. H. Furness, father of the architect Frank Furness, became pastor. Under his leadership, the membership grew so that by 1828, plans were furnished by Strickland for a new church which was completed under his superintendence in the same year.

Style: Greek Revival, with a Doric portico and two Doric columns in the interior, on either side of the altar. The front walls were without windows.

Plan: Rectangular, 61 by 83 feet.

Materials: Pennsylvania marble. For economy, brick and stone from the Octagon church was used in the new building. The columns were taken from the waterworks, formerly in Centre Square, which had been designed by Benjamin H. Latrobe.

Cost: $30,000.

Outstanding feature: The severity of the exterior and interior design.

1828

Steeple of the old State House, now Independence Hall, Chestnut Street between Fifth and Sixth streets. (Plate 22)

Reference: *Hazard's Register of Pennsylvania,* I, (March, 1828). Proceedings of Councils, February 28, 1828, pp. 152-54. Decision of Councils, March 15, 1828, p. 176.

One of Strickland's most interesting commissions in 1828 was to rebuild the steeple on Independence Hall. The original tower was completed in 1751. By 1774, the woodwork was found to be rotting and it was ordered to be torn down and a covering put on. This was done in 1781 when a low hip roof was constructed above the brickwork. In the background of the portrait of N. Gerard painted by Charles Willson Peale in 1778, there is a good representation of the original tower. William Birch in 1800 did an engraving of the State House, as it was still called, which gives an accurate view of the low covering that remained until 1828. In that year, on February 7, a committee was appointed by Councils "to cause the turret in the rear of the State House, to be surveyed, and to procure a plan and estimate of the cost of carrying it up to a sufficient height to place a clock and bell there."

The committee, composed of Francis Gurney Smith, Benjamin Tilghman, J. W. Thompson, and Manuel Eyre, procured estimates from Strickland for the general plan; from Daniel Groves, for brickwork; John O'Neil, for carpentry, and John Struthers, for masonry. Strickland reported that the walls were thick enough to permit the addition of a tower, as they tapered from 3 feet to 18 feet within 69 feet and were 31 feet square trussed. There was a crack in the south wall, but he thought that "one or two stories of brick 18 inches thick and about 28 or 30 feet high might be added with framing and diagonal girders attached by iron clamps" and above that a wooden cupola and spire might "be firmly and easily constructed." With this report, he sent a plan and elevation and an estimate of $8,000.

At the meeting of Councils on February 28, the committee submitted the reports which it had gathered. Lukens was to provide the clock, Willbank the bell, Strickland the architectural work, and the whole cost was to be $12,000. In presenting the drawing by Strickland, it was said to be ". . . in fact a restoration of the spire originally erected with the building, and standing there on the 4th July 1776."

This report precipitated an unusually lively discussion in Councils, although on the need for the clock there was an agreement and Councils resolved that "The time of the citizens of Philadelphia was of so much importance to them, that there ought to be some accurate means of marking its passage." It was the question of aesthetics which troubled the councilmen. Tilghman, a member of the committee, said with great modesty, "I pretend not to taste, and therefore will not say what merit Mr. Strickland's plan may have as an architectural design; but I am well convinced that no arguments that I could use, could persuade my friend opposite that there is either beauty or convenience in a steeple house." His "friend opposite" was Wayne, who had been very critical.

Troth then spoke up and said that he liked the plan of William Strickland; this caused Tilghman to answer, "The plan of Mr. Strickland has been preferred, on account of its being a restoration of the old steeple." Troth hedged by remarking, "Our character is at stake, as men of taste, and as admirers of antiquity, and I hope we will not proceed hastily in this business."

Lowber had very definite opinions on the matter and did not hesitate to say, "So far from being an ornament to the city, it would be a deformity." And later on in the discussion, "The ancient steeple was very handsome—this is a mammouth chimney—so it would be called if it was ever erected—a straight mass of walls—*a shot tower*—there is no beauty, no symmetry about it."

The discussion raged, however, until March 15, when it was noted in the papers, "The Select and Common Councils, on Thursday evening, decided to erect a Steeple on the State House, agreeably to

Mr. Strickland's plan, and appropriated for that purpose, and purchase of a Clock and Bell, $12,000." Work was begun directly and the tower was completed that summer.

Lowber has been proved a false prophet. The tower has not been considered a deformity or a mammoth chimney, but has become a national monument, as familiar to most Americans as Mills's Washington monument or Walter's dome on the Capitol in Washington. Most people are not aware that the tower is not the original one, because it harmonizes with the first building and the wings by Mills. It is not an exact replica of the first steeple, but follows the general design with the three main divisions of brick, wood and cupola. The designs in the form of a half-wreath below the faces of the clock are reminiscent of the design about the clock in the main banking room of the United States Bank. The clock faces are of glass and were illuminated by gas at night, a convenience which was much admired and appreciated by the citizens of the city. For the decoration of the square tower, Strickland used pilasters with Doric, Ionic, and Corinthian capitals; urns, and a balustrade. The surmounting belfry and steeple are close to the original form. The whole is genuinely pleasing and convincingly Georgian. It should be recorded in the architectural annals as one of the first examples of the restoration of a Colonial building, a forerunner of the Wakefield and Williamsburg projects.

1828

Report on the safe condition of Fair Mount Dam to the Select and Common Councils. Letter of William Strickland and Daniel Groves, dated September 18, 1828.

Reference: *Hazard's Register of Pennsylvania,* II, 183.

1828

Cornerstone laid for Leiper Canal on Saturday, August 16, 1828.

Reference: *Hazard's Register of Pennsylvania,* II, 96.

Note: Since Strickland laid the cornerstone for this canal which was to extend from the Leiper quarries on Crum Creek to the Delaware River, and since the canal boat was named for him, it is likely that he was the engineer, or at least the consultant engineer, for the canal.

1828

Arch Street Theatre, near Sixth Street. (Plate 19)

Opened: Wednesday, October 1, 1828.

Front and interior remodeled: 1863.

Reference: *The Philadelphia Album,* notices about the theatre appear in the issues of September 24, October 1 and 8, and November 12, 1828. In the last, there appeared an engraving and a description of the theatre. The engraving was by M. J. Yeager. The comment is favorable: "No pen can do adequate justice to the interior beauties of the building" and practical: "the seats are properly stuffed and covered with calf-skin."

Philadelphia in 1830 (Philadelphia: Carey and Hart, 1830), pp. 142-44.

The front is of marble: a screen of columns projects nearly to the line of the street, supporting a frieze of Doric character, and flanked by marble wings, in which are the staircases to the pit. The entrance to the boxes is by three ample doors beneath the screen. These admit us into a vestibule much resembling that of the Chestnut street house, terminated at the ends by the offices of the treasurer and the box-keeper; and from the vestibule we pass into the lobby, under an arcade corresponding with the doors or entrances. The lobby is not as wide as that in Chestnut street, but it is sufficiently so to insure the safety and comfort of the audience.

The boxes are disposed somewhat in the manner and form of an antique lyre, so that all of them, the stage box included, present a front to some part of the stage. There are no back-boxes. The lower tier is more elevated than is common, and rises as it recedes from the stage, the front boxes being of course the highest. The pit is spacious, and extends with an alcove ceiling, under the boxes.

The columns supporting the boxes are of iron, bronzed with gilt, formed like the festive Thyrsis, with its riband and bullets. They are thrown back several feet from the front line of the boxes, and thus give the idea of hanging galleries. The expansive area of the house, combined with the unusual height of the box ceilings, gives the whole a peculiar air of lightness. The saloon on the second floor extends the whole breadth of the building, and there are commodious coffee-rooms in different parts of the house. The ventilation of the theatre is effected by a large radiating circle in the dome, sixty feet above the floor of the pit. The proscenium is nearly filled by a beautiful painting of the chariot of Apollo, dashing rapidly through the skies, surrounded by the Hours, and followed by the Seasons of the year. In front of the building, at an elevated height, is an alto-relief of the Young Apollo, resting on his lyre, carved by the chisel of M. Gevelot, from a massy stone, walled into the building. Mr. Strickland is the architect of this beautiful theatre, which was first opened on the 1st of October 1828.

1829

Canal Boat named for Strickland.

Reference: *Hazard's Register of Pennsylvania,* IV, 247.

Chester, Pennsylvania, October 9, 1829.
The Leiper Canal.– This Canal, the work of our enterprising and public spirited fellow-citizen, George G. Leiper, Esq., was yesterday filled with water, and his new Canal Boat, the *William Strickland,* passed the whole line of the canal, up to the quarry. The Volunteer Battalion of this country, with their band of music, and a band from the city, we are informed, were present to give life to the interesting scene.

1829

Medical Hall, University of Pennsylvania, Ninth Street between Chestnut and Market streets. (Plate 21)

Reference: University of Pennsylvania, Minutes of Trustees, VII, May 24, 1822–June 7, 1831. University of Pennsylvania Library.

Report on Medical Hall, November 4, 1828. The medical faculty approved Strickland's plan and estimate of about $16,000. (Page 250)

A building committee of the Trustees was appointed and the same committee [was to be] authorized to contract with William Strickland for the taking down of the present Medical Hall and for the erection of a new Hall according to the elevations and plans accompanying this report . . . the work to commence on the first day of March and the building to be completed and fit for use on or before the first day of October next. (Page 252)

Report of Committee on a new Medical Hall, December 2, 1828.

New estimate including fittings of anatomical and chemical departments $23,750 to which adding 5 per cent for the superintendence of the architect $1,187.50 the entire cost of the Building would be $24,937.50 say, $25,000. (Page 260)

Report on February 17, 1829. Contracts with Daniel Groves, bricklayer; John O'Neal, carpenter; John Struthers, marble-mason, and James Allen, plasterer. (Page 272)

Description of ceremonies attendant on the laying of the cornerstone, Saturday, March 21, 1829. (Page 272)

1829-30

College Hall, University of Pennsylvania, Ninth Street between Chestnut and Market streets, Philadelphia. (Plate 20A,B)

Reference: University of Pennsylvania, Minutes of Trustees, VII, May 24, 1822-June 7, 1831. University of Pennsylvania Library.

Faculty of Arts desired a new building, April 7, 1829. Plans made by Strickland and estimated at $22,000. The building would be symmetrical with the Medical Hall, with 90 feet between the two. (Page 278)

Contracts signed on July 1, 1829. (Page 288)

Cornerstone laid on July 31, 1829. (Page 292)

Meeting of the committee on February 16, 1830, to consider increased expenses. "Mr. Strickland is of the opinion that about $9000 more will complete the buildings." Original estimate for both buildings was $50,000 of which about $28,000 would be returned to the University by the medical faculty. The cost of College Hall was set at about $23,000, including Strickland's compensation as architect. "Mr. Strickland estimates that to surround the lot with a dwarf wall and iron railings and gates will cost $2010." (Page 336)

Ibid., p. 371. College Hall was ready for use in the fall of 1830.

Illustrations: J. C. Wild, *Views of Philadelphia* (1838).

Old photograph in the collection of the Historical Society of Pennsylvania.

1829-33

United States Mint, Chestnut and Juniper streets. Demolished: 1907. (Plate 23B)

Reference: Mint Letters, *Index of Letters Rec'd and Sent from Philadelphia, 1792-1835.* Treasury Division, National Archives, Washington, D. C. *Hazard's Register of Pennsylvania,* XII (August, 1833), 68.

On March 2, 1829, Congress passed a resolution and appropriation for a new Mint building in Philadelphia.

A lot for the new building was purchased on the west side of Juniper Street, extending from Chestnut Street to Penn Square, with a frontage of 150 feet on Chestnut and 204 feet on Juniper Street.

On March 19, 1829, Samuel Moore, Director of the Mint, sent letters to William Strickland and John Haviland asking them to send plans and estimates for the new building (#1554).

Strickland answered on the following day that he would prepare an estimate and plans (#1551). There is no reply recorded from Haviland, who at that time was engaged in building the Naval Asylum at Norfolk.

The next day, March 20, Samuel Moore again wrote to Strickland to inquire what his charges would be for the plan. Strickland delayed until the twenty-fourth to reply that he would charge $150 for the plan (#1552).

On April 20, 1829, Strickland forwarded the plans and estimate to Moore (#1553). These were accepted and Strickland was appointed superintendent of the construction. Work on the foundations began immediately and the cornerstone was laid on July 4, 1829.

Style: Greek Revival. Two porticoes, one on Chestnut Street and one on Penn Square, each of the Ionic order with six columns, six feet in diameter, fluted and bound at the neck with an olive wreath. An entablature went all around the building, supported by antae at the corners and surmounted at the ends of the flanks by four pediments.

Plan: Rectangular building, 129 feet wide and 139 feet long plus two porticoes, each 27 by 60 feet, making the total length 193 feet. In the center there was a court, 55 by 84 feet. There were three stories: the basement where the assaying, melting, and refining was done. The main floor with the officers' rooms and space for coining and printing. The attic was occupied by the standards of weights and balances. Some of the dimensions were:

assaying rooms..	50 x 20
Melter and Refiner	95 x 35
melting	37 x 32
gold and silver casting	53 x 32
Chief Coiner 2 rooms each	55 x 40
coinage	120 x 32
printing room (10 presses)	37 x 32

Construction and materials: Marble and brick; copper roof. Basement and main story arched and fireproofed throughout.

Outstanding feature: The use of the court for light and as a means of access to the various rooms and floors by the iron piazzas and staircases.

Cost: $209,230 (according to the *Nashville Whig Banner,* May 27, 1843).

1829-40

Delaware Breakwater, off Lewes, Delaware, in Delaware Bay. Still in use.

Reference: *Reflections upon the Perils and Difficulties of the Winter Navigation of the Delaware,* written and illustrated by Captain William Jones (Philadelphia Chamber of Commerce: 1822).

Manuscript Material, The National Archives, Washington, D. C. Navy Department, General Letter Book XVII #63.

Civil Appointments and Letters from the Department, 1825–Dec. 17, 1829.

Miscellaneous Letters, November, 1828. (#135)

Letter Book, Navy Yard, March 2, 1821–April 22, 1833. (#4, Pages 282, 284, 285).

Topographical Engineers, original manuscript of the Commissioners' Report on the Delaware Breakwater, February 2, 1829. Approved by John Quincy Adams, February 27, 1829. Maps in Map Files, R.9.

Treasury Department, Index Letters Received I, July, 1834–March, 1835. #124 From Strickland at Lewes, Delaware notifying the Treasury Department on September 27, 1835 of the appointment of Mr. Crachen as Revenue officer to be stationed at the Delaware Breakwater.

H.S.P. A drawing and map on one sheet of paper,

entitled "Harbour of the Delaware Breakwater from the Atlantic Ocean."

A.P.S. Triangulation of the Harbour in Delaware Bay print. Library Company of Philadelphia, Ridgway Library. Original working drawings showing the triangulation of the entrance to the Delaware Bay and the deposits made for the breakwater on June 4, and November 1, 1830, signed "William Strickland Engineer/Philadelphia November 12, 1830." One complete drawing and parts of two others have been pasted together. They are now backed with muslin and measure 95 inches long by 30 inches wide.

Tennessee State Library. Drawing of a crane. "Plan & longitudinal section of a Lighthouse to be constructed on the western end of the Delaware Breakwater. W. Strickland Engr. Scale 1/9 of an inch to the foot."

Poussin, Gme. Tell. *Travaux d'améliorations intérieures, projetes ou exécutés par le governement général des États-Unis d'Amerique de 1824 à 1831* (Paris, 1834), Chapter 8.

Hazard's Register of Pennsylvania (Philadelphia, 1828-35), I, 51, 66, 70, 115, 251; II (see Index); VI, 16, 335, 397; X, 311, 334.

Public Works in the United States of America, edited by William Strickland, Architect and Civil Engineer, Edw. H. Gill, Civil Engineer, and Henry R. Campbell, Civil Engineer (London: Weale, 1841).

History: During the eighteenth century and the early years of the nineteenth, Philadelphia was a major port. The approach was through the Delaware Bay and up the Delaware River. The question, therefore, of a breakwater which would provide a safe harbor was a matter of prime importance to the Philadelphia merchants. It is ironic that the breakwater was not undertaken until Philadelphia was a secondary port.

The first printed project was that by William Jones, who had been Secretary of the Navy and Acting Secretary of the Treasury in 1813-14, and president of the Second Bank of the United States from 1816 to 1819. This was presented to the Philadelphia Chamber of Commerce in 1821 and printed by it in 1822. Perhaps as a result of this pamphlet, Congress appropriated $22,000 in March, 1822 for the erection of stone piers which might break the force of the storms which swept up the Delaware and endangered shipping. Jones had suggested a stone breakwater and given designs and estimates; therefore the Chamber of Commerce made an application to the Secretary of the Treasury to have the Bay surveyed with the idea of erecting a breakwater rather than piers. The request was granted and in June, 1823, a commission of United States Engineers composed of General S. Bernard, Lieutenant Colonel J. G. Totten, and Commander Bainbridge made a survey, and presented a report and drawings on July 14, 1823. Congress, however, did not appropriate funds for the Breakwater. Philadelphia sent memorials to Congress in 1824 and 1825. The citizens of Philadelphia held a town meeting on December 28, 1825 at which it was resolved to send a petition to Congress.

Strickland was in Dublin in the summer of 1825 and made a study of the Kingstown Breakwater, and in the *Reports* published by the Pennsylvania Society for the Promotion of Internal Improvement, he made a plate to show how such a breakwater would be adapted to the needs in the Delaware Bay and gave an estimate of $1,380,478.

An Act of Congress on May 24, 1828 appointed a commission to examine the Bay. The commission this time was composed of Commodore Rodgers, U.S.N., Brigadier-General Bernard, U. S. Engineers, and William Strickland, Architect and Engineer. Their report, which is preserved in the National Archives and also printed by Hazard in his *Register of Pennsylvania*, was dated February 2, 1829 and was approved by President Jackson on February 27. It closely followed the report of 1823 and gave the estimated cost as $2,216,950.46.

The letter from Secretary of the Navy Southard to William Strickland, appointing him engineer in charge of the construction of the Breakwater, dated November 24, 1828, and Strickland's acceptance, dated November 29, are both preserved; one, a copy, the other in the original, in the Navy Records of the National Archives.

A short correspondence is also preserved dating from January, 1829, when Strickland purchased a vessel for $2,900 without consulting the Navy Department or requisitioning it through the authorized Navy agent, Clement C. Biddle.

In February, 1829, Southard wrote Strickland that he was to receive the same pay per day that Commodore Rodgers was receiving.

Guillaume Poussin, formerly of the United States Engineers, saw the work in 1831 and commented upon it in his book on public works in the United States, published in Paris in 1834.

L'exécution de ces travaux a été dirigée par M. Wm. Strickland, ingenieur et architecte distingué de Philadelphie, qui, pour cet objet spécial, aurait été nommé membre de la commission qui a donne le plan et prescrit les procédés d'exécution que nous venons de faire connaître.
On ne peut trop admirir la rapitité et le talent avec lesquels cette entreprise a été conduite, puisque déjà le commence de cette baie retire un avantage immédiat des travaux finis jusqu'à ce jour; et cependent, ces travaux n'ont été commencés qu'à la fin de l'année 1829!

By 1840, when Strickland was writing the account of the Breakwater, dated February 12, for the volume on public works in the United States, of which he was one of the editors, he stated, "The Work may be considered now so finished as to have accomplished materially the purposes for which it was projected."

Plan: One breakwater, extending 1,200 yards, ENE, from the point of Cape Henlopen into Delaware Bay. The cross section of the Breakwater shows a batter wall 165¾ feet at the bottom and 22 feet wide at the top with a 45 degree angle slope on either side. The height is 80 feet and stands 5½ feet above high tide. Strickland, in his 1830 report, stated that 23,570 perches of stone were used in 1829 and 29,743.16 by June 23, 1830. The report of the War Department on the Breakwater in 1835 stated that work had ceased because funds were lacking, and that sand was filling up the harbor, making it unusable; hence the report recommended an immediate appropriation of $100,000. In the 1840 report, Strickland suggested a "small casemented tower (estimated cost about $15,000) mounting 6 guns and protecting a temporary battery" as being sufficient defense for the entrance to the Bay and the Breakwater, but it was not constructed. Strickland also projected a lighthouse, with appropriate quarters for the keeper. The drawing and plan are in the Tennessee State Library.

Construction: Cut stone placed according to plan, laid without any binder. Large blocks of great tonnage were used and stability was maintained by inertia.

Cost: About $3,000,000.

Importance: Aid to the shipping on the Delaware River. This benefit was commented upon as early as 1832 in two letters which were printed in *Hazard's Register of Pennsylvania,* X, 311,344. The writer was T. Robinson of the U. S. Brig *Casket.* The first letter was dated Delaware Breakwater, October 26, 1832 and commented upon the absence of wrecks after the recent heavy storms because of the protection afforded by the Breakwater, even in its unfinished condition. To arouse more interest in the undertaking, he sent a sketch of the Breakwater by Traquair with the letter, and added "was this immense pile of stone being got up in New York waters, its advantages would be strongly portrayed in all their prints, and the people would be told in the prettiest manner possible of the utility of the work." Robinson's second letter was dated November 12, 1832 and reported on the state of the Breakwater at that time, "200 yards of 5 foot above high water and a continuence 400 yards at the south part, awash at common high tide."

*1830

Remodeling of the interior of St. Paul's Episcopal Church, Third Street, south of Walnut.

Reference: Hazard's Register of Pennsylvania, VII (January, 1831), 48.

Cost: $11,000. Amount of work done: pulpit decorations, pews, and—in the basement—a vestry room, a lecture room and a Sunday school room.

1830

Report on the route recommended by the Canal Commissioners, advocating bringing the Columbia and Philadelphia Railway into Philadelphia, across the Market Street Bridge and up Market Street.

Reference: *Hazard's Register of Pennsylvania,* V, 191-203.

*1830-34

New Almshouse, Blockley Township.

A part of the original buildings are still in use (1950). (Plates 24 and 25)

Reference: *Hazard's Register of Pennsylvania,* V, 347. Cornerstone laid on May 26, 1830, in the northeast corner of the building. William Strickland, architect; Hugh Scott, stonecutter; Corlies & Copperthwaite, masters; William Gouett, superintendent; John Dicke, clerk.

Ibid., XVI, 302. "A Visit to the New Almshouse," from the *United States Gazette.*

Drawings, Tennessee State Library:

1. "Survey of Land of Alms House and plan from Darby Road to Schuylkill River. Scale 11½ perches to the inch Philadelphia August 1, 1831. Protracted from the Deeds by William Strickland, Archt. and Engr." This drawing shows the topography of the land, the river and creeks; also the wharf on the Schuylkill opposite South Street, roads, and buildings. The land for the Almshouse comprised 187 acres and 60 perches. The ground plan of the Almshouse buildings was 888 by 493 feet and included ten acres.
2. Scale drawing of façade of Almshouse signed "W. Strickland, Archt."
3. Ground plan.
4. Front elevation of Almshouse and adjoining buildings.
5. Operating theatre and ward.
6. "Alms House Detail of Antae & Base Portico."
7. "Alms House Front Andrew J. Binny, Sept. 29th, 1840."

Plan: Four buildings; three and four stories high, about an open square. Interiors with central corridors and rooms on either side, with variations adapted to the needs of the various buildings. Main or east building: central portico of eight Doric columns, central doorway with three windows on either side. Wings, three stories high, with seven windows and a low gable roof, terminated by four-story, transverse ends, with two windows on each floor with pediments. This building housed the offices, the guardian's rooms, the servants' quarters and the men's asylum. The other buildings were plain, without porticoes.

The north building contained the children's asylum with a nursery. On the top of it, there was a reservoir where the water from a 40-foot well was pumped by a 12-horsepower engine which also supplied power to run the machines in the work building.

In the south building, there were the lunatics' ward, medical library, apothecary's shop and laboratory, surgical amphitheatre, and chapel.

The west building was reserved for women. "The northern part of the building is devoted to the accommodation of the lame, the halt, the blind, the idiotic, the convalescent, and the decayed females, classified with care, and, so far as we could observe, provided for with all the liberality that true economy would allow." There were also stores, workshops, and an obstetrical ward. In the center of the square court formed by these buildings was the wash-house, with a steeple, a bell, and a clock with an illuminated dial.

Construction:

The buildings were fireproof throughout. The cellars were arched. The portico was of marble, the remainder of plastered brick.

Style: Rational with a Greek Revival portico.

*1831

Monument to Benjamin Carr, St. Peter's Churchyard, Third and Pine streets. (Plate 28)

Inscription on front:

Benjamin Carr
A Distinguished Professor of Music
Died May 24, 1831, Aged 62 years
Charitable, without Ostentation
Faithful and true in his friendships
With the intelligence of a man,
He united the simplicity of a child.
In testimony of the high esteem in which
he was held, this monument is erected by
his friends and associates of the
Musical Fund Society
of Philadelphia

Reference: *The Inscriptions in St. Peter's Church Yard, Philadelphia,* copied and arranged by Reverend William White Bronson, edited by Charles R. Hildeby, (Camden, 1879).

*1832-34

Philadelphia Exchange (also called Merchants Exchange), Third, Walnut, and Dock streets. (Plates 26 and 27)

Markets have been added to the west front and the interior has been considerably changed.

Reference: *Prospectus of a Plan for . . . an Exchange,* Philadelphia Free Library, Ridgway Branch. *Hazard's Register of Pennsylvania,* XII, 293; XIII, 12,208. J. C. Wild, *Views of Philadelphia and Vicinity* (1838).

Work on the Exchange was begun in 1832. The site is an unusually handsome one, on a slight rise and bounded by three streets, with an open space in front provided by the intersection of Dock and Walnut streets. It was purchased for $75,000. Strickland's original estimate for the building was $159,-435. The new Post Office was opened in the unfinished Exchange on June 25, 1833. In November, 1833, the placing of the capstone was celebrated by a dinner for the 140 men who were employed on the building. At the head table were William Strickland, the architect; John Struthers, the stone-mason; John O'Neill, the master-carpenter; some of the directors, and guests. Many toasts were given of which Strickland proposed two: "The artizans, mechanics and working men engaged in the building of the Philadelphia Exchange. Their good conduct and orderly deportment have been as remarkable as their skill and excellence of workmanship." The second toast was to "Peter and Philip Bardi, sculptors of the capitals." It is especially interesting that Italian sculptors were employed to carve the capitals since the role of the itinerant Italian stonecarver in early nineteenth-century American architecture is yet to be studied. At the dinner, John Struthers gave the following toast, "The merchants and stockholders of the Philadelphia Exchange. It is to their liberality that Philadelphia is indebted for another monument of the Grecian art." J. R. Chandler toasted the architect, "William Strickland, the architect of the Merchants' Exchange. He will realize the boast of the ancient emperor. He found us living in a city of brick, and he will leave us in a city of marble."

The Exchange was opened in March, 1834, earlier than was expected.

Style: Greek Revival in its more ornate expression. The use of Corinthian columns, the rounded portico on Dock Street; the recessed portico on Third Street; the tower in the form of the Choragic Monument of Lysicrates; the full entablature all around the building; and the water-leaf capitals on the ground floor columns all combine to make a richly decorative building.

Plan: Originally the main entrance from Dock Street on the ground floor led to the post office which occupied two-fifths of the floor. On either side of the portico, there are steps which led to doorways to the reading room which occupied the lofty room over the post office. This room was lighted by high French windows which opened on the semicircular portico. J. Coffee was in charge of the reading room when it opened. It has been somewhat changed, but is still an impressive room. Behind this room originally there was a handsome rotunda on the second floor which opened on the Third Street portico. This was the exchange room. The floor "was inlaid with beautiful mosaic work." The ceiling was painted by an Italian painter, Monachesi, who also decorated St. John's Church, Thirteenth Street. On the ground floor, there were five square rooms on each side to be used as offices for insurance companies. The Third Street side on the third floor had a number of small offices, one of which Strickland rented for twelve years.

Elevation: Three stories. The ground floor has recessed doorways; on the sides, the doors are flanked by water-leaf columns taken from the Tower of the Winds in Athens; heavy Tuscan columns flank the entrance on Third Street, while the part under the curved portico on the Dock Street façade is unornamented. On Third Street, the recessed portico rises two stories with four Corinthian columns and two pilasters, crowned by a pediment. The side walls are divided into five bays. In each bay, there is a tripartite opening; on the ground floor this is composed of the door flanked by columns and a narrow window on either side. On the upper stories each bay has a tripartite window. The main façade has a rounded portico which is two stories high with Corinthian columns. These are repeated on the round tower.

Material: Pennsylvania marble. Vaulted ceilings throughout. A minimum of wood was used.

Cost: $159,435.

Outstanding features: Circular portico, tower, interior rotunda, and, formerly, the view from the tower.

Philadelphia Contributionship. Insurance Surveys No. 7442.

I have Surveyed the Exchange Building belonging to "The Philad[a] Exchange Company" situate on Third, Walnut, & Dock Streets. Being 90 feet on Third Street. by 150 feet to Dock Street including the semicircular basement or first story & Portico, thick brick walls faced with marble. Fronting on Third Street from the second story is a portico with four large marble columns fluted & two anties all with richly carved marble capitals. On the Dock Street front is a semicircular portico with Eight columns & two Anties all with capitals &c. as those on Third Street. The first story is divided into Eleven rooms & two halls, one room large, & occupied as the Post office, the other rooms as Public & private offices, seven marble mantles, of neat patan [?], moulded base round, windows cased, & inside shutters to all these. Cornices, fire proof closets with iron doors in seven rooms, the floors of 5/4[in] yellow pine, laid on mortar, the whole of the basement floor is arched under. In the halls is marble wash board, stucco cornice & floored with Italian marble flags. In the large hall are two flights of marble stairs, right & left with large continued hand rail of mahogany & large turn'd ballusters & an opening though the 2nd floor about 12 by 14 feet surrounded by rail & ballusters of the same kind. All the door ways on Walnut Street, Third & part of Dock Street have each two plain marble columns with carved caps. Those on the other part of Dock Street are plain marble folding sash doors, Glass 6½ & 8½ by 15″; a vestibule with each also with folding sash doors. Glass in the windows 12 by 18″. Brick partition walls dividing all the rooms.—The 2nd Story is divided into six rooms, large Hall & Exchange room, one a reading room, two marble mantles, moulded base, windows cased with double architraves, Glass 13 by 18 & 14 by 20″ with panneld inside shutters, the other 5 rooms are occupied as Offices, with marble mantles & neat wash boards, inside Shutters & Stucco cornice. In the Hall is a continuation of the Stairs from the first Story—with mahogany rail & turn'd ballusters to the 3rd Story. In the Exchange room are two marble mantles, moulded base, windows cased, & inside shutters, four large columns of marble with carved caps, similar to those of the Porticos, supporting the roof & ceiling a part of which is a semicircular dome & part flat with a stucco cornice round. The walls & ceiling of this room are ornamented with Fresco painting, outside doors large & folding. The columns in this room also support a circular Lantern of wood, 40 feet high, neatly finish'd outside with Eight columns of wood & with carved capitals, carved roof, covered with copper, ornamented with carved work vane &c. sashes round. The entrance to this room from the Hall has an arch'd head, side lights, venetian door way, & close folding doors. 4 large fluted columns with carved capitals, brick partitions, between the reading room & the North west room, is a flight of open newal stairs such as before described leading to the 3rd Story. The 3rd Story is divided into Seven rooms, & passage, the floor of 5/4″ yellow pine, moulded base, windows cased & pannel'd inside shutters. Those rooms are occupied for public & private purposes, in one is the Magnetic telegraph, operating machine. In this Story is one flight of winding Stairs leading to the Garret, & connecting with a circular Stairs in the Lantern leading to the top of the Same with painted rail, close String & square ballusters. Garret formed in the centre running East & west & plastered stud partitions, floor rough white pine boards, *groved,* two flat sky lights in the roof, the whole of which is boarded & covered with copper.

In the cellar are two Furnaces, safely built in brick work, one for the use of the Post office, & the other for warming the Exchange room, the heat from which passes up through a hollow cast iron column in the hall of the first story into the room, covered by a marble curb with a brass revolving ventilator. A smaller one in the Post office of iron. Marble cornice round the whole building, copper gutterd & pipes.

7 Mo. 3rd 1848. John C. Evans
Surveyor

Liberty of Magnetic Telegraphs in Insured Building. It is expressly understood that this Insurance is not to apply to, nor is the Company to be in any wise responsible for any injury, that may be done

to the Fresco or Ornamental painting in the premises hereby Insured.
Policy No. 7442. Drs. 10.000. at 3 per Cent Drs. 300.–

Agreed to be correct.
John C. Martin
For Phil[a] Exchange Co.

A Furnace in the Cellar (South West Corner) for warming the room above which appears safely constructed.

November 11th 1851 D. R. Knight
Surveyor"

This fire insurance survey was found in the active records of the Contributionship, 212 South Fourth Street, Philadelphia, by Charles E. Peterson.

1833

Second premium in Girard College competition. (Plate 29A)

Reference: *United States Gazette,* Philadelphia, January 3, 1833. The committee appointed to procure plans for the Girard College, reported:

That agreeable to a resolution, passed on the 14th of June, 1832, they caused an advertisement to be published in most of the newspapers of this city, inviting the attention of architects and others to this subject, in consequence of which they have received and examined designs and plans from the following named gentlemen: Higham and Wetherill, New York; Town, Davis & co., do; William Strickland, Thomas U. Walters, W. Rodrique, John Haviland, George Strickland, William B. Crisp, R. W. Israel and Y. J. Stewart of Philadelphia; Mr. Jenks of Germantown; Edward Shaw, John Kutts and Isaiah Rogers of Boston; Lieutenant William M. Mather of West Point and two others.

Hazard's Register of Pennsylvania, II, 126. Award of premiums in competition.

Ibid., p. 154. February 23, 1833.

Mr. Groves's resolution adopted by Select and Common Councils that the Mayor be and is authorized to draw on the Treasurer of Girard Trusts in favor of Thomas U. Walter $400., William Strickland $200., Isaiah Rogers $150., being premiums awarded them at the meeting of Councils February 12. *Ibid.,* p. 314. On Thursday evening, March 14, 1833 at a joint meeting of Select and Common Councils, T. U. Walter was elected architect of Girard College by receiving 16 votes. Mr. Strickland received 13.

Water-color study of three buildings, Girard College, Philadelphia, signed by Strickland, not dated. The main building is a Doric peristyle temple with ten columns on the front and eighteen on the side. Judging by Strickland's comment on the plan chosen for Girard College in his letter to John Struthers, it would seem that his first plan would have been more in keeping with the directions given in Girard's will. This may have been a second attempt, but that is only surmise, as the drawing is not dated.

*1834

Estimate of work needed on grounds of the Naval Asylum.

Reference: Records of the Department of the Navy, PN–Naval Asylum, Philadelphia; construction. 1826-35.
William Strickland to Commodore James Barron, Philadelphia, May 12, 1834.

Estimate of work needed to be done on grounds of the asylum

1200 ft board fencing	820.00
excavating 4000 cu ft of earth on road	800.00
paving and curbing 1200 ft of 60 ft wide street	2900.00
circular gravel walk between the entrance and portico, 20 ft wide by 900 in length	1000.00
ploughing, harrowing and sowing grass on ground in front and purchase and planting 80 trees	580.00
building milk house, ice house and stalls	2800.00
(material from old barn)	8900.00

Also, of the same date, a letter on using Schuylkill water in the Asylum. Fixtures for baths, water closets, sinks with iron piping would cost $3,000, and the annual rent would be $60 a year.

On the same day, May 12, 1834, Barron sent letters and estimates to the Navy agent Rogers who, in turn, on May 16 sent them to Secretary Woodbury in Washington with a request for authorization and for funds from the General Hospital Fund.

There are no letters to show whether the work was authorized and how much was done. The present grounds, roads, and paths suggest that Strickland's plan was carried out, although it is certain that the work was not completed for a year.

A letter (#120) from Rodgers to John Boyle, Acting Secretary of the Navy, dated May 29, 1835, recommends that the old dwelling house on the Asylum grounds be destroyed because, "it prevents grading of land and permits water to settle about the Main Building." It could be sold for $160, he stated, and he concluded by requesting an authorization to sell on the best terms.

1834

"A Great Project for Sixth and Walnut Streets." (Plate 29B)

Reference: A first-story plan signed "William Strickland, Archt." in the Strickland portfolio in the Tennessee State Library. A plan for the prison lot at Sixth and Walnut streets and the adjoining streets and properties. Strickland portfolio, Tennessee State Library.

The plan, drawn on the scale of 12 feet to one inch, is for a building 174 by 224 feet, with an interior open court 61 by 108 feet, and a yard to the east 24 feet wide by 224 long, in which are situated 14 privies. The main entrance was to be from Walnut Street. Double stairways are indicated in the center of the north and south portions of the building and single stairways in the center of the east and west sections. There are eight large rooms and four small rooms, each 16 by 21 feet. The rooms are assigned to the following societies: Academy of Natural Sciences, Foreign Library, Law Academy, Mercantile Library, Pennsylvania Library Company, and Athenaeum.

In the *Early Proceedings of the American Philosophical Society, 1744-1838,* there are several references to a committee on a building for the Scientific and literary Associations of Philadelphia, which appears to have prompted this drawing.

On January 3, 1834, this committee which was composed of N. Chapman, Joseph Hopkinson, J. K. Kane, William Strickland, and John Vaughn made a report and presented a plan and an estimate of $30,000. The committee united "in commending the beauty and commodious arrangement of the Building which has been proposed." They added that the facilities for the library and the museum were "less dangerous than those in the present building." However, the membership of the American Philosophical Society was opposed to a joint building, and on June 27, 1834, all the committees which had been working on the project were discharged (p. 29).

1835

Survey of the route of the Wilmington and Susquehanna Railroad.

Reference: *Franklin Journal,* XV (No. 4, April, 1835), 225-34. Letter from Strickland, giving his opinion of the route, dated Philadelphia, February 11, 1835. The actual survey was made by his pupil, John C. Trautwine, under Strickland's personal supervision.

*1835

"Parsonage" or "Stone House," built for the Reverend Courtland Van Rensselaer. Corner of River Bank and Talbot Street, Burlington, New Jersey. (Plate 30A)

Reference: Owners (1950): Mr. and Mrs. A. Neilson Carter.

Dr. Edward B. Hodge of Philadelphia, a descendant of the original owner, has inherited a perspective view of the "Parsonage" in water color and ink which is signed "W. Strickland Archt et Delint."

Portfolio of Strickland drawings. Tennessee State Library. Front elevation in pencil with a working drawing of the front wall, 1 foot eight inches thick. A front elevation and ground plan with a torn inscription, ". . . age House . . . ton, N. J." which may have read "Parsonage House, Burlington, N. J." The ground plan is similar to the house as it now is, but the elevation is different.

Style: Cottage Gothic or Tudor Villa achieved by hood moldings, casement windows of varying sizes, an arched window, battlements, a front porch and side conservatory roofed with copper with a sloping concave profile, edged with a barge board of tooth pattern, gabled roofs with projecting eaves.

Plan: Symmetrical, central-hall type with two rooms on either side. The small stairs are behind the main hall. At the back is a one room, one-story ell with a three-sided end. The large kitchen and storage closets are in the basement. There are four bedrooms and two small dressing rooms upstairs. Over the front hall was a chapel, 15 by 18 feet, with a vaulted ceiling and a pointed window. The low attic was intended for storage.

Materials: Local stone, plastered and painted yellow, was used for the outer walls and brick for the interior. The trim is all wood, and the roof is of wood covered with copper. The size is 48 feet wide by 39 feet deep, with the castellated one-room wing at the back right, 17 by 18 feet. This was the rector's study, warmed by a large fireplace. The general construction is massive and heavy.

Outstanding features: The hood moldings and the castellated wing.

1835

Plans and estimate of proposed hall for the Franklin Institute, on the site of the Masonic Hall, Chestnut Street between Seventh and Eighth streets.

Project not carried out because of the depression of 1837.

Reference: *Franklin Journal* (n.s.) XV, 380-84. On June 20, 1835, a resolution was passed to sell the Hall of the Franklin Institute, which had been designed by John Haviland in 1825 and to buy the Grand Lodge or Masonic Hall. At the quarterly meeting on October 27, 1835, "The architect of the new hall, William Strickland, Esq., explained the drawings, presented to the meeting by the committee." In the Report of the Committee on Extension of Accommodations of the Franklin Institute, it is recorded that the Masons wanted $110,550 for their hall and land to be paid on June 1, 1842. Strickland's estimate for alterations to the Masonic Hall and land was $175,000, and for the new building which they proposed erecting behind the Lodge, $99,450. The Masonic Hall was to be remodeled with janitor's quarters and classrooms in the basement, a large lecture hall, 60 by 100 feet and 30 feet high, with seating capacity for 1,200 on the main floor, and apartments above. The new building was to be four stories high with a ground area of 30 by 72 feet, with an exhibition room on the ground floor, a library and a manager's room on the second floor, a model room on the third, and more exhibitions on the fourth floor.

1835

Plan of Pennsylvania Hotel, southeast corner of Walnut and Sixth streets. Project not executed.

Reference: *Hazard's Register of Pennsylvania,* XVI, 287.

A ground plan and drawing in perspective of the new hotel to be erected on the site of the old Walnut Street prison, is now to be seen at the Exchange. The Building was designed, and the plan etc. drawn by our distinguished architect, William Strickland, Esq. and is on a scale worthy of the city to which it will be an ornament.

Summary of the article: Favorable site with one side fronting Independence Square and the other fronting Washington Square. Primarily for family lodgings. Frontage of 180 feet on Walnut Street; 423 feet on Sixth Street. Five Stories.

Basement: 5 stores, 24 shops, stage, refreshment and oyster cellar.

Principal story: 1 coffee room, 3 suites of bathrooms, 26 parlors, 1 dining room 56 by 108 feet, kitchen beneath—same size, 1 bar room, 1 barber's shop, 2 baggage rooms, 1 reading room, 1 private dining room, 1 ladies' dining-room, 1 ladies' drawing room, 2 rooms for servants, etc.

Third Floor: 22 parlors, 58 bedrooms, 1 suite ladies' bathing rooms.

Fourth and fifth floors: 22 parlors, 66 bedrooms, 12 servants' rooms.

Total: 29 stores, 82 parlors, 200 bedrooms, 25 miscellaneous rooms; 336 rooms in all.

*1835

Plan and estimate of the Branch Mint, Charlotte, North Carolina. (Plate 30B)

The building was constructed between 1835 and 1840 by Perry and Ligon of Raleigh, North Carolina. It burned on July 27, 1844, but was reconstructed on the same plan, completed in 1846. It was in use as a mint until 1861 and as an assay office until 1913. In 1932, the government ordered it to be destroyed. A group of Charlotte citizens determined to preserve the building by purchasing the material of the Mint building which was then (February, 1933) being torn down. E. C. Griffith offered a twenty-acre lot in Eastover to the Mint Museum Society. It was accepted and through the Public Works Administration the rebuilding was started in December, 1933. The work was completed and the building was opened as the Mint Museum of Art on October 22, 1936.

Reference: Pamphlets of the Mint Museum of Art. Letters of B. Rhett Chamberlain, vice-president of the Mint Museum of Art.

Congressional Record. Acts passed at the First Session of the 22nd Congress, 1835, chap. 39, p. 42– An act to establish branches of the Mint of the United States. IV. Statute at Large, Mar. 3, 1835, p. 774. Executive Documents, 1st Sess., 24th Cong., III, 1825-36, #76; House Documents, 2nd Sess., 24th Cong., #54, 96; House Documents, 2nd Sess., 25th Cong., #110, 273, 457.

The National Archives, Washington, D. C. Mint Documents TD44-20.

Estimate of the cost of the accompanying plan and elevation of a building for a Mint.

Digging cellar and foundation–1107 cub. yds.	$221
Cellar walls–450 perches building stone including laying, lime and sand	1350
Bricks, laying, lime and sand–420,000	4200
The 1st story to be arched in the front alone	
Carpenters work	4500
Lumber	5200
Plastering including materials	2800
Painting and Glazing	2500
Ironmongery, nails, screws, etc.	800
Cast iron columns for Piazzas	400
Blacksmiths work	1750
Zinc covering for roof. . 6000 sq. ft.	1200
Stone window sills, steps and door sills and heads	800
Rough casting	844
Gutters and Conductors	460
Stone water table all round the building 5 ft in height	1688
Total cost	$28,713
Add for difference of labor and materials, hauling etc.	5,000
	$33,713

respectfully submitted,
W. Strickland, Architect

Philada. July 11th, 1835

Strickland's plan and estimate were accepted. He was not the superintendent in charge of the building the Mint at Charlotte, North Carolina, but he was consulted when any problem in the interpretation of the plan presented itself, as is shown by the following letter, also in the National Archives.

Philada. June 3 1836.

Dear Sir,

In answer to your letter of the 2nd inst enclosing the profile of the cornice of the Branch Mint now building at Charlotte, N. C. I enclose you the same profile with the method marked, upon which the Architrave, frieze and Cornice is to be finished and then rough cast.– The projection of the cornice must of course be sustained by means of *flag stones* laid *in* and *out* of the walls of the building.– The cyma is to be supported by the flags, and the Eve course of the roof will project over the cyma to protect the whole.

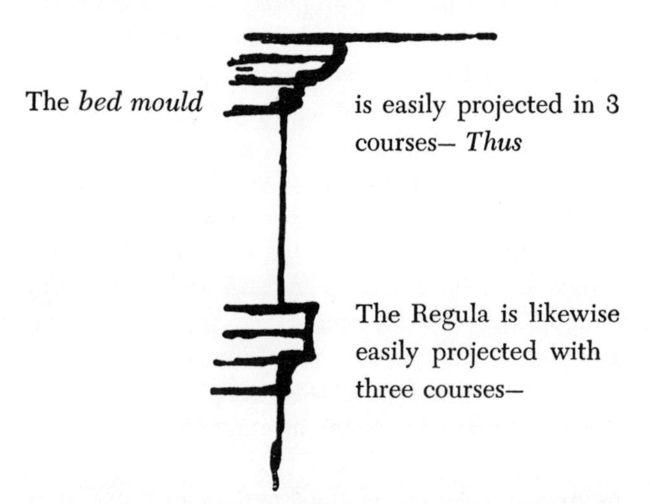

The flags may be rough and 3 feet in length by any breadth which they happen to have.

Very truly
yours.
W. Strickland

To/
R. M. Patterson Esqr
Prest. of the U. S. Mint.

One of the earliest descriptions of this Branch Mint is to be found in Turner and Hughes' North Carolina *Almanac* for 1840, the year in which the building was completed. The account follows:

The edifice is beautifully located on the street leading to Lincolnton and has a commanding appearance. It has a front of 125 feet with a rear building of fifty-three feet. It was designed by Mr. Strickland, a distinguished Architect of Philadelphia, and executed by Messrs Perry & Ligon, under the Supervision of Major Samuel McComb of Charlotte. In addition to the regular mint edifice are the Quarters of the Superintendent who resides in the Mint; the out-houses of which were contracted for and built by Mr. Jonas Bost of Lincolnton.

As yet no print of the building as it was before the fire in July, 1844, has been found. The Mint was rebuilt according to the original plans, but it seems likely that there were various changes in the façade. Strickland's estimate did not indicate the present porch with Tuscan columns although it did include an item for cast-iron columns for piazzas, which are no longer present. Also, there is not a cornice, frieze, and architrave, as indicated by the sketch in Strickland's letter to Patterson of June 3, 1836.

The building, as it now stands, is an exceptionally pleasing example of the Classic Revival, but until further information is available, it is impossible to determine how much credit for the present building should be given to the Strickland design.

*1835-36

Plan of the United States Mint, Esplanade and Decatur streets, New Orleans. (Plate 31)

In use as a Mint: 1838-62, 1879-1910.

Used by the Veterans Bureau: 1927-30.

Converted into a federal prison in 1931 by Diboll and Owen, architects. Large dormitories and cell blocks were added to the rear of the wings, the smokestack was removed, and the rear courts enclosed by high walls.

Offices of the Coast Guard occupy it at present (1950).

Reference: The Strickland drawings are preserved in the Notarial Records in the Court House in New Orleans.

The New Orleans Association of Commerce supplied information and photographs.

House Documents #462, Second Session, Twenty-seventh Congress.

The Nashville Whig Banner, May 27, 1843.

Style: Greek Revival. A front central portico with a high entablature and a flat roof with corner piers and four Ionic columns. Doorways with pilasters and an entablature over the main entrance. An entablature all about the building. Pediments at the ends of the central building and the ends of the wings.

Plan: Symmetrical with cross axes. Three stories: Basement, main story, and attic.

Construction and materials: River mud brick, stuccoed and trimmed with granite. Vaulted and fireproof. The walls, which are offset both inside and outside, range in thickness from 3 feet on the ground floor to 18 inches on the upper story. The roof was originally copper. In 1856, a 20-gauge galvanized iron roof was laid and is still in good condition.

Outstanding feature: The main vaulting is supported by piers and not tied into the walls, thus eliminating the danger of settlement to the exterior.

Cost: Estimate, $182,000. Expenditure by 1843, $254,740, including an item of $818 for finishing water closets.

1836(?)

Drawing of an Egyptian Revival gate, flanked by obelisks, with "Laurel Hill" on the lintel. Signed "W. Strickland, Archt." (Plate 32A)

Laurel Hill Cemetery Company founded: November, 1835.

Grounds purchased: February, 1836.

Incorporated: 1837.

Reference: Drawing in the Library Company of Philadelphia, Ridgway Library.

R. A. Smith, *Smith's Illustrated Guide to and through Laurel Hill Cemetery* (Philadelphia, 1852).

In manuscript on file at the Department of Art, University of Pennsylvania, a term paper by John Batz "Egypt in Philadelphia," pp. 14-15.

In Ridgway Library, beside the Strickland drawing, there is a drawing of an Egyptian pylon gate for Laurel Hill by Thomas U. Walter, dated May 14, 1836. In the minutes of the Cemetery Company, no mention of Strickland has been found. It would seem that both Strickland and Walter made drawings on their own initiative. By 1837, the Roman Doric gate which is still standing (1950) was completed under the supervision of John Notman, architect of the company.

*1836

Providence Athenaeum, 251 Benefit Street, Providence, Rhode Island. (Plates 33A, B)

Plans dated: November, 1836.

Cornerstone laid: April 4, 1837.

Dedicated: July 11, 1838.

Interior alterations: 1868 (by James C. Bucklin); 1894-98, 1906.

Wing added: 1914.

The present Providence Athenaeum was chartered in 1836, the result of the union of the Providence Library Company, which was started in 1753 and an earlier Providence Athenaeum, founded in 1831. Also, in 1836, the library received an offer from Nicholas Brown, Moses B. Ives, and Robert H. Ives—executors of the estate of the late Thomas P. Ives—of the lot at the corner of College and Benefit streets, valued at $4,000; of $6,000 to be spent on "an edifice to be erected of stone or brick for the suitable accommodation of the Athenaeum, Historical and Franklin Societies—the lot and building to be owned by the Athenaeum"; and of $4,000 for the purchase of books on the condition that $10,000 was subscribed by others towards the building and $4,000 for books.

The offer was accepted, the money raised, a building committee appointed, and plans procured from the Providence architect Russell Warren. His project was too expensive and, since he was in Nova Scotia at that time and thus unable to revise his plan, another architect was sought. The committee "having ascertained that Willian Strickland of Philadelphia, had a reputation second to none in this country in his profession," invited him to Providence, "expressly for the purpose of surveying the site for the Library, and of drafting a plan which should not be beyond the pecuniary ability of this Corporation to execute."

Strickland visited Providence in November, 1836, and furnished a plan which, with one major change, was carried out. The original drawings, which are still in the Athenaeum, call for a building with a frontage of 48 feet and a depth of 98 feet. The building as completed is 48 by 78 feet. The proposals from carpenters, masons, and quarry owners are preserved in the Athenaeum and explain why the change was made. The first estimates added up to more than the allotted $16,000. The building committee inquired whether the other societies which were to be housed in the same building would mind a revised plan. The Franklin Society agreed to shortening the building by not more than twenty feet. The building committee then got proposals on the revised plan. This time the total was within the permitted amount. The proposals date from September 29 to March 13. Nathaniel Potter provided the granite for the front section from his quarry at Quincy, Massachusetts. The granite for the other walls came from the quarry of Amasa Sweet at Johnston, Rhode Island. The stonemason was Samuel B. Durfee of Providence. The carpenter was Ebenezer Carpenter. Proposals or estimates were also received from Joseph A. Andrews for the masonry work, and from J. H. Sprague, and E. Martin, and Tallman and Bucklin for the carpenter's work.

Strickland provided three drawings all of which are signed, but not dated. One sheet, 22½ by 27 inches, has a small-scale front elevation in the upper center, a plan of the basement on the left, and a plan of the principal story on the right. There is an unsigned copy of this sheet drawn to the same scale. Various indications suggest that the copy may have been drawn by Strickland's son, Francis. The inked lines are thinner and less sure, the masonry walls are indicated in mulberry instead of pink-gray, and the Roman lettering slopes slightly to the right. There are a few minor inaccuracies in the copy such as an additional step and variations in indicating the masonry work.

The second sheet has a transverse section on the scale of ¼ of an inch to one foot. At the bottom of the sheet is the silhouette of the washboard outlined in ink and drawn at the actual scale. The construction of the roof, supported by king-and-queen posts is shown, and notations on the side give the sizes of the rafters and girders. Notations are also given as to the size of the windows: in the basement, 4 feet 9 inches by 6 feet 7 inches; in the principal story, 4 feet 7 inches by 10 feet 7 inches; 4- by 6-inch lights, "frames revealed with Quirk ovolo and bead." A door is also shown which is typical of the doors used throughout the building; double doors with vertical panels recessed twice. Three of the original interior doors are still in place.

The third drawing is of the longitudinal section, scaled ½ an inch to one foot, and is drawn on a double sheet. Again the construction of the roof is carefully given with the size of the purlins (6 inches by 8 inches), rafters (6 inches by 12 inches), and jack rafters (3 inches by 7 inches). In the façade, the nineteen steps are indicated, but not the acroteriun. Eight windows along the side are shown. Under the brick piers of the basement there is a note in Strickland's writing, "cast iron columns may be here used instead of brick piers." The ceiling of the basement is at present supported by simple cast-iron columns with rounded capitals. Perhaps the most interesting feature of the drawing is the heating system. Fireplaces were still generally used in the 1830's, but this building was to be entirely heated by hot air. The system was the same as the one which Strickland described in 1818 for the heating of the banking room of the Second Bank of the United States, but on a larger scale. In the front of the basement under the portico was, and still is, a storage place for coal, then a cellar with an opening for the stove and a large air chamber with a circular opening at the top for the passage of the warm air into the reading room above. The flue from the stove went straight to the level of the ceiling and was then turned at right angles and extended to the front wall by the door and bent about it to rise straight to the apex of the pediment where the chimney was disguised by the carved acroterial block.

Besides the original drawings, Strickland's specifications are also preserved in the Athenaeum on one folded sheet of paper. They cover three and a half sides of the sheet in his neat, legible handwriting. There is also another set of specifications in a clear but unknown hand, evidently that of an older man since there are long *s*'s and *Doric* is spelt with a *k*, old-fashioned usages. The copy gives the specifications for the building as completed with the shortened length of 78 feet and there are a number of minor variations throughout.

The basement plan, as designed by Strickland, called for two main rooms for the accommodation of the Franklin Society. The front section was reserved for the heating system. In the middle of the building, there was a room 34 by 44 feet, heated by a stove, which was to be used for experiments. A narrow stairway, parallel to the division wall, rose to the Athenaeum, behind which was another room, 31 by 44 feet. The basic divisions of the ground floor are the same, but the small stairway has been removed and a large stairway put in the central room. The Franklin Society remained in these quarters for ten years and the basement was then taken over by the Athenaeum and the front room is now used for a periodical reading room and the back room for book stacks and storage.

The principal floor was planned to house both the Athenaeum and the Historical Society, but the latter never moved in. The door from the portico led into a narrow vestibule, 7 feet wide with a small room, 13 by 18 feet, on either side. The one to the left was for the use of the librarian, and still is. In the space between the portico and the front wall, there was to be a fireproof closet. The closet is still there, but is not fireproof. The main reading room was 34 by 44 feet, and behind it there were to be two smaller rooms for the Historical Society. This is now one large room lined with alcoves of bookshelves and a skylight has replaced the sturdy rafter-roof designed by Strickland.

The exterior has been slightly changed from the original drawing. A door has been added at the back from College Street and a wing on the other side, but, otherwise, the walls, doors, and windows are as they were originally built. The granite walls are now covered with ivy so the clear-cut form of the building is lost in summer. The cornice, entablature, and pediment are of wood. The recessed portico is roughcast to simulate granite and the floor is of enormous flagstones. The main architectural embellishment is the two Doric columns, 14 feet high, with a diameter of 2 feet 4½ inches at the bottom and 1 foot 9¾ inches at the top. The capitals are of the simplest type with a single filet band for necking.

One other rather important change was made by the building committee. Strickland's specifications called for 24-inch walls in the basement and 20-inch walls in the upper story. These were not considered thick enough and two inches were added.

The Athenaeum is an excellent example of Greek Revival at its best. It is simple, well-proportioned, of excellent construction. Utility was not sacrificed for appearance. The classic features were used with restraint; the central axis in the length of the building, the gable roof, and the recessed portico with the two Doric columns.

1836-37

Capitol of North Carolina, Raleigh, North Carolina. Strickland called in as consultant.

Reference: Two letters from Strickland in the North Carolina Department of Archives and History. One dated Philadelphia, November 4, 1836, addressed to David Paton, at that time the supervising architect of the Capitol which had been designed by Town and Davis in 1833. The other letter is addressed to General Beverly Daniel, Chairman of the board of commissioners for building the Capitol, dated Philadelphia, November 10, 1837.

1837

Philadelphia Bank, between Fourth and Fifth streets on Chestnut Street. (Plate 32B)

Reference: Proceedings of the American Philosophical Society (1854), XVI. Letter and memorandum among the Etting papers, H.S.P. The original envelope is also preserved and Strickland's round seal of light red wax is intact. The impression is of a cockleshell with a twisted bar below and a semicircular banner above inscribed "coeur ouvert." The envelope is addressed to

The Cashier of B.U.S.
To/Messrs Lippincott, Neff &
Vanderkemp —— Copperthwaite
Bank United States

Also there is the following note on the envelope:

Wm Strickland's account
Building–East of BUS

$35.249 c

Sept. 28, 1837

Note: The following letter and memo do not conclusively show that the building here referred to was the new Bank of Philadelphia. The old Gothic-style building, designed by Benjamin H. Latrobe and built in 1809 under the superintendence of Robert Mills, was at the corner of Fourth and Chestnut streets. The new building was illustrated in *Views of Philadelphia* by J. C. Wild, 1838, Plate II. It is a handsome building with stores on the lower floor and the bank in the main story with a central portico of six columns which appear to be composite.

Philada Sept 28th 1837

To/

The Building Committee of the United States Bank.

Gentlemen,

I have the honor to enclose you my account for building the new Banking house and stores adjoining the Philadelphia bank on Chesnut street, as there are several bills remaining unpaid I will thank you to place to my credit the balance of the account, in order that I may settle them and furnish you with a release for workmanship & materials.

Very respectfully
Your obdt servt
William Strickland

To/

Messrs Lippincott, Neff & Vanderkemp
The United States Bank
To William Strickland Dr.

For amount of estimate for building on Chestnut Street in conjunction with the Philadelphia Bank	27,000
For Mr. Struthers bill of marble and workmanship for the flank next the Bank U.S. including cornice, coping and watch box	7,220
Two fire proofs with iron doors in the shops of basement story	250
Mr. McClures bill of extra work in flooring the ceilings over the Prest & Directors rooms, including balustrade & Jas. Allens bill of extra plastering	479
For brick wall to the alley south side of building, including capping etc.	200
For 10 Tons of coal for heating the building during the last winter	100
	35,249
Cash received at sundry times	24,000
Balance due	11,249

1837

Design for the Sarcophagus of Washington at Mount Vernon, Virginia. (Plate 49A)

Reference: *The Pennsylvania Inquirer,* Monday, September 18, 1837. "The design, we understand, was furnished by that gifted artist, Mr. Wm. Strickland, but the execution is by an exquisitely delicate chisel, from the hands of a workman, Mr. John Hill, in the employ of Mr. Struthers."

The Tomb of Washington at Mount Vernon (Philadelphia: Carey and Hart, 1840). This small booklet apparently was edited by Strickland, at least he signed the dedication to Henry Clay and made the drawing of the tomb and the burial plot at Mount Vernon. The booklet includes the correspondence between Lawrence Lewis, to whom Mount Vernon had descended and John Struthers, the English marble-mason, who had settled in Philadelphia and built up a reputation for carving funereal monuments. In one letter (p. 17), Struthers wrote of "My friend, William Strickland, who gave the design." There is also a description of the transfer of the body to the new sarcophagus and the "Farewell Speech."

1838-39

Consultant Engineer for the Cairo City and Canal Company. (Plate 35)

In the autumn of 1838 Strickland made a survey of the site of the city of Cairo, at the confluence of the Ohio and Mississippi rivers in Illinois, with Richard C. Taylor, engineer and geologist. They prepared a map of the site and a cross section to show the relation of the proposed city and the levees and also a five-page report. They were employed by John Wright and Co. of London which issued and sold bonds amounting to £287,600 for the Cairo City and Canal Company. Strickland was retained as a consulting engineer by the company of which Darius B. Holbrook was president. Both Strickland and Taylor were among the six advisory people listed in Philadelphia.

Reference: John M. Lansden, *A History of the City of Cairo, Illinois* (Chicago, 1910), pp. 42, 48, 112, 116, 162.

Cairo Business Mirror and City Directory for 1864-65. Compiled by Thomas Lewis (Cairo, 1864). *Cairo, Illinois* (American Guide Series, 1938), p. 19.

There is a tradition in the family that Strickland was paid for his services to the Cairo City and Canal Company by a grant of land and that part of the city of Cairo still bears his name.

1838

Plans for the Episcopal Church of the Holy Trinity, West Chester, Pennsylvania.

Reference: Two plans in the Strickland portfolio, Tennessee State Library. One plan is titled "Church on Gay Street" and signed "William Strickland Archt & Engineer," with the notation "Scale 8 ft to the Inch." It shows a rectangular plan with central projecting steps before an entrance distyle-in-antis portico. On the interior, there are four blocks of pews, a semicircular recess for the altar, with choir seats on either side.

The other plan is unsigned but inscribed "Trinity Church West Chester Pa. Scale 8 ft to the inch." This plan is also rectangular with a projecting distyle portico in front and a slight projection behind the pulpit. There are stairs from the vestibule. In the auditorium, there are three blocks of seats of seventeen rows each. The chancel is eighteen feet wide; there is a reading desk and pulpit in the center of the back wall with seats for the choir on either side. The width of the building is 56 feet. In the history of the church which was published in honor of its centennial celebration in 1938, no reference is made to Strickland as the architect of the first church, started in 1838, built by Benjamin F. Haines for $3,695 and consecrated on July 12, 1839. The church was on the north side of Gay Street between Darlington and New streets.

1839

Strickland tried, unsuccessfully, to procure an American patent for a propeller, designed by a Mr. Smith.

Reference: Two letters from Strickland to Dr. Thomas P. Jones, Patent Office, Washington, D. C., are preserved from the correspondence between them on the subject of Smith's propeller. Dr. Jones formerly edited the *Franklin Journal,* and taught mechanics at the Franklin Institute when Strickland was teaching architecture there. Smith was evidently an Englishman whom Strickland had met during his visit to England, the previous year.

The first letter is in the Manuscript Collection of the New York-Historical Society and follows:

Phila., June 8th, 39.

Dr. Thos. P. Jones
Patent Office, Washington
Dear Sir,
Yours of the 6th came duly to hand and I am glad to learn that the model of Mr. Smith's propeller has arrived, and been deposited in the Patent Office. Many thanks for your disposition to urge its early examination.
I will send you the fee of $20. upon the arrival of the steam ship Liverpool, which will be in about 3 weeks.
I have received a letter from one of the agents of the *screw ship* in London in which he says, "*Our ship* has arrived at Portsmouth after a cruise in the Channel, she goes 10 knots with ease, and has beaten one of the Government steamers.— She has encountered bad weather and met it beautifully.— She has astonished the naval men in steering. She *turns* in *double her own length.* Goodbye to paddle boxes for the Ocean, as a *tug* it is believed no power will equal the screw under water."

With great respect, Sir
Your obdt Servant,
W. Strickland.

This letter is postmarked June 10 and was sealed with Strickland's seal, the shell and *coeur ouvert* motto. On the back there is a note in Jones' handwriting, "Wrote to Mr. Strickland June 15th & sent on Mr. Smith's specification with the objections of this office, and proposed to confine their claim to the location in the deal wood."

Strickland replied, giving the exact position of the propeller as "in the stern under water above the keel," and reiterating that he would send the fee later. The letter is preserved in the Manuscript Collection of the Historical Society of Pennsylvania, Simon Gratz Collection (Box 25, Case 7).

An examination of patents issued shows that Strickland was not able to obtain a patent for Smith's propeller.

1839

Plans of a proposed hotel at the southwest corner of Chestnut and Ninth streets, extending to Sansom Street. (Plates 34A, B, C)

Reference: Three drawings in the Harold E. Gillingham collection in the Historical Society of Pennsylvania. "Drawn by Wm. Strickland, arch. for Edward Shippen Burd about 1839-40." (The date has been crossed off and "1848" substituted.) Paper is watermarked "J. Whatman 1837," which suggests the earlier date.

Note: There is no indication of who was responsible for dating the drawings. Since Strickland was in Nashville in 1848, it seems unlikely that he did them there. And since during the winter of 1839-40, he was doing little architectural work but was making plans and projects, the earlier date seems the more probable.

Drawing 1. Elevation of the Ninth Street façade. Signed "Wm. Strickland. Scale ½ inch to one foot." Length, 235 feet. Height, 46 feet. Four stories: first and second, 12 feet high; third, 11 feet; fourth, 9 feet. A plain rectangular building with a low hip roof and no adornment. Twenty-three windows across the upper stories, 14 doors on main floor, one of which is the main entrance to the hotel, and 7 entrances to stores which have large, square display windows.

Drawing 2. Elevation of the George (Sansom) Street façade. Length, 101 feet. Six stories high. Eight windows across the upper stories. Two arches, each 10 feet wide, at the central entrance to the hotel; 4 store entrances. Large square windows.

Note: A blue wash was used for the roof, probably indicating slate. White was used for cornice and trims of doors and windows, indicating wood; and pink was used for the main body of the building to indicate brick.

Drawing 3. A large sheet with plans for the first, or basement, story and the second, or main, story. Scale, 8 feet to the inch. On the basement floor in the center of the Chestnut Street front, the main entrance to the hotel is shown through an open vestibule with eight columns; a porter's lodge and a bar are beyond, and then stairs to the main part of the hotel. The street fronts are flanked with stores. There is a small court in the center and a 10-foot passage beyond, leading to Sansom Street. To the east there is a row of privies for the stores and to the west a group of 6 privies for the service. The west back central portion is allotted to the kitchen, scullery, and washroom. To the north are a group of small rooms for the barber shop, housekeeper's room, laundry, pantry, boot-room, and porter's room. The walls are two feet thick.

The basic divisions of the basement are carried out in the second floor also: the court, the central back passage, and the row of privies. The largest room is an exhibition room 22 by 100 feet at the corner of Ninth and Chestnut streets, reached by private stairs. At the other side is the dining room 25 x 90 feet. Between the two, there are four large chambers and the front stairs. At the end of the dining room, there is another flight of stairs, beyond which is a double row of seven chambers, 12 by 15 feet, each with two windows flanking a fireplace. There is a central passage and two bathrooms with four baths each at the ends. Behind the exhibition room on Ninth Street, there are a series of private drawing rooms, most of them 20 by 19 feet, two with private stairs. At the George Street end, there is the large public drawing room and two large private ones with stairways.

1839

Plans of a proposed Hall at Sixth and Walnut streets.

Reference: Plan of basement story, plan of principal story, and specifications are in the Historical Society of Pennsylvania.

Specifications

Proposed Hall 75 by 70 ft Area–5259
Philosophical Hall 50 by 70 ft Area–3500

Increased difference 1750

This design comprehends 3 Stories in height, with cellars under the whole.

Basement Story 10 ft containing
Four offices of 2 Rooms each
Estimated at a rent of 500 $ pr annum, = 2000.
Three single offices – 300 pr an 900.

Principal Story 16 ft in height, containing
A Library – News-room – Directors, –
and a room for the Librarian. –

Attic Story 12 ft in height, containing
Four Rooms, the same as in the principal story, which may accommodate
Engravers, Pointers, etc.: average rent – 300$ pr annum *1200*

The Pilasters and Entablature on each of the fronts to be constructed with marble.
The body of the building brick, rough cast with hydraulic cement.
The steps of the Basement and the Architraves of the windows and doors to be of marble.
The roof covered with copper.
Estimated cost of the building above described– $42,000

William Strickland Archt.
Philadelphia Novr 27th 1839.

1840

Drawing of a monument to Fulton in the portfolio of Strickland drawings in the Tennessee State Library. An obelisk on a rectangular base. On the base is the inscription:

To
Fulton
The people of the West
Have erected this obelisk
At the City of Cairo
In commemoration of the
Great benefits which have
Followed the invention
of steam navigation
on these waters
1840

Note: It is assumed that this monument was never erected since it does not exist now and there is no record of it. Probably the failure of Wright and Co. on November 23, 1840, and the subsequent failure of the Cairo City and Canal Company, prevented its erection.

1840

Drawings for St. James' Church, Richmond, Virginia.

Reference: Drawing in the Strickland portfolio,

Tennessee State Library, Nashville, labeled "Design of a pulpit and Reading Desk for St. James' Church. William Strickland Archt."

William and Mary College Quarterly, II, No. 2 (October 1893), 136. A letter from B. B. Minor to the editor states, "The record of St. James' Church shows that Genaro Persico, John Williams, and Dr. James Beale were its building committee, and Persico endeavored to interest in its behalf Mr. Wm. Strickland, a prominent architect of Philadelphia."

(There is no proof that this drawing was for the church in Richmond.)

1842-53

Member of the Institution of Civil Engineers, London.

Reference: *Institution of Civil Engineers, Minutes of Proceedings, Session 1843* (London, 1843). "May 3, 1842. The following were balloted for and elected:—Robert Thomas Atkinson, Francis Giles, and William Strickland, as Members, . . . John Struthers as Associates."

Minutes of Proceedings, XIII (1853-54), 133. ". . . following resignates and permitted to retire, Colonel George Landmann and William Strickland, Members; John Struthers and 24 associates."

1842-43

Architect and superintendent in charge of alterations at the Naval Asylum.

Reference: Records of the Department of the Navy. Navy Department, General Letter Book, No. 31, October 6, 1842—April 3, 1843 (Letters #70, 80, 214, 263); General Letter Book, No. 35, March 22, 1845—January 21, 1846 (Letter # 147); Miscellaneous Letters, November 1842 (Letters #114, 115).

On November 7, 1842, Secretary of the Navy Upshur wrote to Strickland (#70) requesting a plan and estimate for dividing the Philadelphia Asylum, pursuant to the conversation in Washington. He suggests that the division be in the middle, unless Strickland has another line of division, and that the arrangements for changing the building be as desired by the Bureau of Medicine and Surgery.

Strickland's answer (#114) follows:

Philadelphia, November 10, 1842.

Sir,

I have the honor to acknowledge the receipt of your letter of the 7th inst. requesting me to partition off the building of the Naval Asylum in two equal parts, so as to assign the Southern portion exclusively to the purposes of an Hospital, and to make an estimate and report on the probable cost.

In conformity with your wishes I have visited the building and examined into the best mode of performing this work, and find that your object can be perfectly and substantially attained without changing or disturbing any of the symmetry of the present plan; Indeed sir, in the original design of the building this kind of separation was contemplated.— There is simply nothing more to do than to preserve the principal entrance hall at its present width; This leads from the front Portico and will form a vestibule for general entrance, and where the longitudinal lobby or passages crosses this vestibule to construct a permanent partition in the centre of the building East and West, on each side of which doors may be, the one to enter into the *South* or Hospital lobby, and the other into that of the North, or Pensioners lobby:— The gallery leading across the stairways for the lobby to the rotunda or Chapel to be also partitioned off on each side, having a door of access from the Southern as well as one from the Northern lobby into the Chapel; These partitions will completely separate the two stairways, going one flight to each division of the building. This is all that will be required on the principal Story.

In the Basement the longitudinal passage or lobby may be also separated by a *bulkhead,* and the East and West passage leading at right angles from the foot of the stairways to the Kitchens and dining rooms should have a similar *bulkhead* forward in the centre of the passage, and be continued past the kitchens to the dining rooms, where two partitions should be constructed forming a lobby of separation between the kitchens, so that a wide outlet may be made into a passage to the grounds at the rear of the building.—

The stairways, kitchens, dining rooms, storerooms, closets, coal vaults, furnaces etc. by this plan of separation will be all in one place, and the one suite being exactly the ditto of the other in each compartment of the building, and I need only add that each will have more than ample space in cooking and dining rooms, together with the necessary apart-

ments for the accommodation of at least 100 persons.
In the third story the partition must also extend across the longitudinal passage in the centre of the building as below, as well as in the centre of the gallery which crosses the head of the stairways, leaving sufficient space to enter upon the roof.—
There will be required to carry out the plan 8 circular sash over the doors and partitions for the purpose of light and ventilation, besides 6 doors and doorway fittings, which will cost, including partitions, carpenter's work and materials,—Plastering, painting and glazing=————$700.
In the extreme southern end of the building or *Hospital division* there is a large room in the third story fitted with a skylight in the ceiling, which room was originally intended for a surgical hall, and which may now at a moderate expense, be finished with the necessary fixtures for Medical and surgical purposes—say $250.
In my examination I found the Joist and floor of one of the rooms of the Basement on the N.E. angle of the building somewhat decayed from the dampness carried through the foundations by the external pavement; this ought to be examined and if found necessary, the whole floor may be renewed at an expense of $100.—
The skylights on the roof are out of repair, owing to the expansion and contraction of the metal gutters, as well as the capillary attraction of the water under the lap of the glass, but with these exceptions the whole building is in good substantial order, being very clean and neat throughout.—
I would suggest the propriety of fitting up the Rotunda as a Chapel.— The walls ought to be draped on the 4 angles of the room, where the arch springs from, in order to check the effect of the echo which prevails in it:— The floor carpeted, and otherwise finished as a place of worship.— This portion of the building will not cost more than————$600.
In conclusion sir, it will give me great pleasure to furnish you with any further information which you may require upon the subject of the Asylum, as well as expeditiously to carry out the plan of alteration which you propose.

With great respect
Your obdt servant
William Strickland.

The honorable
A. P. Upshur
Sec. of the Navy.
Washington.

Upshur answered this letter promptly on November 12, 1842. There are two copies of his answer (#80, 115). He wrote in part,

You will please proceed with the work on the Asylum as sketched in your letter of the 10th day of November with the exception of so much as relates to the chapel and surgical hall. You will have regard to the necessary accommodation of the several classes of people in the asylum, with reference to dining room, kitchen and other such arrangements keeping each class to itself. The small repairs which you mention, must be made.

Strickland began work immediately as a letter of Upshur to Strickland dated January 5, 1843, shows:

Your letter of the 2nd stating progress of work at the Naval Asylum is received.
You will put up the necessary shelving and cases which may be required by the Surgeon in rooms designated for the purposes of a Dispensary, Apothecary's shop and storeroom.

The work was evidently completed by the end of the first week in January.

The work of partitioning the Naval Asylum proceeded promptly during November and December. A further correspondence took place between Upshur and Strickland in January, 1843.

Reference: Navy Department, General Letter Book (#31), October 6, 1842-April 3, 1843 (#214, 263); Miscellaneous Letters, January, 1843 (#9, 67).

Strickland wrote to Secretary of the Navy Upshur on January 2, 1843, stating that in compliance with the instructions to proceed on the work at the Naval Asylum, a partition had been constructed which divided the several stories of the building exactly in halves, so as to assign the southern portion for a hospital and that the work was completed according to the estimate. The expenses were for labor and materials, furnished by contracts with the carpenter, plasterer, painter, etc.

The whole of which, including repairs in the N.E. portion of the building amounting to . . $900
In addition to which you will please to allow me for my professional services as superintendent, and for drawing the plans which have been furnished to D. Barton 50
$950

He added that the surgeon required shelving in the dispensary, apothecary shop and storeroom. The building required paint and repairs to the skylight. The dimensions of all the rooms were on the plans of the principal and second stories which he added that he was mailing the same day.

Upshur replied on January 5 and requested that all the necessary shelving and cases be constructed.

Strickland answered on January 7 to say that the "fitting up shall be done beginning Monday," and to request that the money be sent.

Upshur delayed his reply until January 19, 1843, when he stated that the bills for work and materials furnished to the Naval Asylum at Philadelphia should be sent to the Bureau of Navy Yards and Docks for approval.

1842-44

Drawings for the War and Navy Department Building, Washington, D. C.

Not constructed.

Reference: Topographical Bureau, Letters Received, II (Letters #158, 171, 198, 204, 406).

Topographical Bureau, Letters Issued, VI, November 2, 1842-October 31, 1843; one letter, November 28, 1842; VII, November 2, 1843-October 16, 1844 (#194); VIII, October 17, 1844-August 11, 1845; one letter, December 13, 1844; the National Archives, Washington, D. C.

House of Representatives (#267), 28th long, 1st Sess., I, Mar. 7, 1844. Report of Mr. Pratt, Chairman of the Public Buildings and Grounds Committee, and in appendix, Strickland's estimate and specifications for the War and Navy Building and report thereon presented to the House.

In the letters of the Topographical Bureau part of the correspondence between Strickland and Colonel Abert, Chief of the Topographical Bureau, regarding the proposed building for the War and Navy Department is preserved.

It begins with a letter from Strickland, dated Philadelphia, October 10, 1842, in which he wrote that he had heard that a new building for the War and Navy Department was to be constructed and he wished to be considered as a possible architect. On November 22, he proceeded to submit an estimate for the construction of a building for the War and Navy Department and with his letter he enclosed the bill of lading for the box containing the drawings of the proposed building. These were acknowledged by Abert in a letter of November 28, 1842, sent to Strickland at Burlington, New Jersey. Abert added that the Secretary of War would notice it particularly in his report to Congress.

Since Strickland heard no further news of the matter, he again wrote to Colonel Abert on March 7, 1843, to inquire about appropriations for the new building. No answer to this letter is preserved. Abert probably stated that there were no appropriations, because on March 29, 1843, Strickland wrote asking to be refunded for the expense incurred by him in coming to Washington and preparing a plan for the construction of the buildings.

Two letters from Strickland to John Struthers, now in the manuscript collection of the Historical Society of Pennsylvania, indicate that Strickland went to Washington about January 5, 1844, and remained there until at least the middle of February to lobby for an appropriation for the War and Navy Building. He was optimistic and in his first letter of January 11, he wrote: "I think there is a chance of getting an appropriation for the War and Navy Building." In the postscript of the second letter, dated February 9, he concluded, "We will, however, have an appropriation for the war office buildings."

On February 12, 1844, Strickland presented his report to the House, printed with his specifications and estimate for the building in the appendix to the report of the Committee on Public Buildings and Grounds. He added,

In conclusion, sir, permit to urge upon you the necessity of draughting a bill for this one building for the accommodation of the War and Navy department. You are in possession of all the facts and specifications, as well as the estimates, and no more light can be thrown on the subject which you are not now perfectly acquainted with, and again permit me to add, that the construction of the work should be placed in charge of the Secretary of War, through the superintendence of the chief of the Topographical Bureau (Colonel Abert) who knows perfectly well all the theory and practice of the building art, and who also knows what will accommodate the department of which he is the Chief engineer.

On April 5, 1844, Colonel Abert wrote Strickland that the wants of the War Department's Committee of Buildings had changed and requested that Strickland come as soon as possible to give aid and co-operation in the examinations and estimates which would be required.

There is no record of whether Strickland went to Washington in April, but he probably did, since he was called upon again in December, 1844.

On December 13, 1844, Colonel Abert wrote as follows to Strickland:

I have been requested by the Hon. Mr. Pratt, Chairman of the Committee on public buildings, to furnish the drawings and estimates for the New War and Navy Department Buildings. These refer to the plan which has been lost or mislaid, and upon which we had agreed. In conversation with Mr. Pratt, I told him that you only could renew the drawing, and that it would be necessary to require you to come on for that purpose. Upon which I was fully authorized by him to write you and to desire your attendance at Washington as soon as convenient.

Strickland answered promptly on December 14, 1844, that he had received the letter desiring his attendance at Washington and that after preparing the drawing required from a rough sketch in his possession he would immediately proceed to Washington with them.

Description of the proposed building:

Site: On the Potomac River.

Estimate: $119,774; portico, $16,000.

Plan: 3 stories, each 14 feet high; attic 10 feet high; arched cellar.

Construction: Fireproof throughout; no wood.

Walls: Marble and granite outside; brick and stucco inside. Floors, flagstone; washboards, stone; joists and frames, iron.

Outstanding features: Windows in the blank space of the frieze.

. . . all the glass of the lower sash to be ground, so as not to transmit the direct rays of the sun into the south portion of the rooms; this will prevent the necessity of resorting to blinds and boxes outside of the sash, which are extremely ugly in a public building, and which are always slamming about in the windy district of Washington.

1843

Consultant architect for proposed alteration of the Capitol; a new Hall for the House of Representatives, Washington, D. C.

Reference: Topographical Bureau, Letters Received, II (#275,283).

Letters Issued, VII, November 2, 1843-October 16, 1844 (#66). The National Archives, Washington, D. C.

House Documents (#51), 28th long, 1st Sess., III, Jan. 8, 1844.

On November 13, 1843, Strickland wrote Colonel Abert that he was preparing plans and an estimate for the new Hall of Representatives and that he would forward them to the Bureau by December 1.

On December 6, 1843, Strickland submitted drawings and an estimate for enlarging the south wing of the Capitol and constructing "a new Hall for the better accommodation of the House of Representatives." Colonel Abert acknowledged the arrival of these on December 14. The estimate was printed in the House Documents.

On March 1, 1843, the House passed a resolution to provide a new room for the House of Representatives. Colonel Abert in his report to the House gives an account of Strickland's connection with the proposed room:

After the dimensions of the additions and their position had been determined, and the drawing of the plan and elevation completed, an opportunity offered of consulting that eminent architect, W. Strickland, esq. of Philadelphia, and accordingly the whole was submitted to his inspection. It gives me great pleasure to say that it met with his entire approbation, and, in conformity with your desire, he was also employed to make an estimate of the cost, and to give a view of the interior, method of making the roof, and of admitting the light. Our views on these points do not differ materially, as the drawings furnished by Mr. Strickland and from this office will more fully show; the principal difference being in the space assigned to the spectators. Mr. Strickland, in his plan, extends the gallery space to the outer walls of the building; while in that from this office, this space is limited to the dimension of the hall.

Our estimates agree to within 13,500 dollars—the larger being the one from this office—the difference arises chiefly from the different prices assumed for the brick work.

Strickland gave an estimate of the total cost at $282,789.20. He suggested that the height of the Hall should be one-third of the width as low ceilings furnish the best acoustics as demonstrated in the Musical Fund Hall in Philadelphia and the Capitol in Harrisburg. For the roof, he advocated a trussed design with a descent of 8 feet in 76 feet and with the ridge-pole on the level with the top of the balustrade. For the spectators' gallery, he suggested the use of iron rafters and columns, also cast-iron window sashes.

1843

Estimate of addition to hospital building at Marine barracks, Navy Yard.

Reference: Records of the Department of the Navy, Navy Department, Miscellaneous Letters, January, 1843 (#361).

On January 31, 1843, Strickland wrote to the Secretary of the Navy that at the request of Dr. Barton, he had visited the Hospital building at the Marine barracks for the purpose of making an estimate of the cost of making it

a story higher and thereon to finish 4 additional rooms and garrets.
I have the honor to submit the following for the purpose: viz.

50,000 Bricks	$600
Carpenters work in raising the roof	150
10 windows and frames	200
10 doors with locks and hinges complete	150
Plastering	160
Lumber	200
Painting and glazing	90
	$1550

1844

Strickland's Letters to John Struthers in H.S.P.

Fullers Hotel
Washington, Jan 11/44

Dear John,

I have been in Washington now nearly a week and have just entered into the threshold of my business— In this City of Magnificent distances you can't find a man without a mile, and as Paddy would say, and then he is sure to be out.— Congress do not sit till 12 oClock everyday, and the Members do not dine till 6 or 7 oClock.—

President making is the order of the *day* and frolicking that of the *night*.— The *motto* is every man for himself, and God for us all.— All *the holes* of office *are stopped*, in other words, John, there are a great many more *pigs* than *teats*.— Tyler is between *two stools* and you know the rest.— But we Tyler men are to turn to *Clay* as sure as fate.

The Treasury is M.T. and the Committee of *Ways and Means* are hard at work to find out the way to create the *almighty dollars*.— I think there is a chance of getting an appropriation for the War and Navy buildings, but this will not be until the close of the session, and yet it is necessary to talk, and coax and wheedle them into doing what is right and proper— Col A[l]bert is my friend here, and so is the Sec[y] at War, and I can depend upon them I think in any emergency with reference to those buildings.

When Rob[t] Tyler comes to town he has promised to fix up some office for me *ad interim*.— Tyson is also friendly, but here there is no such thing as getting an office, without cutting off *some man's head*, and that you know, John, is a bloody business—

I have paid a visit to your friend Brown, who arrived here from Scotland last October.— He looks as fat as a whale, but complains of having nothing to do; but I believe John, he is pretty well off in this "worlds gear"— I do not think he has any influence with any of the members of Congress, the most of which are new hands. However he looks like a good fellow and he is disposed to befriend me.— He sends his best respects to you, and made many enquiries about your health and business—

Farewell! and believe me to be
Yours always truly,
W. Strickland

My respects to Mrs. Struthers, William and all the family. w.s.

Washington Feb 9th/44

Dear John,

Many thanks for your book upon the Washington disinterment and the sarcophagus.

The Secretary of War wishes to have another copy and will take much pleasure in having one for his own particular use.— Be good enough to direct one to him from yourself, that is, say on the back or cover of the fly leaf,—presented to Judge Porter Sec[y] of War by John Struthers of Philad[a]—

The affairs of Congress are rather tardy, inasmuch as very few of the regular committees have as yet reported their proceedings to Congress.— Next week, however, we may expect some substantial business to be taken up.—

Mr. Binney & Mr. Sergeant have just concluded their speeches on behalf of the trust of Stephen Girard.— Daniel Webster begins in the morning against the Trust as exercised by the City, and it is expected, will make one of his best constitutional speeches.

The Daniel will have a large contingent fee if he succeeds in breaking the will,—and I think, as far as I can hear that the whole Trust is in danger.— I have heard some of the argument, but it is all about the legal question whether the City corporation can receive and administer a Charitable trust.— The main point, whether the City of Philadelphia has been guilty of a breach of Trust by the construction of a *Palace or Temple* instead of a College as described in *Girard's Will,* is not yet touched, but the *almighty* Daniel, or, in other words, *as you Whigs say, the Godlike man,* is to have a large share of the spoils!— He is running a Crusade for fees.— What does he care, he has a retaining fee, and the promise of a contingent one of three hundred thousand dollars.—

Shakespeare says, or rather Fallstaff, "Master Shallow I owe you *a thousand pounds.*" He will advocate the cause of the Devil for Money, and care not if he makes the "*worse* appear the *better* part."

My respects to your family, and believe me always truly

W. Strickland.

P.S.
The business of making a sale of the Bank of the U.S. for a Custom house is in a very good train for accomplishment.— As for getting an office from John Tyler;— That is neither here nor there— We will however, have an appropriation for the war office buildings.—

1844

Application for superintendency of the Dry Dock, New York.

Reference: Records of the Department of the Navy. Navy Department, General Letter Book (#34), July 10, 1844-March 21, 1845 (Letters #70, 120).

S. Warrington, for the Secretary of the Navy, wrote to Strickland at Philadelphia, August 17, 1844 (#70), "Your application, dated 15th inst., for the situation of Superintendent of the Dry Dock, at New York has been received and will be brought to the notice of the Secretary on his return to Washington."

J. Y. Mason, Secretary of the Navy, wrote to Strickland at Philadelphia, September 16, 1844 (#120), "Should a Superintendent of the Dry Dock at New York be needed, Mr. Strickland's application would be respectfully considered."

Navy Department, Miscellaneous Letters, August, 1844 (Letter #118).

Strickland's letter of application concludes:

I am familiar with the building art in all its branches and have examined and made drawings of all the best Docks in Europe, particularly those at Toulon, London, Liverpool, etc.—and have all the details in my Portfolio.— I have some years ago, sent to Washington through Commodore Stewart designs for a Dock at this station sufficiently capacious to contain the *Pennsylvania* all of which has met his approval and most decided approbation:— Should you, sir, think proper to confide this stone dock at New York to my care I am very sure of giving you as well as the country the utmost satisfaction.

1844

Plans and estimate for changing the library room of the Capitol into a Hall for the House of Representatives, Washington, D. C.

Not used.

Reference: Topographical Bureau, Letters Issued, VII, November 2, 1843-October 16, 1844 (Letter #194); Letters Received, II (#319).

War Department, Division of Architecture, Records of Committee of Buildings, Strickland's report.

All material in the National Archives, Washington, D. C.

Colonel Abert wrote (April 5, 1844) to Strickland to inform him that the Committee of Buildings of the War Department had abandoned the idea of building a new wing for the House of Representatives and requested Strickland to come to Washington as soon as possible to make estimates and plans for the new proposal of changing the library room of the Capitol into a hall to accommodate the House of Representatives.

Strickland was in Washington on April 21, and had evidently been there for some time, since on that day he was able to submit plans and an estimate. The next day he wrote his report which was received by the War Department on April 24, 1844.

This report is preserved in the original manuscript and since this plan is not mentioned in histories of the Capitol, it is included here in full.

Washington, April 22, 1844.

To/

Col[l] J. J. Abert, Chief Top[l] Engineers,

Sir,

In conformity with your instructions that I should visit Washington and examine into the practicability of modifying the present Library room of the Capitol according with a proposed plan to adapt that room and its adjacent passages to the purposes of a Chamber of Representatives, I have now the honor of reporting to you plans and estimates exhibiting the effect of such an alteration in an Architectural and Mechanical point of view.

1st. You will perceive by the plan that the semicircular wall coloured *red*, and marked A.A.A. must necessarily cross all the Arches of the rooms in the Basement story in a diagonal line with their axes of direction, and upon the supposition that this wall is to be founded on the top of these arches, it would contain, including the flat arch of the ceiling, or segmental Dome, 275,000 Bricks which is about 1100 Tons of weight including mortar, and if it is intended to found the wall on the solid earth it would require upwards of 300,000 additional bricks, not including a total new arrangement of the walls of the Basement and sub-basement stories.

2nd. The span of the arched ceiling of the proposed design is 92 feet, with a rise of only 11 ft. from the springing line to its apex or base of the skylight: B.B. represents in the section this flat arch without any apparent means of forming a sufficient abutment of resistance, as the springing line is 5 feet above the level of the floor of the attic story, and its thrust for nearly one third of the semicircle would be in the direction of the two open spaces, or, *Courts,* as they are termed in the proposed plan:— This flat segment of a Dome would contain 125,000 Bricks which is equal to the weight of 350 Tons:—

I am of the opinion that so flat an Arch with so great a span could not be constructed to stand without great danger, and even within any reasonable limits of adequate abutments.

3rd. You will remark, that in the plan and section the flues of Chimneys, or stacks in the main wall of the Library room, marked C.C.C. would be cut off from the fire places of the Basement stories, and a great portion of this wall would have to be taken down, as it now stands at least 12 ft. within the periphery of the wall contemplated in the proposed alteration, and I cannot perceive how these stacks are to be disposed of, unless it is intended to let them stand in the Chamber under cover of some ornamental pier or column.

4th. The main flight of stone stairs leading from the Gallery of the Library to the Committee and Documents rooms if the Attic story, marked D.D.D. would have to be torn down to make room for the entrance Lobbys to the Chamber, and in its stead two Spiral stairways are proposed to be placed in the spandrils of the semicircular wall, similar in size and in every other respect to that marked E, now leading from the south lobby of the centre building to the Basement Stories, which has in an eminent degree, darkness and inconvenience and are entirely unfit as approaches to the Attic story.—

5th. Those parts of the plan and section colored with *light Indian ink* represent the situation of all the walls of the centre building facing the West and surrounding the proposed position for the new Chamber, as well as those of the Basement under the Library room, and which form its entire support, and although I believe these walls to be strong enough to receive the weight of the persons of the Members and auditory, I am decidedly aware that they would be incapable of sustaining the pressure of the semicircular wall and arch of the proposed room, and that nothing short of founding them upon the solid earth should be entertained:— As this cannot be done without removing the principal interior walls of the lower stories and cellar, or in other words, taking them all out beneath the Library floor and reconstructing new forms of support, which would be attended with great expense, and even when is done, the Library room and gallery space would afford but an inferior and circumscribed area for the accommodation of the present number of members of the Chamber of Representatives and the proposed form of room would, when executed, produce all the difficulties of speaking and hearing, which necessarily accompanies rooms upon circular plans with arched ceilings.— In conclusion sir, from a thorough examination of this portion of the centre building and comparing the plan of the proposed modifications with it, I am of the opinion that it would in no way be effectual or expedient to attempt to convert or adapt the present Library room into a Chamber of Representatives.—

I also subjoin an approximate Estimate of the cost of tearing down the Library and division walls of the Basement stories, together with the roof, and of constructing others according with the proposed plan of modification.

Viz:

Laborers work in removing wall arches, stairway and roof	$4,000
Excavation, and building up new foundations and walls in the cellar and Basement	11,800
Bricks and workmanship from the floor of the proposed Chamber, including the arched ceiling	6,500
Constructing a new roof, Plumbers work etc.	5,000
Carpenter & lumber, centering, scaffolding etc.	10,000
Plasterers work & materials	4,700
Painting & Glazing	3,500
Blacksmiths work in roof in banding & keying up the flat arch	1,500
Stone & workmanship in circular stairways, sills, Architraves etc.	5,000
	$52,000
Add for contingencies 7 pr Ct	3,640
	$55,640

respectfully submitted,
by your Obdt. servt.
William Strickland
Architect

*1844

Two residences on the grounds of the Naval Home, Gray's Ferry Road. (Plates 36 and 37)

The one built for the Governor is still in excellent condition and only slightly altered.

The one for the Chief Medical Officer has been remodeled and made into two apartments.

Reference: U.S. Naval Home, Philadelphia. Two drawings, front and side elevations, signed and dated Philadelphia, July 28, 1844. (The finished buildings follow these drawings in almost every detail.)

Records of the Department of the Navy, office of Naval Records and Library. Captains' letters, January, February, 1845. National Archives, Washington, D. C.

Style: Classic Revival of the simplest type with verandas supported by cast-iron pillars instead of columns. Well-proportioned entablature. Plain rectangular windows.

Plan: Two-story building with basement and attic. There is a central hall with a vestibule in front and stairs at back; to the left a drawing room with two columns near the walls at the center; to the right, a study and dining room. An ell at the back contains a kitchen, pantry, storerooms, and servants' quarters above. Four bedrooms, each with a fireplace, are on the second floor. They have high ceilings and large windows.

Materials: Brick, plastered and white-washed; wood trim. Cast-iron pillars and railings on the verandas.

Outstanding features: Iron work with appropriate designs of anchors, ropes, and dolphins. Large drawing room. In a letter dated February 12, 1845, Captain Morgan stated,

> The Drawing room-parlors of the house are thrown into one large saloon with a column on either side—making the partitions, when completed in this style—are generally separated by a curtain, suspended between the two columns, which when well selected will require as little, probably less, repairs for ten or fifteen years, than the double doors on rollers or hinges.

1844

Examination of grounds of the Depot of Charts in Washington and plan of buildings for officers' houses.

Report and plan approved by Secretary of the Navy Mason, September 10, 1844.

Reference: Records of the Department of the Navy. Navy Department, General Letter Book #34, July 10, 1844-March 21, 1845 (Letters #41, 51, 66, 127).

Navy Department, Miscellaneous Letters, August, 1844 (Letters #24, 29, 83, 97).

On July 31, 1844, Secretary of the Navy Mason wrote to Strickland (#41), "If convenient to proceed immediately to Washington to examine the grounds around the Depot of Charts, and prepare a plan for their improvement in reference to suitable buildings hereafter to be constructed."

Strickland replied on August 4 (#24) that he would do so, and hoped to be in Washington on August 5.

Strickland arrived as planned since on that day S. Warrington, acting for the Secretary of the Navy, wrote him a letter at Washington stating that upon presentation of the letter to Lieutenant Gillis, "he will show you the grounds to be graded and enclosed around the new Depot of Charts in Washington. After examination, you will be pleased to report to the Department a plan for the proposed improvement."

Also on August 5, 1844, Strickland wrote to Warrington (#29) that he had made a partial examination of the grounds and would require a week or ten days to do the report.

Strickland completed his report more quickly than he anticipated and sent it from Philadelphia on August 10, 1844 (#83). He reported that he had visited the Depot of Charts and suggested cutting the ground at the corner of E and Twenty-third streets to the city grade and terracing the area with circular esplanades. He sent a ground plan and sectional drawings and an estimate of the amount for excavation. For the enclosing wall, he suggested a stone foundation at least 2 feet deep, with a brick wall 13 inches thick and piers 22 inches square placed 10 or 12 feet apart. For the plan of two houses to accommodate the chief of the Depot and his assistant, he designed buildings two stories in height and 46 feet square which would cost about $6,000 each. In conclusion, he stated that the terrace plan was a good one viewed either from a distance or at close range. He added a note suggesting an alteration of the base of the dome of the Depot, namely, the addition of a circular colonnade and enclosed a "drawing to that effect."

On August 13 (#97), Strickland wrote again, enclosing "bills for professional services in drawing plans for the Naval Asylum at Philadelphia, and for plan for enclosure and grading the grounds around the Depot of Charts and expenses to and from Washington."

Warrington acknowledged this on August 14 (#66) and stated that the two bills submitted by Strickland on the thirteenth were enclosed and approved for the sum of $210 and that the Navy agent in Philadelphia would pay them upon presentation.

J. Y. Mason, the Secretary of the Navy, wrote Strickland September 18, 1844 (#127) that he had received the report of the examination of the grounds at the Depot of Charts, etc., dated August 10, with the plan for the officers' houses. "The report and plan are approved, with the exception of that part relating to the dome, which is reserved for further consideration."

*1845-47

St. Mary's Church, formerly the Cathedral of the Blessed Virgin of the Seven Dolors, southeast corner of Cedar and Fifth streets, Nashville. (Plate 41B)

Reference: V. F. O'Daniel, *The Father of the Church in Tennessee, or the Life, Times, and Character of the Right Reverend Richard Pius Miles, O.P., the first bishop of Nashville* (Washington, D. C.: Dominicana, 1926), p. 426. "William Strickland, an architect of no mean reputation and builder of the Tennessee State capitol, is reported to have considered it his finest ecclesiastical structure."

Daniel F. Barr, *Souvenir of St. Mary's Cathedral, 1847-1897.*

Republican Banner, Nashville, Friday, November 5, 1847. Description of the dedication of the cathedral on Sunday, October 31, 1847. "It is a neat and chaste specimen of Grecian Architecture, which reflects credit upon its architect. Its external dimensions are 110 feet in length, 60 feet in breadth, and 32 feet in height, besides a basement story."

The façade of Tennessee marble is in its original condition, but the side wall and the interior have been altered.

*1845-59

Tennessee State Capitol, Nashville, Tennessee. (Plates 38-41A)

Cornerstone laid: July 4, 1845.

First legislative session held in the building: October 3, 1853.

Last stone laid on tower: July 21, 1855.

Last stone laid on terrace: March 19, 1859.

Reference: Primary sources: Volume of minutes of meetings of the board of commissioners superintending the construction of the State House, from February 12, 1844, through January 3, 1861; Archives of Tennessee Historical Society. (Typewritten copy in the Tennessee State Library.)

Acts of Tennessee. Laws of the General Assembly of Tennessee which concern the commencement of the Capitol:

1843/44—Chapter CCV p. 235.

1845/46—Chapter XLIX p. 102f.

1847/48—Chapter LXXIX p. 127.

1847/48—Chapter XLV p. 77f.

Tennessee Senate Journal, 1845-46—1857-58.

Reports of the Commissioners appointed to superintend the construction of the State House.

1845/46—Appendix pp. 52-55.

1847/48—Appendix pp. 17-20.

1849/50—Appendix pp. 322-23.

1851/52—Appendix pp. 101-2.

1853/54—Appendix pp. 105-7.

1853/54—Appendix pp. 141-44.

1855/56—Appendix pp. 41-45.

1857/58—Appendix pp. 275-78.

Reports of the Architect:

1845/46—Appendix pp. 55-56 date of report May 20, 1845.

1847/48—Appendix pp. 21-22 date of report Oct. 4, 1847.

1849/50—Appendix pp. 324-26 date of report Oct. 12, 1849.

1851/52—Appendix pp. 163-64 date of report Oct. 17, 1851.

1851/52—Appendix pp. 175 date of report Oct. 29, 1851.

Note: The last report which William Strickland presented to the Building Committee in 1853 was presented to the Legislature on Monday morning, November 14, 1853, and referred to the Committee of Ways and Means, but it was not printed.

1855/56—Appendix pp. 45-48 date of report Oct. 1, 1855.

Note: This report was by Francis W. Strickland, who succeeded his father on June 3, 1854, as architect of the State Capitol. Francis was dismissed on May 1, 1857; consequently, this was his only report.

Tennessee State Library—canceled checks, vouchers, papers, letters, accounts, scrapbook of miscellaneous items about the Capitol.

Nashville newspapers, 1845-April, 1854.

Drawings: Tennessee State Library, two sketches in the Strickland portfolio.

Tennessee Historical Society; working drawing, probably by Francis Strickland, of arrangement of marble in basement story.

Tennessee Capitol, attic; wooden model of the Capitol tower. Made in 1850 by Messrs. Spain and Coleman in the shop of Messrs. Vannoy and Tuberville after drawings by Strickland. Height 60 inches, width at base 26 inches.

Engravings: A large number in all media. One view was used on Confederate paper money. First engraving was a woodcut by Daniel Adams after Strickland's drawing, first printed in the *Republican Banner,* Nashville, June 22, 1846.

Secondary sources:

George Dardis, *Description of the State Capitol of Tennessee* (Nashville, 1859). Dardis, the porter of the building, was also employed to act as guide for Capitol visitors. Since he had access to all the papers concerning the construction of the building, this account, which is the first lengthy description of the Capitol, gives an excellent history of the building. There are errors in the account of the life of Strickland, since it was copied from an article written by Mrs. Jesse Hartley Strickland which appeared in a Philadelphia newspaper.

Nell Savage Mahoney, "William Strickland and the Building of Tennessee's Capitol, 1845-1854," pp. 99-153. *Tennessee Historical Quarterly,* IV, 2 (June, 1945). This is an excellent, recent account of the Capitol. Mrs. Mahoney had access to the same material which Dardis used. The article was first written in 1939 as a thesis for a Master of Arts degree, Vanderbilt University.

Charles P. White, "Early Experiments with Prison Labor in Tennessee," *The East Tennessee Historical Society Publications,* No. 12 (1940), pp. 45-69. Discussion of the use of slave labor on the Capitol including a table of the total prison population and the number engaged on the Capitol from 1845 to 1857 (p. 64).

Note: There are hundreds of descriptions and accounts of the Tennessee State Capitol, but since they are repetitious, only the most inclusive accounts are given.

History: Nashville was chosen as the permanent capital of Tennessee by an Act of the Legislature of October 7, 1843. The citizens of Nashville, to show their appreciation at the selection of their city, bought Campbell's Hill, the highest eminence in the city, just south of the City Square for $30,000 and offered it to the State as a site for the Capitol building. It was accepted and a Board of Commissioners to superintend the construction of the State Capitol was appointed on January 30, 1844, including William Carroll, William Nichol, John M. Bass, Samuel D. Morgan, James Erwin, and Morgan W. Brown. On May 14, 1844, Nichol, Armstrong, and Erwin resigned and James Woods, Joseph T. Elliston, and Allen A. Hall were appointed to replace them. John M. Bass was the chairman until he resigned on March 31, 1854, when Samuel D. Morgan was appointed. It was largely because of Morgan's efforts that the Capitol was completed and that the accounts and records were kept. In appreciation of Morgan's services, the state voted that he should be interred in a niche in the wall of the basement story.

By June 16, 1844, the board had learned of Strickland's willingness to make plans for the Capitol, but he did not arrive in Nashville until May, 1845. The first report of the Commissioners stated their regrets that the plan had not been obtained by competition, but that had been precluded by an Act of the General Assembly. It also states that the board learned of Strickland after extensive correspondence with persons in the East, and described him as

> a gentleman who had devoted a life, now somewhat advanced, to this profession (architecture) . . . That while on all occasions he had displayed the utmost good taste in the buildings erected by him, he never sacrificed solidity for show—the useful, for the merely ornamental; and that his estimates of cost were to be implicitly relied on.

Strickland's plans were accepted on May 20, 1845, and he was employed as State Architect in charge of the construction of the State Capitol at the salary of $2,500 a year.

The other problem with which the Building Commission had to deal was the supply of marble. It had been decided, as a means of economy, to use the convict labor at the Penitentiary. A quarry was bought adjacent to the Penitentiary and the able-bodied and skilled prisoners were used for quarrying the stone and cutting it. The Mechanics Association wrote a memorial to the General Assembly of Tennessee on November 29, 1845, complaining of the use of convict labor as "a direct interference and infringement upon the rights and interest of the Mechanics of the State of Tennessee." Prison labor was used only at the quarry; not at the Capitol where Negroes were used for the heavy labor and white men for the skilled work. James Birth was appointed foreman, or superintendent of the work at the Penitentiary, on October 19, 1847, with a salary of $250. George Creighton was the master-mason and W. Stickell, the plasterer.

The secretaries of the Board of Commissioners were: June 18, 1844, Edward G. Steele with a salary of $50 a year; February 26, 1849, H. A. Gleaves, $100 a year; April 3, 1854, James Plunkett, secretary and general superintendent, $1,200 a year.

The cornerstone was laid on July 4, 1845, with due Masonic pomp and ceremony and a long procession. An excellent account is to be found in the *Republican Banner*, July 7, 1845.

The first account of the work done in 1845 was written by Strickland for his friend Wilkins Tannehill and appeared in the newspaper which Tannehill edited, *The Nashville Orthopolitan*, on December 2, 1845. By then the rough stone masonry and most of the cut work of the basement was in place and the arches under the porticoes and over the windows completed. An oak platform around the building upon which the hoisting machinery was to be placed was almost finished. Strickland took the opportunity of recommending that the Legislature appropriate sufficient funds so that the work could continue without delay in the spring and also to provide for "devoting the entire competent force of the Penitentiary towards the cutting of stone for the main body of the building."

By May, 1847, the first capital for the porticoes was carved and an eulogistic description of it appeared in the *Republican Banner* on Wednesday, May 26, 1847, written by William Wales, the editor, probably at the instigation of Strickland.

In October, 1847, when Strickland presented his first report to the Commissioners on the work completed, the subbasement was finished and five courses of the basement, rusticated and tooled on the outside, with rubbed stone on the interior. The elevation of the building above the rough stone foundations was about thirteen feet. The cost of the work to date, including the carving of the Ionic capital, totaled $90,720, figuring the price of the ashlar at the prevailing price in an eastern city and the prison labor at the rate charged by good stonecutters. The Pentitentiary force was found to be inadequate and twenty to thirty Negroes were hired to quarry the stone. Strickland concluded his report by saying that if sufficient funds were appropriated for one hundred and fifty stonecutters to be employed, the work could be finished in three more years.

Small boys had been playing in the unfinished building and marking the walls. As a result the General Assembly passed a law on January 11, 1848, making it a misdemeanor to deface or damage in any way the State House or any building belonging to the State, "punishable by a fine not exceeding fifty dollars or imprisonment not exceeding ten days, or by both fine and imprisonment, within said limits."

When Strickland made his next report on October 12, 1849, the State House was half completed; the basement story was finished both inside and out, and the walls, both interior and exterior, of the main story were partly in place, to the height of nine feet on the exterior and more on the interior. Up to that time, 144,000 superficial feet of stone had been wrought and set in the building. An average of 233 men had been employed daily, engaged as follows:

50 cutting and rubbing stone
45 quarrying, rolling and loading wagons
112 of the Penitentiary force
- 47 cutting and rubbing
- 45 sawing and rolling
- 20 quarrying

26 at the Capitol (stone-setters, trimmers, riggers, and masons)

Bricks, numbering 643,130, had been used in building the arches, filling in the walls and spandrils, all of which were laid by thirteen bricklayers and forty tenders and mortar-makers, employed from May to July, 1849.

During the summer of 1850, the wood model for the iron roof was made and exhibited at the Capitol. (*Daily Evening Reporter*, Nashville, September 10, 1850.)

On September 9, 1850, Strickland inserted an advertisement in the Nashville papers requesting sealed proposals from iron founders on the price of iron for the roof of the Capitol before October 1. In all, about two hundred tons of iron were required, consisting of cast discs and rolled bars.

Strickland, in his report of October, 1851, stated that the iron was procured from the Cumberland Iron Works (210 tons at a cost of $15,790) and was delivered and ready to be put in place within the next three weeks.

At that time, the main story was completed as far as the roof. The stones of the cornice were cut and the copper for the roof (27¼ tons at the cost of $12,267) was also ready at the site. The porticoes, roof, tower, and cornice, and the screen and speaker's chair, which were to be carved out of East Tennessee marble, were still to be done. He concluded by saying that the building would be ready for the next General Assembly if a generous appropriation was granted and commended the work of James Birth, the superintendent of the stonecutters, and the coöperation of Mr. McIntosh, superintendent of the Penitentiary.

The question of money came up biennially at the meetings of the Legislature and criticisms of expense and length of time came also. In the *Republican Banner* for December 6, 1851, a long letter signed "Vindex" appeared which answered these complaints by pointing out the magnitude of the building, the permanence of the materials, the excellence of the decoration, and length of time which comparable buildings took to complete.

No one complains, either, that the able Architect has not always been prompt with his draughts—that he has not done all that the means furnished him by the State enabled him to do! Let the State then chide its own impatience, rather than his want of zeal; And, I think too, with all due deference to the opinion of others, that so far from being *censured* by any act of Legislature, he should receive its cordial *approval* for his skill and fidelity.

On Monday, October 3, 1853, the Tennessee State Legislature met for the first time in the Capitol which was complete except for the tower, the terrace, the balcony, and committee rooms in the Hall of Representatives, the fittings of the library, the chandeliers, and various other fittings of the interior. The newly-appointed Speakers of the Senate and the House made appropriate references to the "new and magnificent Capitol." In the Governor's message on October 8, William B. Campbell remarked, "All around, you have daily presented to your view and contemplation models of all that is pure and beautiful in architectural taste."

Soon the words of praise ceased and criticism began instead. The acoustics of the Senate Chamber were found to be poor and a committee was appointed to confer with the architect to seek a remedy. They decided to curtain the windows and carpet the floor. Because the Hall of Representatives was unfinished, it was difficult to hear there too. Sawdust was put under the carpeting and curtains were also purchased for those windows.

On November 14, 1853, Strickland's last report was presented by Mr. Reid, a Senator from Davidson County, and referred to the Committee of Ways and Means, but the printing of the architect's report was not ordered, hence there is no record of it.

On the first of January, William Strickland addressed a petition to the General Assembly of the State of Tennessee on behalf of his son Francis, who had been engaged as an assistant architect for the past five years without pay. Strickland asked that his son might be recompensed, and pointed out that his services had greatly facilitated the progress of the work and that it was customary to have a paid assistant to make drafts and specifications and aid in the supervision of work.

The petition was not granted. Instead a resolution was introduced to remove the architect (House Resolution #145). However, it was indefinitely postponed, and when the Building Committee was questioned on the subject, the reply was that such an action was inexpedient and that the salary was not excessive.

Strickland died on April 6, 1854, and was interred in the wall of the north entrance to the basement on Saturday morning, April 8.

Francis W. Strickland was recommended to succeed his father in a letter addressed to the Building Committee on April 21, 1854, signed by Augustus Heiman, G. C. Creighton, superintendent of the State Capitol; Alvah Mitchell, foreman; H. C. Marcell, civil engineer; James Sloan, Warren and Moore, and William Stockell, plasterer. He was appointed architect in charge of the State Capitol on June 3, 1854, and served until May 1, 1857.

Samuel D. Morgan who became chairman of the Building Commission on March 31, 1854, upon the resignation of John Bass, continued to act in that capacity until October, 1861. It was because of Morgan's efforts that the library was equipped and the grounds graded and landscaped.

Description: The best description and the one most often copied first appeared in the *Republican Banner and Nashville Whig* on November 15, 1853, and was signed "F.W.S." It was used again for the report to the Building Commissioners in 1855 and it is to be found in the appendixes of the Senate and House Journals for the session 1855-56.

The Tennessee State Capitol is a rectangular, temple-type building with side porticoes and a tower. It covers three-quarters of an acre. Its length is 239 feet 3 inches; width, 112 feet 5 inches at the ends, and 138 feet 5 inches at the center, including the side porticoes, each 13 feet wide. The terrace about the building is 17 feet wide and the steps at the ends are 16 feet 10 inches.

The total height of the building is 206 feet 7 inches; height from the terrace to the top of the entablature, 64 feet 8 inches; height of the stonework of the tower, 79 feet 2 inches; height of the roof and the iron finial ornament, 34 feet.

There are four stories: a cellar or crypt, designed to house the state armory; the basement story which is rusticated on the exterior and has round-arched entrances was designed to house the offices of the Governor and the Secretary of State and courtrooms. The main story, which is reached by a central staircase on the west side of the building, contains the Hall of Representatives; at the south end—a room 61 by 97 feet with a series of five committee rooms on either side under the spectators' balconies, each committee room being 16 feet 8 inches square. The central lobby on the main or second floor is lighted by large windows behind the side porticoes. On the west side there are small stairs to the spectators balcony in the Hall of Representatives and to the attic. The main stairway which rises to a platform and then divides and reaches the upper floor has two stairways leading to the large lobby. In the northeast corner is the Senate Room, 34 feet 8 inches by 70 feet 3 inches. In the northwest corner is the library, 34 feet square, and a room for book stacks, 16 feet by 34. The hall between the library and the Senate Room is 24 feet 2 inches.

The attic is unfinished but the south end has been floored and walled in and is used for the storage of archives, papers, and maps, and as an annex to the library. There are stairs to the tower and a door which opens onto the roof of the tower. Formerly, climbing the tower of the State House was a great attraction because the view is excellent in all directions. It is now (1941) open only to the porter who puts up and takes down the flag, and to visitors with special permission who are accompanied by a porter.

The decoration of the Senate Room and the Hall of Representatives is especially handsome. In the Senate Room, the Speaker's dais is in the center of the long side of the rectangle. On the other three sides, there is a balcony for spectators which is supported by Ionic columns of red Tennessee marble, 10 feet 3 inches high and 3 feet 5½ inches in diameter, of which there are twelve in all. The bases are of black marble and the architrave of red and white marble. In the Hall of Representatives, the columns are of gray marble and support the ceiling over the side galleries. They are Corinthian and arranged in three pairs with single columns at the ends on each side. On the wall behind the Speaker's chair and the opposite wall, there are pilasters which extend the height of the room.

The lobby is extremely impressive because of the great height of the ceiling, the beautiful finish of the marble, and the massiveness of the four piers, each 10 by 12 feet, which support the tower and which are decorated by niches.

Style: Greek Revival. The Ionic capitals of the porticoes, the most striking external feature, were copied consciously and conscientiously from a Greek model. In this case, the model was the illustration of the capitals of the north and east porches of the Erechtheum in Athens as shown in Stuart and Revett, *Antiquities of Athens*, II, chapter 2. The other dominant feature of the building is the tower which was copied from the plates in the same work, Volume I, chapter 4, which illustrated the Choragic Monument of Lysicrates.

A building is an example of revival architecture, if its outstanding features copy models of another style. Otherwise, the building need not have either the plan or the structure of the architectural style of which it is called a revival. In this case, there are various Roman and Renaissance features in the building also; for instance, the lower or basement story with the rusticated stonework and the round arches, the hanging stairway, and the fine niches in the central lobby of the main story.

Plan: Cross axis with transverse halls leading from the four porticoes. The building is almost symmetrical in a longitudinal section, but asymmetrical in a transverse section. The ceilings are high, forty-three feet in the main story, and the proportion of the rooms is nearly square. The plan is utilitarian, but impressive.

Materials: The building is almost completely constructed of blue-gray Tennessee marble from a local quarry. The brown ornamental marble in the Senate Chamber and Hall of Representatives is from East Tennessee. The brick was fired locally. The iron came from the Cumberland Iron Works and the copper for the roof from Pittsburgh.

Cost: The minutes of the Board of the Commissioners appointed to superintend the erection of the State House gives the total expenditure from January 3, 1845 to October 7, 1861 as $925,639.02.

This total takes the lesser estimate for the work done at the Penitentiary. There were differences of opinion between the Board of Commissioners and the superintendent of the Penitentiary as to the value of the work done by the convicts. Samuel Morgan, in a letter to James Plunket, the Secretary of the Board, dated October 1, 1857, said that the Penitentiary was charging $363,072.12 for the work done and that he was allowing $91,200 for the same work as he contended that the State should not be charged quadruple profits by her own institution.

Strickland, in his estimate given on May 20, 1845, said that the cost of the building would be $340,000 if the work were done by contract, but if prison labor were used, the cost would be reduced to between $240,000 and $260,000, to which 7½ per cent should be added for incidental expenses.

Outstanding features: On the exterior, the most impressive features are the porticoes of eight columns each on the north and south and six columns each on the east and west. They are thirty-six feet high and four and one-half feet in diameter. The capitals which are the type of Ionic capital with the wide necking of the anthemion motif are particularly handsome. The tower with the eight Corinthian columns is another unusual feature of the exterior. On the interior, the stone walls and floors, the height of the ceiling of the main story, the central lobby lighted by the high windows of the east and west porticoes, the hanging stairs, and the arrangement of the Hall of Representatives are specially noteworthy.

*1845-54(?)

Small city houses, Nashville.

These houses may have been designed by Strickland, but there is no proof. Stylistically, they are mid-century and therefore might, more likely, be the design of Francis Strickland.

Style: Italianate, early Florentine Renaissance with cornice, arched hood moldings and curved tracery in the windows.

Plan: Entrance hall running the length of the front part of the house with a parlor and bedrooms leading off it. At the back, a dining room, kitchen, and open porch.

Elevation: One story, flat roof, door at the side with steps leading to it and an arched opening, two arched windows, and the whole façade topped by a cornice.

Materials: Wood or brick.

1846

Plans for a Monterey Monument, Nashville.

The only information concerning this design is to be found in an article which appeared in the *Republican Banner*, Nashville, Wednesday, November 18, 1846.

The Monument–It having been esteemed of great importance to the accomplishment of the object had in view, by the Public Meeting in Nashville on the 26th day of the last month, in reference to the erection of a suitable *Monument* to the Memory of the Tennessee Volunteers who fell at the storming and capture of Monterey, that a *Plan* should be adopted, and something like an estimate of the probable *Cost* obtained, before subscriptions were applied for, that portion of the committee residing in Davidson county have agreed upon the following, submitted to them, by the State Architect, W. *Strickland*, Esq.

Description of a BATTLE MONUMENT to the Memory of the Citizen Volunteers of Tennessee who fell in the seige of Monterey.

The design embraces a pedestal of ten feet square and 14 feet in height, surmounted by an obelisk of 36 feet by 6 feet square at the base, *in one solid block*, weighing about 42 tons, making the whole height 50 feet; the whole to be constructed of the white compact limestone of the Nashville quarries.

The pedestal rests upon two steps of 2 feet rise each, and is embellished, on the four corners, with the Roman Fasces and battle axe, supporting funeral vases at the base of the obelisk, while the American eagle is perched upon its apex.

The names of the slain are to be inscribed upon the shaft as well as upon the panels of the Pedestal;–The counties from which they came are also to be inscribed.

The whole cost is estimated by the Architect at $8500, including a substantial enclosure of spear railings of wrought iron.

It is intended to erect this monument on the top of the hill immediately in front of the State Capitol.

Mr. Strickland has furnished the committee with

a drawing of this plan, and it is their intention to have at least a dozen copies of it taken as soon as possible, so that they may be sent to the different parts of the State. Our own citizens will find the original drawings at the Bookstore of Mr. *Wm. T. Berry.*

Subsequent newspaper entries record that the committee was unable to raise subscriptions; that a monument was erected at Gallatin, Tennessee (which is still standing), but that one was never erected in Nashville.

*1846

Walker Monument, City Cemetery, Nashville, Tennessee. (Plate 43)

Reference: Inscription on base, "Des'd by W. Strickland."

Nashville Orthopolitan, July 6, 1846. The following description which appeared in the newspaper on that date was probably written by Strickland himself, as he was a good friend of Wilkins Tannenhill, the editor of the *Orthopolitan.*

The monument to which we have alluded, is tasteful in its design and admirable in its execution. We are indebted to a friend for the following description: "The very elegant Mausoleum which J. W. Walker, Esq. has recently built to the memory of his wife in the Cemetery of Nashville is constructed of pure white marble from the quarries near Baltimore. The design consists of a rectangular rusticated Pedestal or Die upon the top of which rises two Piers that support a semicircular arched superstructure entirely open from front to rear; the piers are enriched with the egg and dart moulding upon their capitals, and the external angles of the arched superstructure are ornamented with double consoles richly carved and supporting a Cornice, the bed mould of which is decorated with a band of Dentils. The cornice is surmounted by a crowning device consisting of a double scroll supporting a Hymeneal torch.

The *Die* of the pedestal supports a Lacrymal vase, that stands in the center immediately beneath the arch, and which is an exact copy of the form of the vases found in the ruins of Pompeii.

In the center of the front of the Pedestal there are raised panels upon one of which is the following neat and unostentatious inscription:

Sarah Ann Gray
wife of
Jno W. Walker
Died on Sunday morning 16th day
of March 1845,
In the 28th Year of her age.

The whole structure stands upon a base course and two steps: Its dimensions are 9 feet by 7 and 20 feet in height. The plot is surrounded by a very handsome cast iron railing which encloses a space of 20 by 40 feet.

1848

Plan of New Hotel, Public Square, Nashville.

Project never executed.

Reference: *Republican Banner,* Nashville, October 5, 1848.

The New Hotel. Through the politeness of Jas. Walker Esq. we had the opportunity afforded us of examining the drawing of a new hotel which it is proposed to erect on the site of the Nashville Inn. The drawing is executed in a most elegant manner by Maj. Strickland, the Architect of the New State Capitol, and if carried out as designed, the building will be a grand addition to the architectural beauty of our city. It can be seen at the office of the Nashville Insurance and Trust Company.

1848

Strickland consulted by Major A. Heiman about a proposed suspension bridge across the Cumberland River at Nashville.

Reference: A. Heiman, "Report on the Construction of a Suspension Bridge across the Cumberland River at Nashville, 1849." Heiman made a copy of the report for the Tennessee Historical Society, Nashville. He stated that after seeing the designs for the bridge in the spring of 1848, he objected to the sandy base to be used for the abutments.

Having submitted the foregoing views to my friend, Mr. Wm. Strickland, whose judgment in all such matters is admitted to stand preeminent, and who having kindly examined with me the premisses in question, and considering as he does with me in the substance and matter of this Report in all its details

I confidently submit the same to the inspection and scrutiny of the Board, Respectfully,

Your obedient Servant
A. Heiman.

*1848-51

First Presbyterian Church, Church Street and Fifth Avenue, Nashville. (Plates 44 and 45)

Cornerstone laid: April 28, 1849.

First service in basement: January 5, 1850.

Dedicated: April 20, 1851.

Used as a hospital by the Federal Army: December 31, 1862-June, 1862.

Rededicated: July 2, 1865.

Reference: Church Minutes, 1828-52. Accounts of the building of the church, microfilm copy in Vanderbilt University Library, Nashville.

The First Presbyterian Church burned on September 14, 1848. On Saturday, September 16, a meeting was called and a committee of six: John M. Bass, William Nichol, A. W. Putnam, John M. Hill, Alexander Allison, and William Eakin, was appointed to solicit subscriptions and authorized "to procure a plan or plans for a building to be submitted at a future meeting of the congregation."

By October 24, John M. Hill, the treasurer of the committee and a leading grocer of the city, reported subscriptions in the amount of $13,000; the sale of old material, $400; fire insurance, $8,000; a total of $21,400.

On December 15, William Strickland's plan was selected in preference to that of Briscoe Vannoy. On April 19, 1849, Strickland notified the committee that all was in readiness for the laying of the cornerstone. April 24 was chosen for the ceremony, but owing to the inclement weather, it was postponed until April 28.

On June 29, 1849, Strickland reported that the foundations were completed to the floor level. The basement was ready for use by the end of the year and the first service was held there on January 5, 1850.

On February 23, 1850, "A plan of the plastering of the main body of the Church edifice having been submitted by Maj. Strickland, the same with some modifications was adopted."

The accounts for the year 1850 have been preserved in full, and in that year the checks numbered 38, 55, 59, 67, 87, and 125 were paid to William Strickland, totaling $429.

Rev. Robert F. Bunting, *Manual of the First Presbyterian Church, Nashville, Tenn. with a brief History of its Organization November 1814 to November 1868.* Description of the church, p. 101.

The general style of the architecture is Egyptian, but the front, never having been completed, presents an unfinished appearance. A tower 104 feet in height is built on each of the front corners commencing 22 feet square at the base, diminishing by offsets as it rises, and finishing in the shape of an octagon. Between the two towers are the steps, 36 feet in length, ascending to the main floor or body of the church, the entrance to the vestibule being by three doors, finished in the Egyptian style.
The vestibule is 70½ feet long, 16½ feet deep at the center and 9½ feet deep at the ends. From the vestibule four doors lead to the Audience-room which is 101¼ feet long and 70½ feet wide. The pulpit is at the south end, opposite the entrance, and the organ and choir are elevated in the rear of the pulpit. There are 168 pews ranged in three double rows—10 pews of the total number being placed on each side of the pulpit. 1100 persons can sit in the pews and 200 in the gallery over the vestibule. Within the towers, on the main floor, are stairways leading to the gallery, which is 70 feet long and 29½ feet deep across the front of the Audience-room and covering the vestibule.
The basement story is divided into 5 smaller rooms, for the various services of the Church, with the necessary coal-house, passages, etc. The principal one is the large Lecture-room, which is 70½ x 54½ feet in size; the smaller Lecture-room 44½ x 28¼; the Pastor's study 28 x 15. There are also 2 rooms 13½ x 23 used at present as a boys' school by W. Bryce Thompson. . . . The walls of the basement story are of stone, and well built. The body of the church and towers are of brick.

Style: Egyptian Revival owing to the use of cavetto moldings, globe and wings motif, batter jambs of doors and windows, papyrus and palm capitals, and the painted front wall of the interior which suggests an Egyptian temple.

Plan: Two-story rectangular building with square towers on the façade. The basement is divided into rooms for Sunday school, with one large auditorium.

The main floor has a vestibule with stairs leading to the balcony and to the towers. The church auditorium is rectangular, reminiscent of the plainest of meeting houses, despite the exotic decoration. Behind are rooms for the minister and choir. The church has been added to at the rear.

Materials: On the exterior, brick, stone, and metal, all painted gray. On the interior, painted plaster walls, wood and metal half-columns.

Cost: The final entry in accounts of the building is the amount spent on the church up to February 3, 1854, which was $37,191.28.

Outstanding features: The heavy solidity of the construction and the Egyptian features of the ornament.

*1850

Polk Monument, Capitol grounds, Nashville; formerly on the Polk estate grounds, Nashville. (Plate 42A)

Reference: *The Daily Centre-State American*, Nashville, May 21-23, 1850. *Nashville Daily Union*, May 23, 1850.

Anson and Fanny Nelson, *Memorials of Sarah Childress Polk* (New York). The epitaph was prepared by A. O. P. Nicholson.

Polk was the eleventh president of the United States, defeating Tyler as the successful Democratic candidate in 1844, and winning over Henry Clay in the national election. Andrew Jackson voted for him, but his native state as a whole voted against him. He was born in 1795 and died in June 1849, just three months after the expiration of his term of office. His presidency marked the first important steps in American imperialism. The Oregon dispute was settled, Texas was admitted, and the Mexican War fought and won. Tariffs were greatly reduced, much to the annoyance of Protectionist Pennsylvanians, including Strickland's good friend, Judge Kane, who published a pamphlet remonstrating with Polk's tariff policy and accusing him of breaking pre-election commitments.

In his will, Polk left instructions that he should be buried on his own grounds, and that a simple monument should be erected. Strickland carried out his wishes for simplicity. There is a plain sarcophagus in the center of a marble platform, above which, supported by four unfluted Doric columns, is a plain entablature surmounted by a low two-step attic. On the architrave, the name and dates are cut in Roman letters. A longer inscription is cut on the sarcophagus.

May 22, 1850, was the day chosen for the transfer of the remains of Polk from their temporary resting place in City Cemetery. At seven in the morning, Strickland was there with Mr. McCombs, the undertaker, to direct the exhumation of the body. The coffin was found to be in an excellent state of preservation; it was "placed in a black walnut shell, beautifully polished, which was delivered by Colonel Strickland to the Committee appointed to escort the body into the city." Major Heiman was one of the escort, who as a Knight Templar was on horseback. The escort went to the Masonic Hall where, at eight-thirty, the Masonic fraternity, the Fire Companies and the citizens generally began to form into a procession. On arriving at the vault on Polk Place, cannons were fired, prayers were offered by John B. McFerrin, a requiem with music by Ruppius was sung, and the sermon was delivered by Bishop Otey. "The remains of the late ex-president were then placed in the vault with Masonic ceremonies, under the direction of Colonel Strickland. The whole affair was accomplished with successful solemnity."

*1850

John Kane Monument in City Cemetery, Nashville. (Plate 42B)

Inscription on front: KANE.

Inscription on back:

Erected
by the Stone Cutters
of the State House
to the Memory of
John Kane
Died June 18, 1848
in the 38th Year of his Age

Reference: *Daily American*, Nashville, Friday, May 3, 1850. "City Intelligence."

The State Quarry. A monument cut and designed at the quarry—and intended to be placed over the remains of 'John Kane,' a stonecutter who had at

the time of his death been employed on the Capitol, was shown us. It is a tribute of the Stone Cutters employed on the State Capitol, to the memory of their deceased companion, and much credit does it do them. The design is beautiful. On the top of the monument are the "banker blocks" and on the blocks, a stone in the act of being finished for the "capstone." This represents the last job on which the deceased worked. On it is cut in a style that would do credit to any sculpture, the tools as left by the workman when he left his job to return no more. . . .
We learned since the above was in type, that Wm. Strickland, Esq., the talented architect of the Capitol, was the designer of the monument.

*1850

"Belmont," Nashville. (Plates 46 and 47A)

Now one of the buildings of Ward-Belmont School; additions have been made, but the original building has not been altered.

No source material has been found to authenticate the tradition that "Belmont" was built by Strickland for Joseph Acklen and his wife Alicia Hayes Acklen. Stylistically, it seems permissible to do so.

Style: Italianate with Greek Revival details. The Corinthian distyle-in-antis portico, the tower and wings, ornate decoration, ironwork and balconies make the general effect that of the late Renaissance. The classic attic, Greek moldings, and crossets are Greek Revival. The Corinthian columns and rich cornice with acanthus leaves and eagles on the interior are Italianate.

Plan: From the central, recessed entrance, one enters a vestibule, with parlors on either side at the front; and a large room, the entire width of the central building behind, with a double colonnade of Corinthian columns and a free-standing stairway. Upstairs, there are a large transverse hall with stairs to the tower and four master bedrooms.

Materials: The walls are of stone and brick, plastered and painted. The trim and roof are of wood.

Outstanding features: The Corinthian portico, the tower, the large wings with iron balconies, and —on the interior—the large drawing room with colonnades and a rich cornice, and the stairs, especially those to the tower.

The *Annals of the Army of the Cumberland* by an Officer [John Fitch] (Philadelphia, 1863).

An account based largely on the police records of the occupation of Nashville by the Union Army. It contains a description of "Belmont" which is interesting in that it shows the impression that the building and its gardens made upon someone of unsophisticated taste.

The police record contains a description of Acklin's premises; for they are rather a specialty in the way of extravagance. The place is situated two miles out of the city, and comprises about one hundred acres of land. His buildings are gothic-ified and starched and bedizened to perfection. Serpentine walks, shrubbery, and all that sort of thing, abound in great quantity and profusion. A tower, one hundred and five feet high, is built near a spring a fourth of a mile distant from the buildings, and a steam-engine within its base forces water to its top, whence it is piped in every direction over the grounds. The improvements upon this place, such as the buildings, statuary, walls, etc. cost over a quarter of a million of dollars. Looking over it from adjacent high grounds, the white marble fountains, emblems and statues cause the place to resemble somewhat a fashionable first-class cemetery.

*1850(?)

Judge Caruthers' House, Lebanon, Tenn.

There is no documentation to substantiate the tradition that it was designed by Strickland.

In Lebanon, Tennessee, thirty miles to the east of Nashville, there is a house on Main Street attributed to Strickland, built for a Judge Caruthers. The house is still standing and is now used as an undertakers' establishment. It is a wooden house, clapboard, now painted white, with a handsome pediment in front. It has been changed, added to, and altered so that it is impossible to get a clear idea of the original plan, design, and decoration of the house. Also, there is no other wooden house that is definitely attributed to Strickland which makes it more difficult to determine whether this might have been his design. The deeds in the courthouse give no additional clues because the land was owned by Robert Caruthers long before Strickland came to Tennessee. It seems to have originally been a handsome house with the central doorway and interior plan which one finds in the other houses by Strickland, but much of the interior has been renovated so that none of the mid-nineteenth century decoration remains. It has been plastered and papered inside and, at present, is very undistinguished in appearance.

*1852

"Lynnlawn," built for Thomas E. Stratton, 1845-52 (now owned by Mrs. Edgar M. Foster), Gallatin Pike, East Nashville. (Plate 47B)

Reference: Family tradition, according to Mrs. Foster who is a descendant of Thomas E. Stratton, credits William Strickland with the design for the front portion of "Lynnlawn," which is also the most recent.

Internal evidence: Solid construction; square, two-story, central-hall design; high ceilings, classic motifs in plaster work of hall frieze, simplicity of upper story, and the use of gray brick.

While there is nothing in the construction, plan, or decoration which proves the house to have been designed by Strickland, these features are, nevertheless, in accordance with his work elsewhere.

1853

Union Bank, Nashville, Tennessee.

Reference: Secretary of State. Legislative papers. Tennessee State Archives (#417, Box #144).

Letter to John M. Bass from Francis W. Strickland in relation to pay for services rendered in building the Union Bank (1853).

Nashville 8th July /53

To/
John M. Bass, Esqr
Dear Sir.—
I called on Mr. G. M. Fogg yesterday to ask of him the propriety of writing a letter to the President and Directors of the Union Bank respecting the payment of a just claim I am entitled to for my services at the building of the Union Bank, he advised me to call and see you on the subject; having had an interview with you sometime since respecting this matter I thought it proper to address a letter to you. There was no agreement made with me, you asked me what my father and myself would charge for superintending the Bank. I told you I would see him and let you know on what terms we would agree upon. I proposed to him to make a written agreement charging 5 pr Ct. on the cost, the usual percentage; he, my father, said it would be all right, so the matter ended, I being under the impression that I was to be paid. I am willing to receive any amount that you may think proper in the matter, your attention to this will confer a great favour on your Obdt Servt.

Francis W. Strickland.

*1853

"Belle Meade," Harding Road, Nashville. (Plate 48A)

Built for John Harding, it has been continuously occupied and is now owned by Mr. and Mrs. Meredith Caldwell.

There is no source material to support the tradition that the house was designed by Strickland. Stylistically it seems permissible to do so.

Style: Greek Revival with a handsome white marble portico, six square piers supporting an entablature, the central part of which is crowned by a pediment decorated with acroteria, as are the corners of the entablature. J. Frazer Smith (*White Pillars,* [New York, 1941]) suggests that the façade may have been inspired by the plates of the Choragic Monument of Thrasyllus (Stuart and Revett, *Antiquities of Athens,* I, Chapter 4, Plate IV). The doors and windows have crosset moldings. The downstairs interior has rich cornices and ceiling decorations, but they are not Greek Revival.

Plan: Central axis with hall and stairs; drawing room on the left, parlor and dining room on the right; kitchen and servants' quarters in a separate ell to the right. Upstairs, there are four bedrooms in the front part of the house. The ceilings are seventeen feet high; the walls about two feet thick, and the windows are large.

Materials: Walls of stone and brick, plastered and whitewashed, marble portico. Wooden window frames, door jambs, and roof.

Outstanding features: Portico, proportion of house and portico, plaster cornices, stairway.

*1853(?)

Harding Tombs, Harding Road, Belle Meade, outside Nashville.

Note: Tradition assigns these tombs to Strickland. No documentary evidence has been found, but the design and construction are similar to Strickland's work. They are low masonry vaults supported by heavy, unfluted Doric columns.

1854(?)

"Burlington," Nashville. (Plate 48B)

Demolished: 1931.

Miss Josephine Farrell showed me photographs and plans of the house and told me of the family tradition that it was designed by William Strickland and built by his son Francis. There is no documentary evidence for this tradition.

It was a two-story, flat-roofed building with a kitchen ell behind. The side wings were later additions. There were stone foundations and brick walls, stuccoed and painted, and the roof was covered with tin. Again, as at Belmont, if one looks carefully enough, there are classic features present although the general effect is Italianate.

The classic features were the central motif of a triumphal arch crowned with a low pediment above an entablature, the center of the arch, or keystone, ornamented by an acanthus console, the spandrils and pilasters decorated by sunken panels edged with half guilloche moldings (this vertical line was repeated by setting back the side walls two feet and repeating the sunken panel and molding), and the general proportions. The windows were early Florentine Renaissance with two round-headed lights divided by an engaged Corinthian column with a circular motif containing a shield design above. Over the windows were hood moldings, ending on rich corbels and with baroque shields standing out over the keystones, and two rows of heavy, rich ornament in the molding. These foreshadowed the seventies and may have been Francis Strickland's contribution to the coming neo-baroque style.

The interior was of the usual Strickland plan with a central hall and stairway, and rooms on either side on both floors. It was said to be a comfortable house.

Houses near Nashville attributed to William or Francis Strickland:

Rebuilding of "Melrose."

Addition to "Kingsley."

"Clover Bottom."

"Riverwood" (attributed to Francis).

"Two Rivers Farmhouse" (built by Francis for David McGavock in 1859).

Town houses attributed to Strickland (all demolished):

The houses of: William Stockell, H. R. W. Hill and a Mr. Kirkman.

APPENDIX B

STRICKLAND PORTFOLIO OF DRAWINGS, TENNESSEE STATE LIBRARY, NASHVILLE, TENNESSEE

Seventy-three items are in this black portfolio with cloth sides and leather back, 22 by 30 inches. All are mounted and have been bound together.

In this collection, few drawings are signed, fewer are dated, and almost half bear no identifying notation.

Seventeen items are signed "William Strickland, Archt." or "Archt. and Engineer":

1. Project for Sixth and Walnut streets.
2. Survey of land for Almshouse. (Plate 24B)
3. Lighthouse for western end of Delaware Breakwater. (Plate 49C)
4. Design for a pulpit and reading desk for St. James Church.
5. Gothic window, perhaps for the "Parsonage," Burlington, New Jersey.
6. Elevation and plan of a house. Caption torn, leaving ". . . age House . . .ton, N. J."
7. Scale drawing of the façade of the Almshouse, Blockley township.
8. Church on Gay Street (probably the Church of the Holy Trinity, West Chester, Pennsylvania).
9. Second Presbyterian Church (perhaps a preliminary sketch for a church in Nashville in Greek Revival style).
10. Mantel, Second Bank of the United States. (Plate 49B)
11. Estimate for the Second Bank of the United States.
12. Scale drawing of a basement (perhaps Second Bank of the United States).
13. Unidentified plan, scale ½ inch to the foot.
14. Unidentified façade of a house. (Almost square with gable roof, central door with porch, and balcony above. Two windows on each side of the two stories. Similar to design for James A. Hillhouse.)
15. Unidentified sketch of a ground plan of an edifice with an octagonal core, and four square wings enclosed in a quatrefoil.
16. Unidentified north front of a house (octagonal with two wings).
17. Answers to thirty-one questions dealing with the problems of a water supply system in an unidentified city. Examples:

10. The city rates are $5 per house fronting all the streets and 2.50 in Courts and Alleys. Baths $3. water closets $1 per annum Private Stables $5–
11. No, some few dwellings have it and some Hotels introduced into all the rooms and Attics.

* * *

21. The poorer classes are supplyed by a Hydrant placed in a Court or Alley.

* * *

23. Frost is the only inconvenience in piping.

Three drawings are signed by Francis Strickland.

1. Diagram of metal construction labeled "Scale drawing by F. W. Strickland Archt."
2. "Scale drawing of fireplace–drawn by Francis W. Strickland Archt." Evidently for fireplaces in Senate room, Tennessee State Capital; details are identical but proportions vary.
3. The Second Bank of the United States, dated April 20, 1833.

One drawing is signed by Jesse Hartley Strickland. An elevation and ground plan of a small house signed "J. Hartley Strickland Archt." "Engineer" is crossed out. The plan shows no particular ability. Chimneys are placed in the outer walls and extend like rabbit ears above the roof.

One drawing is signed by William Camerer. An unidentified project, perhaps a fort, with notation "Drawn by Wm Camerer 20 ft to an inch."

One drawing is signed by a Mr. Martin, evidently a pupil of Strickland's. A two-story elevation of a building in the Italianate style with corbels, moldings, string courses, a round-headed door, and double windows above. No roof identified. The plan of the first story (scale 8 feet to the inch) shows a large octagonal central part containing a hall and four wings. Comment in pencil in Strickland's writing on the side is the following: "Elevation to be drawn over again. Mr. Martin will please draw the plan over again and put the Pyramid in the Centre of the Room— Take a fresh piece of paper WS[d]"

Four drawings are signed by Andrew J. Binny.

1. Almshouse front, September 29, 1840. (Plate 24A)
2. Corinthian order, October 23, 1840.
3. Plan of the Second Bank of the United States, October 31, 1840.
4. Halls of Justice and House of Detention, New York; designed and erected by John Haviland, architect, 1837; November, 1840.

Five drawings for the benefit of students.

Eleven labeled but unsigned.

1. Projection of a house.
2. Plan of cranes in use at Liverpool Docks.
3. Plan of Broad Street Station for Columbia and Philadelphia Railroad, Philadelphia. (Plate 49D)
4. East elevation of the Timber Shed, Washington (not by Strickland).
5. Front elevation of Almshouse and adjoining buildings.
6. Almshouse, detail of antae and base, portico.
7. Fulton monument for Cairo, Illinois.
8. Plan of a hotel on Third Street, Philadelphia.
9. Trinity Church, West Chester, Pennsylvania.
10. Plan of Tennessee State Capitol and adjoining lots.
11. Transverse Section through Banking Room, Bank of the United States, State of Pennsylvania. Fragmentary note on bottom "When I begin work at Harrisburg perhaps I will draw. . . . I think it would not be useful for. . . ."

The remaining thirty drawings are unsigned, undated, and unlabeled. Some appear to be by Strickland, others look like the work of his son Francis. The less skillful may be by Jesse Hartley, or other pupils. Three can be identified. Two are preliminary sketches for the Tennessee State Capitol. Another is an elevation of the "Parsonage," Burlington, New Jersey. There is an elevation and ground plan of a church. The rest are elevations and ground plans of houses which range from very simple to extremely ornate designs. All the ground plans have a central entrance and hall.

The following information was gathered from the portfolio of drawings:

1. Confirmation of the impression that friendly relations existed between Strickland and Haviland.
2. Some of the grandiose house plans seem to give assurance that Strickland was the architect of the handsome Nashville houses attributed to him.
3. The number of drawings of churches suggest that Strickland designed more than those of which we have records.
4. The drawing for the second floor of the hotel on Third Street brings the number of hotel designs by Strickland to four. As yet there is no evidence that any of them were built.
5. Another drawing of a building with a choragic monument tower confirms Strickland's predeliction for that form.
6. In view of the current interest in octagonal house designs, it is noted that Strickland used the octagonal arrangement as the core for a house, but always with two or four wings added.

APPENDIX C

OILS, WATERCOLORS, DRAWINGS, PRINTS AND ARCHITECTURAL DRAWINGS

Oils:

Christ Church, 1811 (48 by 52) Historical Society of Pennsylvania. (Plate 3)

Watercolors:

Sketchbook of watercolors made on the European trip, 1838, Tennessee State Library.

Wash drawings:

Views of naval engagements of the War of 1812, later reproduced in the Naval and Analectic Magazine.

Nine drawings, New-York Historical Society. (Plate 4)

Pencil drawings:

Two views of New York, New-York Historical Society. (Plate 2)

Landscape sketches, Historical Society of Pennsylvania.

Maps and Surveys:

American Philosophical Society Library.

Tennessee Historical Society Library.

National Archives, Washington, D. C.

Prints:

Strickland did aquatints, lithographs, engravings, and etchings. Good collections of his work are to be found in The Historical Society of Pennsylvania and the Print Room, New York Public Library. Listings of his work are found in:

Carl W. Drepperd, *Early American Prints*, pp. 13, 116.

David McNeeley Stauffer, *American Engravers on Copper and Steel*, Part I, pp. 262-63; Part II, pp. 503-8.

Architectural Drawings:

Tennessee State Library.

Historical Society of Pennsylvania.

U. S. Naval Home, Philadelphia.

The National Archives, Records of the Navy Department.

Yale University Library.

Athenaeum, Providence, Rhode Island.

Notarial Records Office, Court House, New Orleans.

Girard College, Philadelphia.

Philadelphia Free Library, Ridgway Branch.

Philip Strickland Harper, Chicago.

APPENDIX D

PUBLISHED WRITINGS OF WILLIAM STRICKLAND

1813

Catalogue of the Third Annual Exhibition of the Columbian Society of Artists and the Pennsylvania Academy, 1813. #96 "Description of a Great National Monument, Commemorative of the Illustrious Washington."

1813

Decatur's Victory, a song published by G. E. Blake, Philadelphia.

1815

The Art of Landscape Painting. Baltimore.

1819

Analectic Magazine. March, 13:3. "Description of the New Bank of the United States."

1820

A Proposal for Altering the Eastern Front of Philadelphia by Paul Beck, Jr., with an estimate by Strickland.

1821

Port Folio, September, XII. "New Bank of the United States in Philadelphia."

1823

Communication from the Chesapeake and Delaware Canal Company; and a Report and Estimate of William Strickland, to the President and Directors.

1824 (?)

National Gazette. Philadelphia, August 21. Communication signed "S." Concerning the Hall of the Musical Fund Society, possibly by Strickland.

1824

Come Honor the Brave. Song in honor of Lafayette, published by G. E. Blake, Philadelphia.

1826

Franklin Journal, I:1. "A description of the Hetton Railroad in England."

1826

Reports on Canals, Railways, Roads and Other Subjects, Philadelphia.

1833 (?)

Outline of a Plan for the Administration of the Girard Trust.

1835

Report of Survey for Wilmington and Susquehanna Railroad. Philadelphia.

1835

Address upon a Proposed Railroad. Philadelphia.

1840

Tomb of Washington at Mount Vernon. Philadelphia: Carey and Hart.

1840 (?)

An Appeal to the Citizens of the City of Philadelphia Against the City Councils.

1841

Editor, with Gill and Campbell, of *Public Works in the United States of America.* London: Weale.

1844

House Document #51. 28th long First Session III. Ja. 8, 1844, 20 pp.

1844

House Report #267. 28th long First Session I. Mar. 7, 1844, 11 pp.

1845

Nashville Daily Orthopolitan. December 2. "State Capitol."

1846

Nashville Daily Orthopolitan. July 6. "Description of the Walker Monument in the City Cemetery."

1846 (?)

Nashville Daily Orthopolitan. September 16. Article entitled "Fine Arts" and signed "S."

1846

Nashville Republican Banner. November 18. "The Monument," a description of the monument to be erected to the memory of those who fell at Monterey.

1846

Nashville Daily Orthopolitan. May 22-June 24. Series of eleven articles entitled "Sketches of Roman Architecture" signed "S."

1848

Port Folio. Nashville, May, I:11, 321-23. "The Three Orders of Architecture—Wisdom, Strength and Beauty," signed "S."

1850 (?)

The Naturalist, Nashville, August. "Rural Taste."

Note: When the date is followed by a question mark, the following item is attributed to Strickland on stylistic grounds and subject matter, but there is no proof. More reports by Strickland are to be found in the sixteen volumes of *Hazard's Register of Pennsylvania,* 1828-35. "On the Use of the Thermometer in Navigation" by William Strickland in the *Transactions* of the American Philosophical Society, V, has been incorrectly attributed to the architect.

APPENDIX E

PORTRAITS OF WILLIAM STRICKLAND, HIS FATHER AND HIS WIFE

1826

Hugh Bridport exhibited a small portrait in the annual exhibition of the Pennsylvania Academy of Fine Arts (history unknown).

1829

John Neagle painted a portrait, shown in 1830 at the annual exhibition of the Pennsylvania Academy of Fine Arts. It was engraved by John Sartain, a print is in the H.S.P. The painting is now in the possession of Mrs. Norvin H. Green, Tuxedo Park, New York. (Frontispiece)

1838

Bronze bust by Nicholas Gevelot, now in the Tennessee Historical Society. It is said to have been executed in Paris. Gevelot, however, also worked in the United States. In 1828, he carved the statue of Apollo for the Arch Street Theatre, Philadelphia, and in 1833 was working on a life-size statue of Stephen Girard.

In the possession of Philip Strickland Harper of Chicago, there is a portrait by an unknown artist which is said to be of William Strickland. It is a large painting of a young man with dark brown hair and sideburns, seated, holding drawing materials with a landscape background in which there is a colonnade, the columns of which appear to have been intended to have Corinthian capitals.

Mr. Harper also has an oval photograph of William Strickland as an old man. It appears to have been enlarged from a daguerreotype.

The late William Strickland Harper of Hamden, Connecticut, had two photographs of Strickland, one as a young man, the other as an old man. He also had a small oil portrait of Strickland as a young man seated by an easel. The painting was originally rectangular, but has been cut to an oval of about seven by ten inches.

In the Tennessee State Library, there are two portraits of Strickland, both representing him in his old age. One is twenty-five by thirty inches and was the work of an unknown artist in Philadelphia, according to the library records. The other was taken from a daguerreotype made by S. W. Shaw, of Nashville, which was photographed by C. C. Hughes and painted by William Cooper, one of Nashville's most noted and prolific portrait painters of the ante-bellum decade. It is a small oval.

There is a family tradition that Mrs. Strickland was also painted by Neagle, but the whereabouts of the painting is unknown.

In the collection of Mrs. Walter S. Jennings of Cold Spring Harbor, Long Island, there is a portrait of Mrs. Strickland, formerly attributed to Gilbert Stuart, but now attributed to Jacob Eichholz by Lawrence Parks, the biographer of Gilbert Stuart. (Plate 1)

Mrs. Kendall Wyman has a small oval painting of a woman in a white dress. The family tradition is that it is a portrait of Mrs. Strickland by Sully.

A Register of Portraits painted by Thomas Sully 1801-1871, edited by Charles Henry Hart, Philadelphia, 1909, lists:

1600	Mr. Strickland Senr.	Head	1809
1601	William Strickland	Bust	1820
1602	William Strickland	Head	1836

The portrait of John Strickland, the father, is now in the possession of Mrs. Kendall Wyman of Cincinnati, a direct descendant. The whereabouts of the Sully portraits of William is unknown.

APPENDIX F

WILLIAM STRICKLAND'S FAMILY, RESIDENCES, AND OBITUARIES

The name Strickland is derived from the word *stirks,* which means "young cattle." Rich lands south of Penrith were called Stirklands, that is, pasture lands. The name was originally "de Sterkeland" or "Stirkland." The present form was first used in the fifteenth century. (Daniel Scott, *The Stricklands of Sizergh Castle* [Kendal, 1908].)

Most of the information concerning Strickland's family came from the late William Strickland Harper of Hamden, Connecticut, a grandson of the architect, and from Mrs. Bertha E. McGeehan, genealogist, of Philadelphia.

William Strickland was the son of John and Elizabeth Strickland. His father was born in 1757. During the Revolution, he owned a farm at Navesink, New Jersey. William is said to have been born there. The family came to Philadelphia before 1790 because in the census list of that year, there is an entry, "Strickland, John—free white man, two free white males under sixteen years, one free white female. Seventh family down Spruce Street—South Side."

Strickland had a brother named John, Jr. (1791-1835), who became a carpenter like their father. He married Jane Hurst (1787-1872) in Christ Church on May 9, 1815, and had at least three children: a daughter Alicia Jane, baptized at Christ Church on November 5, 1818; a son Edward who died in 1894; another son, William Hurst, whose daughter Mary married Colonel E. P. Pearson, U.S.A.

William's other brother George was born in 1797. He was well known for his drawings and engravings of Philadelphia, a number of which appeared in C. G. Childs' *Views in Philadelphia.* He received his art training from his brother William. He also tried to obtain architectural commissions, but was unsuccessful. He submitted plans for the Girard College competition and for the United States Naval Asylum. William was architect of the latter building and George became clerk of the works. He taught drawing at the Franklin Institute. His later years were spent in the employ of the United States Patent Office in Washington, D. C. This position may have come from his earlier connection at the Franklin Institute for the first editor of the *Journal* of the Institute was Thomas P. Jones who later became director of the Patent Office.

William Strickland married Rachel McCollough Trenchard on November 3, 1812, in Christ Church with Dr. James Abercrombie officiating. Rachel Trenchard was born in 1789 in Woodstown, New Jersey. She was the daughter of Thomas Trenchard and sister of Mary Trenchard who married Anson More. Rachel was the granddaughter of George Trenchard, of Salem, New Jersey, who served as an officer in the Revolution and who married Mary Sennickson, the daughter of Andrew Sennickson, a Swede, who fought in the Revolution and then retired to Salem.

The following notice of the wedding appeared in *Poulson's Daily Advertiser,* Thursday, November 5, 1812:

Married, on Tuesday evening, the 3d inst. by the Rev. Dr. James Abercrombie, Mr. William Strickland, Architect, of this city, to Miss Rachel M. Trenchard, of Bridgetown, West New Jersey.

William and Rachel Strickland had six children who lived to maturity and at least two who died in infancy.

William Hall Strickland was buried in Christ Church burying ground, August 18, 1813, aged nine days.

Mary (1814-81) married Thomas Large of Philadelphia and had at least one daughter Elizabeth, 1839-72.

Elizabeth (1816-85) did not marry.

Francis (c. 1818-95) was trained as an architect by his father. He did not marry. In 1839, he went to Europe with John Struthers, carrying a letter of introduction to Andrew Stevenson, American minister at London. Fought in Civil War. Francis was buried in the Arlington National Cemetery.

Thomas was buried in Christ Church Cemetery, Philadelphia, December 21, 1822, aged seven days.

Emily Maria (1824-1909) accompanied her parents to Europe in 1838 where she saw the coronation procession of Queen Victoria. She married Charles Augustus Harper in St. Stephen's Church, Philadelphia, 1849. He was an officer in the Civil War and later became a judge of the Supreme Court of Arkansas.

Jesse Hartley (c. 1826-99) was named for an English engineer. He studied with his father. He married a girl from Murfreesboro, Tennessee, and left Nashville about 1859 to be an officer in Civil War. He later went to Washington, D. C., where he was employed by the Post Office Department. He was buried in Arlington National Cemetery.

When his youngest daughter Jane Hall (1828-46) died, Strickland bought Lot 47, Section D in Laurel Hill Cemetery, Philadelphia, on March 30, 1846. His daughters Jane, Elizabeth, Mary, his granddaughter Elizabeth Large, and his wife were buried in this lot. The dates are determined from the cemetery records. Rachel Trenchard Strickland was interred on September 23, 1866, aged seventy-seven years.

His father died in 1820, according to the Christ Church records and *Poulson's Daily Advertiser*, Wednesday, July 5, 1820: "Died suddenly on the third instant John Strickland, senr, Carpenter of this City, aged 63 years." He died intestate. Letters of administration were granted to Elizabeth Strickland, March 1, 1824. Sureties, $2,400, William Strickland, City Architect and Philip Justus, City House Carpenter. She never filed an inventory of the estate and an attachment was filed against her (No. 65) March 17, 1826, at the instigation of her son John. She was living with William at this time and until her death.

From the Philadelphia directories, one learns that Strickland lived at a number of different addresses in Philadelphia. His name first appears in 1809 when he was listed as a landscape painter. In 1813, he is listed as an architect and engineer, a title he used until he went to Nashville, where he was listed as state architect. The addresses are:

1809 262 Mulberry Street
1811 262 Arch Street
1813 22 North Eighth Street
1814 181 Cherry Street
1816 47 Filbert Street
1819 5 North Eleventh Street
1820 14 North Ninth Street
1823 117 South Ninth Street
1830 Northwest corner of Ninth Street site of University of Pennsylvania buildings (upon which he was engaged at that time)
1837 11 South Ninth Street
1841 Spruce Street above Broad Street
1843 Northwest corner of Ninth and Pine streets

The last Philadelphia entry was for the year 1846 at the above address. His address in Nashville was City Hotel, Public Square.

No family paper or contemporary record gives the date of Strickland's birth. The date formerly given was 1787. That date appears in a footnote in Scharf and Westcott's *History of Philadelphia*, II, 979. Since the information contained in the footnote relies upon the memory of a correspondent, it is not infallible.

It seems likely that he was born in 1788 because he became a Mason in 1809, and no one is permitted to become a Mason until he is of age. At that time he was engaged on the building of the Masonic Hall, and it might be assumed that he would become a member at the first possible moment. Judge Kane added to his obituary of Strickland, "aged about sixty-five" (manuscript in library of the American Philosophical Society). If Strickland was born in November, 1788, he would have been sixty-five when he died in April, 1854.

Since the stone which marks his vault in the north entrance to the Tennessee State Capitol gives April 7 instead of April 6, which the following obituaries will show is the correct date, the inscription giving Strickland's age as sixty-four years may be incorrect also. Since Strickland wished to appear as young as possible in Nashville as he was considered rather old for the job, he may have dropped a year from his age.

Obituaries from three Nashville and two Philadelphia newspapers:

Republican Banner and Nashville Whig, Saturday, April 8, 1854.

Death of Mr. Strickland

It is with very deep regret that we have to announce the death of WILLIAM STRICKLAND, Esq., the Architect of Our State Capitol. Mr. Strickland was for many years a resident of Philadelphia, where various public buildings attest his skill as an Architect. For the last eight years he has been a resident of this place, engaged in superintending the erection of the noble edifice which has been the creation of his genius. He died at 4 o'clock on Thursday morning last after a short illness.
The funeral will take place this morning at 11 o'clock, at the Capitol. Divine service by Rev. J. B. Ferguson.

Daily Union and American, Nashville, April 8, 1854.

Died in the city yesterday, after a short illness, Wm. Strickland, State Architect. His friends are invited to attend his funeral at 11 o'clock at the State Capitol. Divine Service by Rev. J. B. Ferguson.

(This notice implies that he had died on Friday, but probably the item was given to the paper and perhaps set up on Friday.)

Nashville Daily Gazette, April 8, 1854.

Major Strickland, Architect on the Capitol, died at the City Hotel on Thursday night. He will be buried today at 11 o'clock, in a vault at the Capitol which was set apart and designed for that purpose by an act of the late Legislature.

Public Ledger, Philadelphia, Saturday 15, 1854.

Mr. William Strickland, Architect, died on the 6th instant at Nashville. Mr. Strickland was well known over the country for his architectural skill, and he designed many of the principal public buildings of Philadelphia. He was the architect of the State capitol at Nashville, in which he is to be buried—a vault, in the basement, having been reserved for that purpose.

North American and United States Gazette, Philadelphia, April 15, 1854.

Mr. William Strickland, the well known Architect, formerly of this city, died at Nashville, Tennessee, on the 6th inst. Mr. Strickland has, for some time past, been engaged in superintending the erection of the State Capitol at Nashville, a work which is said to furnish an eminent proof of his taste and skill in his difficult art. He is remembered by his Philadelphia friends as a man of genial temper and varied accomplishments and his loss will be unaffectedly regretted by them.

Strickland died intestate. The administration of his estate is recorded in Book R, page 614, year 1862, City Hall, Philadelphia. On April 22, 1862, Mrs. R. M. Strickland, 703 Spruce St., Miss Elizabeth Strickland, and Francis W. Strickland were appointed administrators of the estate of William Strickland with a bond of $50. Mrs. Strickland affirmed "that the whole of Goods, Chattels, Rights and Credits of the personal estate he died possessed of, in the aggregate, did not in value exceed the sum of Twenty-six dollars to the best of her knowledge and belief."

INDEX

PLATES

(Plate 1) MRS. WILLIAM STRICKLAND

(Plate 2) St. Paul's, New York *Drawing by Strickland*

(Plate 3) Christ Church *Oil painting by Strickland*

(Plate 4) ENCOUNTER OF THE *Wasp* AND THE *Frolic*, WAR OF 1812 *Wash drawing by Strickland*

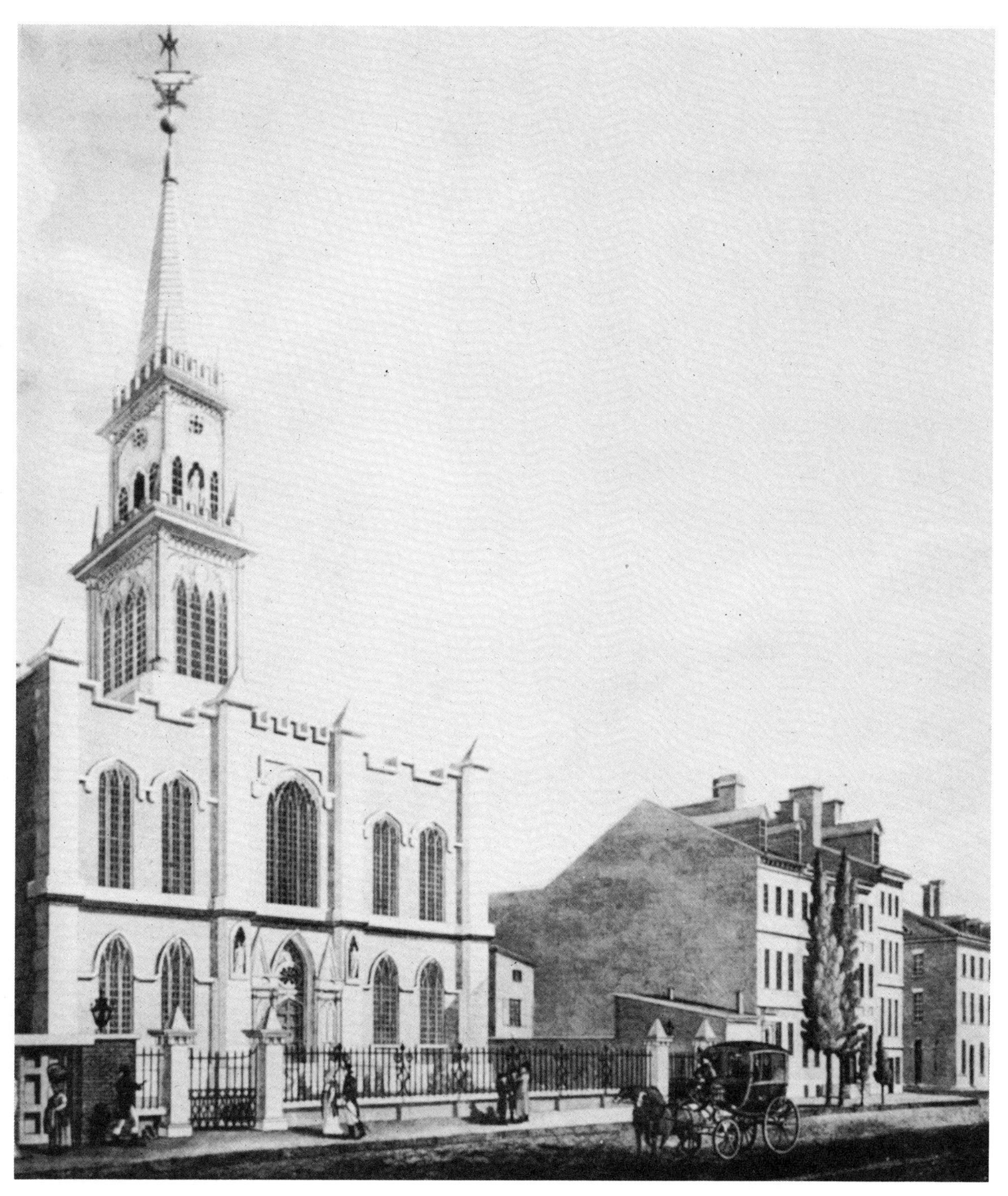

(Plate 5) MASONIC HALL *After a drawing by Strickland*

(Plate 6A) SECOND BANK OF THE UNITED STATES
Chestnut Street façade

(Plate 6B) THE SAME, SIDE VIEW

(Plate 7A) SECOND BANK OF THE UNITED STATES *Library Street façade*

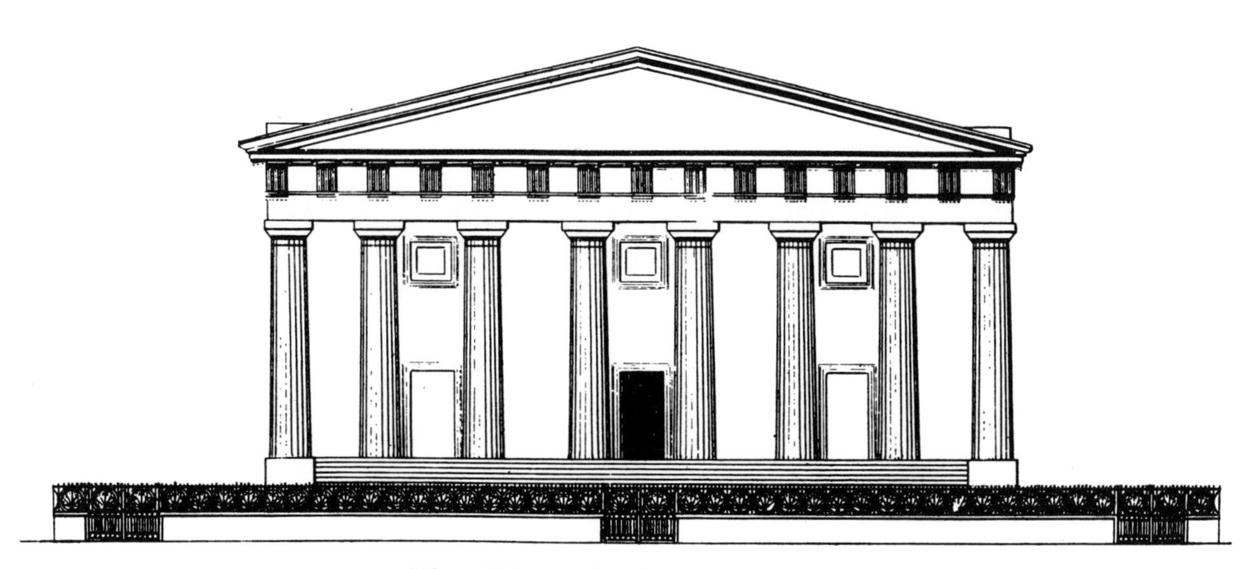

(Plate 7B) THE SAME, ELEVATION

(Plate 8A) SECOND BANK OF THE UNITED STATES
Banking Room

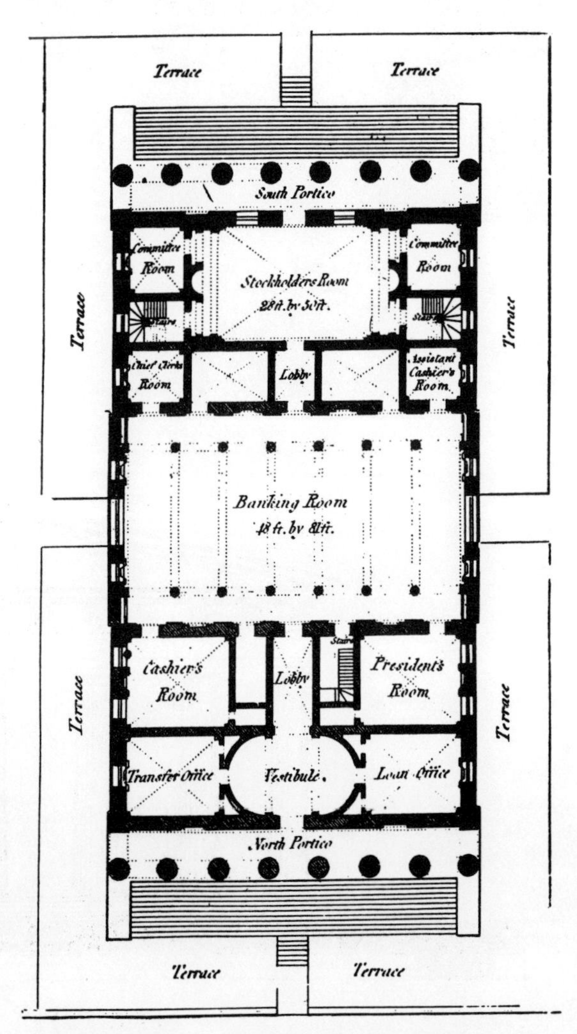

(Plate 8B) THE SAME, FLOOR PLAN

(Plate 9A) FRIENDS' ASYLUM FOR THE INSANE

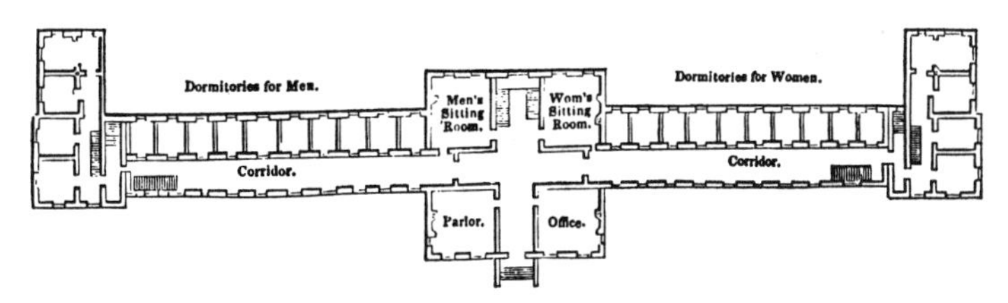

The Same, floor plan

(Plate 9B) FIRST UNITED STATES CUSTOM HOUSE

(Plate 9C) MORAVIAN CHURCH

(Plate 10) St. Stephen's Church

(Plate 11) MASONIC HALL

(Plate 12A) CHESNUT STREET THEATRE

(Plate 12B) ENGRAVING OF THE CHESNUT STREET THEATRE

(Plate 13) Orphans' Society Building and the Indigent Widows' and Single Women's Home

(Plate 14A) MUSICAL FUND SOCIETY HALL *Rear view*

(Plate 14B) CRAWFORD COUNTY COURTHOUSE

(Plate 15) United States Naval Home

(Plate 16) UNITED STATES NAVAL HOME *View of a wing*

(Plate 17A) United States Naval Home

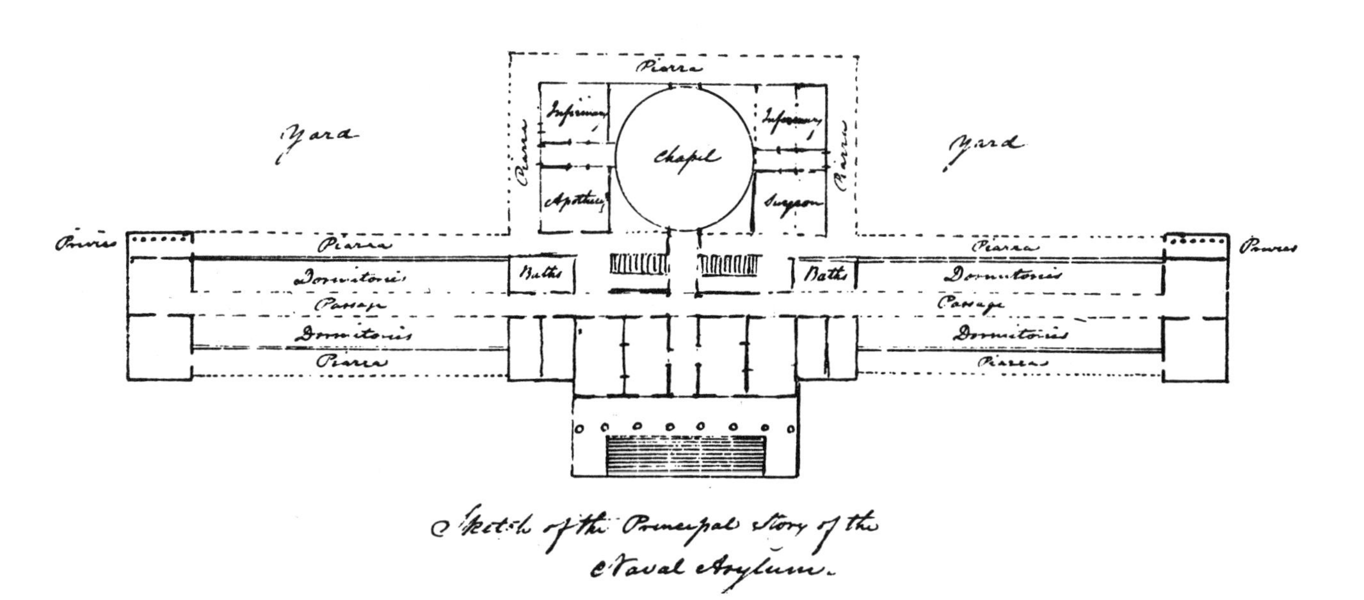

(Plate 17B) The Same, Plan of the Main Floor

(Plate 18A) TEMPLE OF THE NEW JERUSALEM, LATER ACADEMY OF NATURAL SCIENCES

(Plate 18B) MIKVEH-ISRAEL SYNAGOGUE

(Plate 19) ARCH STREET THEATRE

(Plate 20A) UNIVERSITY OF PENNSYLVANIA

(Plate 20B) LITHOGRAPH OF THE UNIVERSITY OF PENNSYLVANIA

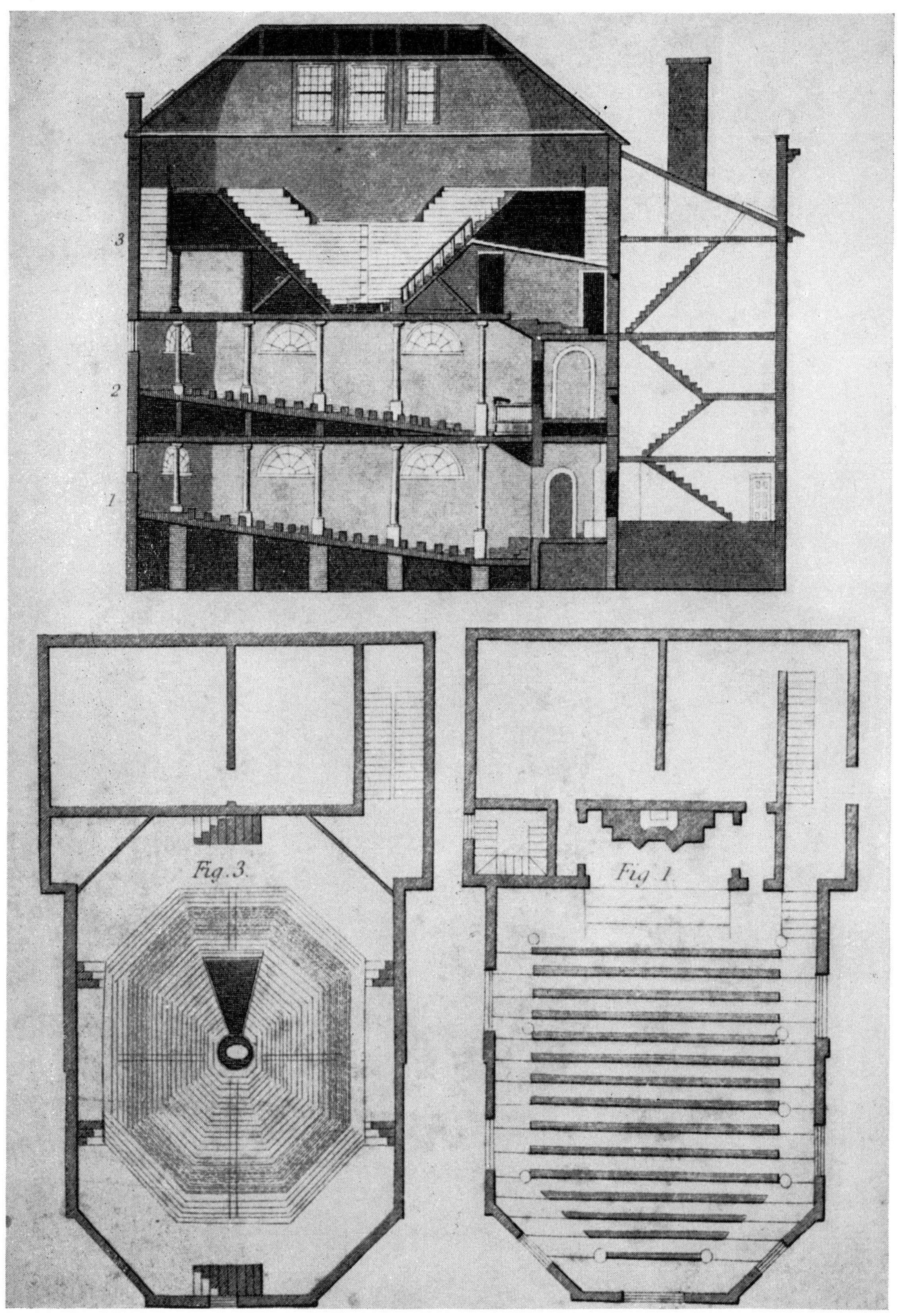

(Plate 21) UNIVERSITY OF PENNSYLVANIA MEDICAL SCHOOL

(Plate 22) Tower of Independence Hall

(Plate 23A) First Congregational Unitarian Church

(Plate 23B) United States Mint

(Plate 24A) NEW ALMSHOUSE, BLOCKLEY TOWNSHIP
Elevation

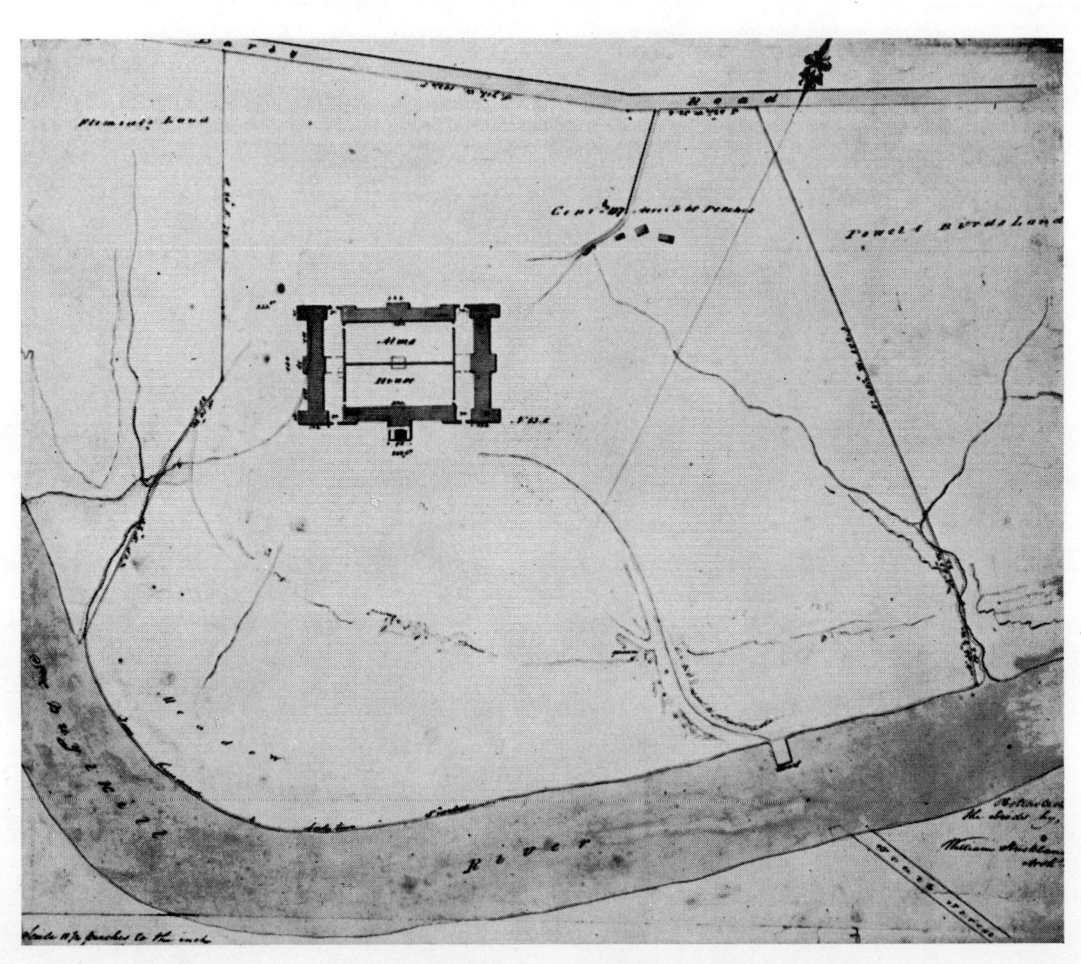

(Plate 24B) NEW ALMSHOUSE *Plan of buildings and grounds*

(Plate 25) New Almshouse, Now the Philadelphia General Hospital

(Plate 26A) THE PHILADELPHIA EXCHANGE

(Plate 26B) TOWER OF THE PHILADELPHIA EXCHANGE

(Plate 27) THE PHILADELPHIA EXCHANGE *Third Street façade*

(Plate 28) Benjamin Carr Monument

(Plate 29A) DRAWING FOR THE GIRARD COLLEGE COMPETITION

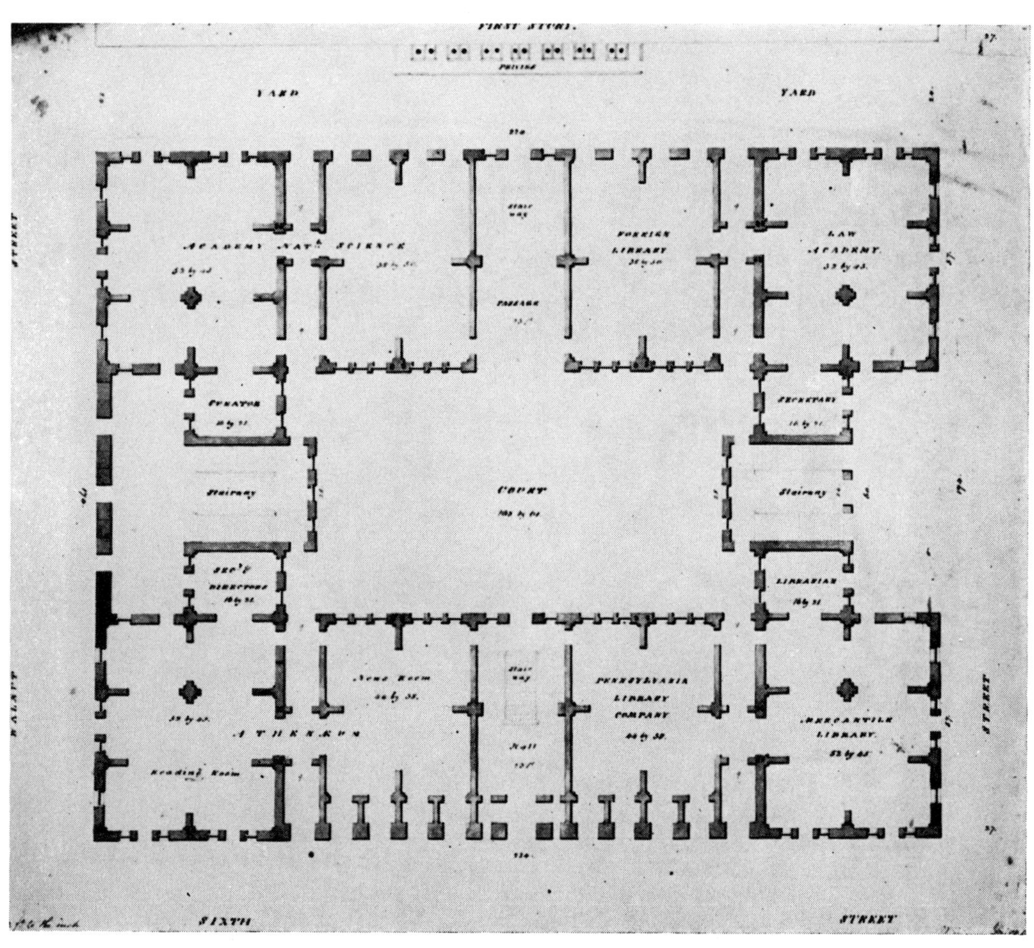

(Plate 29B) PLAN FOR A JOINT LIBRARY BUILDING

(Plate 30A) "PARSONAGE," BURLINGTON, NEW JERSEY

(Plate 30B) BRANCH MINT, CHARLOTTE, NORTH CAROLINA

(Plate 31A) BRANCH MINT, NEW ORLEANS

(Plate 31B) THE SAME, ANOTHER VIEW

(Plate 32A) PROPOSED GATE TO LAUREL HILL CEMETERY

(Plate 32B) BANK OF PHILADELPHIA, ON LEFT

(Plate 33A) PROVIDENCE ATHENAEUM

(Plate 33B) LITHOGRAPH OF THE PROVIDENCE ATHENAEUM

(Plate 34A) Proposed Hotel, Ninth and Chestnut Streets *George Street façade*

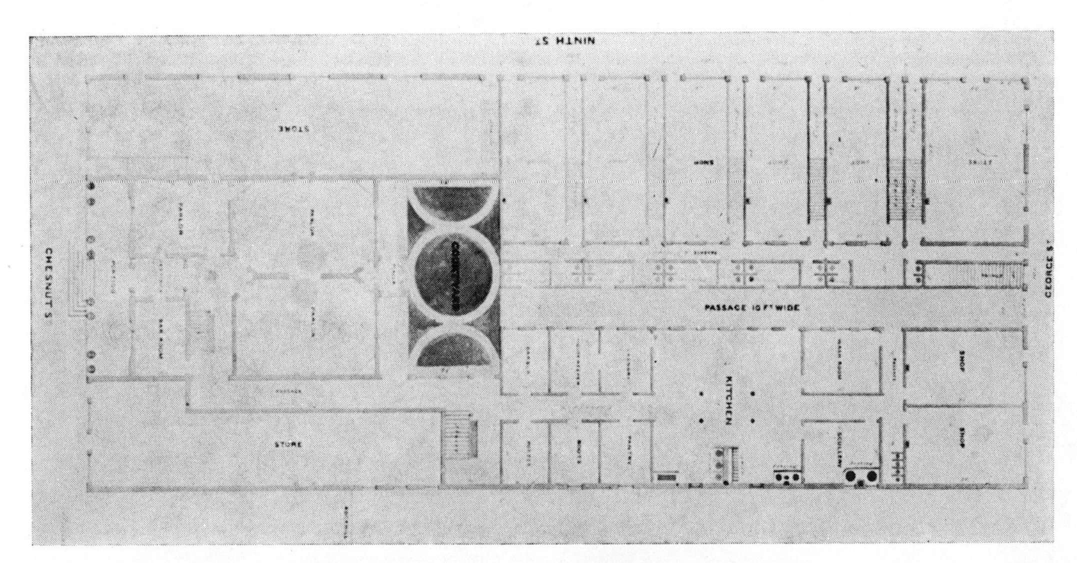

(Plate 34B) Floor Plan of the Hotel

(Plate 34C) Ninth Street Façade of the Hotel

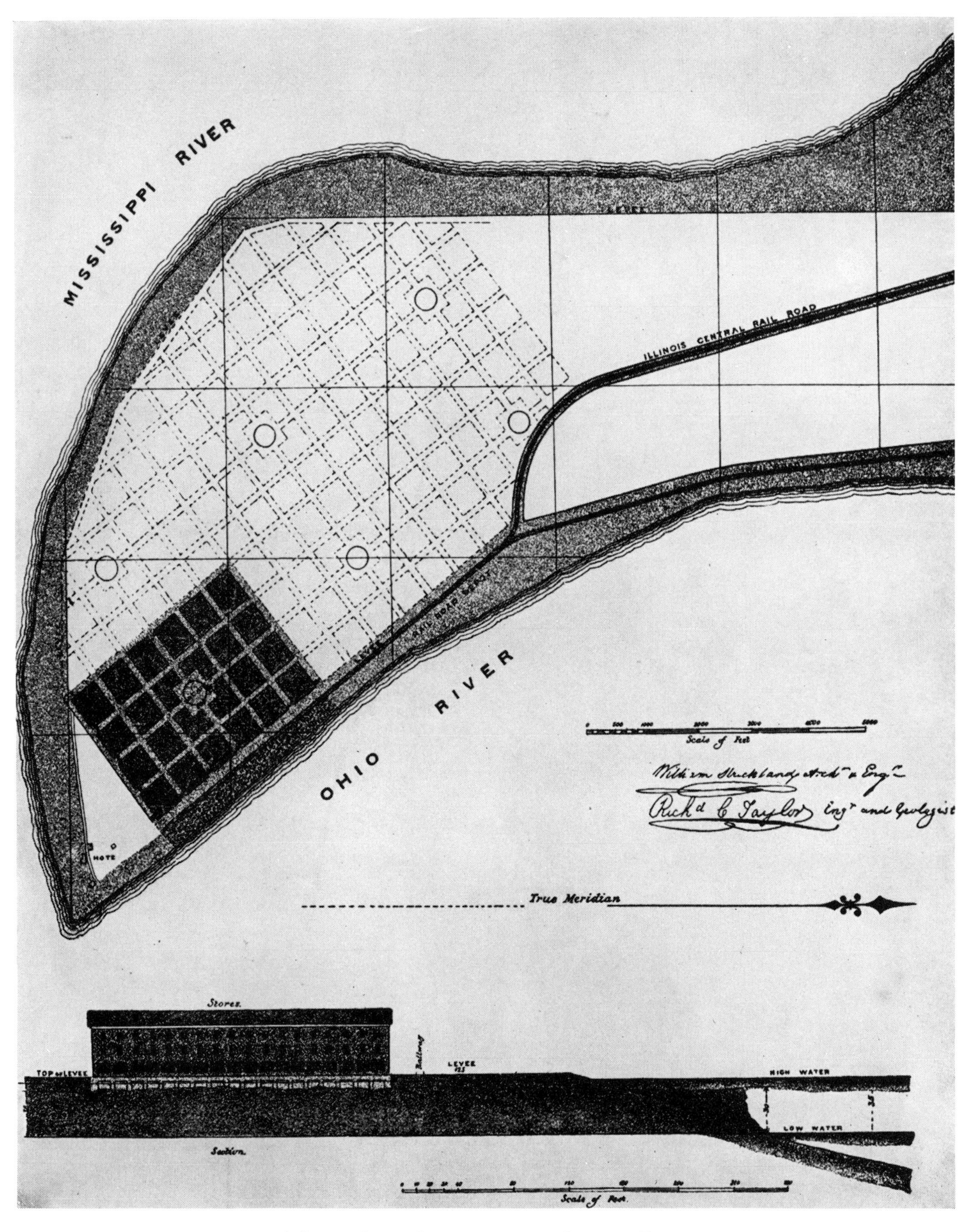

(Plate 35) SURVEY OF THE CITY OF CAIRO

(Plate 36) Governor's House, United States Naval Home

(Plate 37) Drawing Room of the Governor's House, United States Naval Home

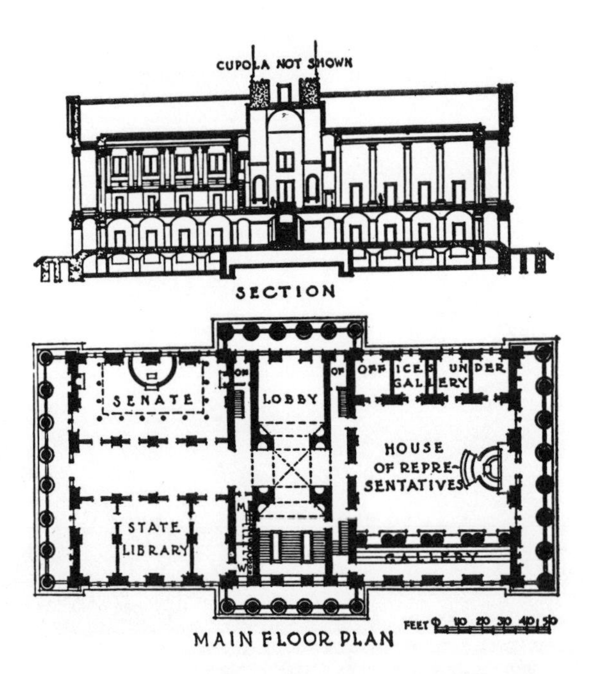

(Plate 38A) TENNESSEE STATE CAPITOL *Elevation and floor plan*

(Plate 38B) THE SAME, EXTERIOR

(Plate 39A) TENNESSEE STATE CAPITOL
Model of the tower

(Plate 39B) THE SAME, ELEVATION

(Plate 40A) TENNESSEE STATE CAPITOL *Stairway*

(Plate 40B) THE SAME, SENATE CHAMBER

(Plate 41A) TENNESSEE STATE CAPITOL
Southeast portico

(Plate 41B) ST. MARY'S CHURCH, NASHVILLE

(Plate 42A) POLK MONUMENT, NASHVILLE

(Plate 42B) KANE MONUMENT, NASHVILLE

(Plate 43) WALKER MONUMENT, NASHVILLE

(Plate 44) FIRST PRESBYTERIAN CHURCH, NASHVILLE

(Plate 45) INTERIOR OF THE FIRST PRESBYTERIAN CHURCH, NASHVILLE

(Plate 46A) "BELMONT," NASHVILLE
South elevation

(Plate 46B) UPPER STAIRWAY AT "BELMONT"

(Plate 47A) GREAT HALL AT "BELMONT"

(Plate 47B) "LYNNLAWN," NASHVILLE

(Plate 48A) "BELLE MEADE," NASHVILLE

(Plate 48B) "BURLINGTON," NASHVILLE

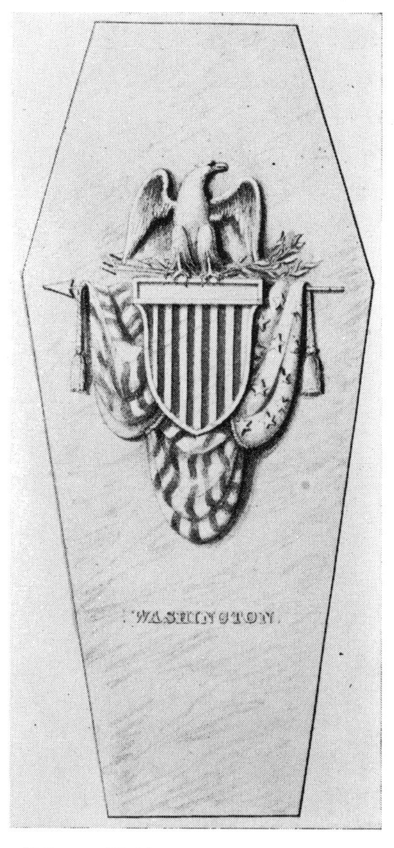

(Plate 49A) SARCOPHAGUS OF GEORGE WASHINGTON

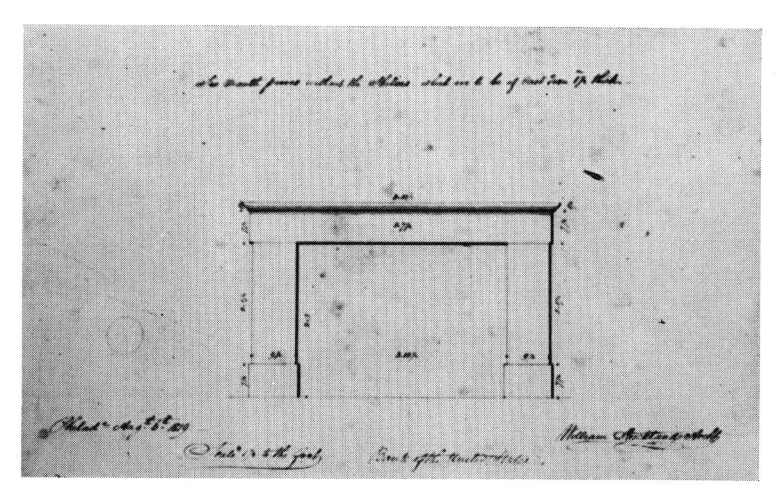

(Plate 49B) MANTEL, SECOND BANK OF THE UNITED STATES

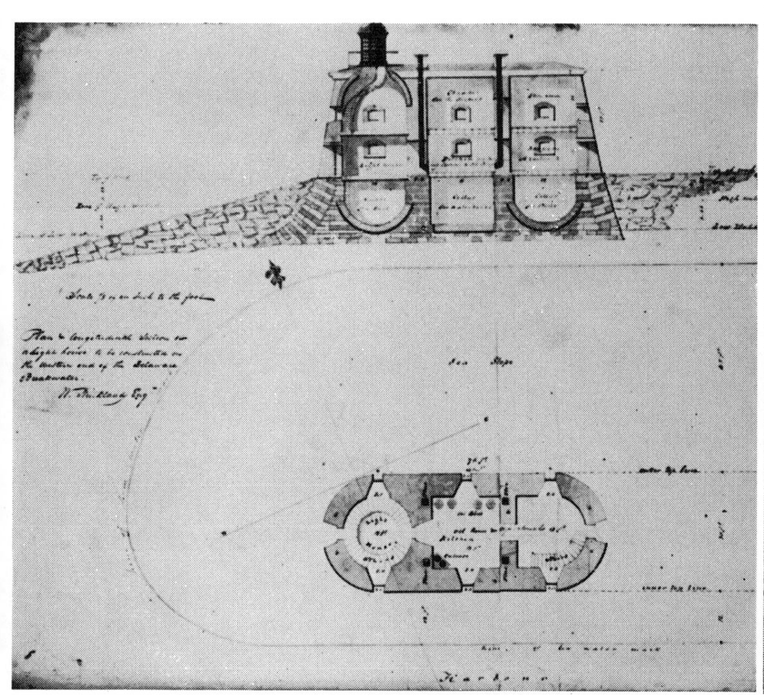

(Plate 49C) LIGHTHOUSE FOR THE DELAWARE BREAKWATER *Plan and section*

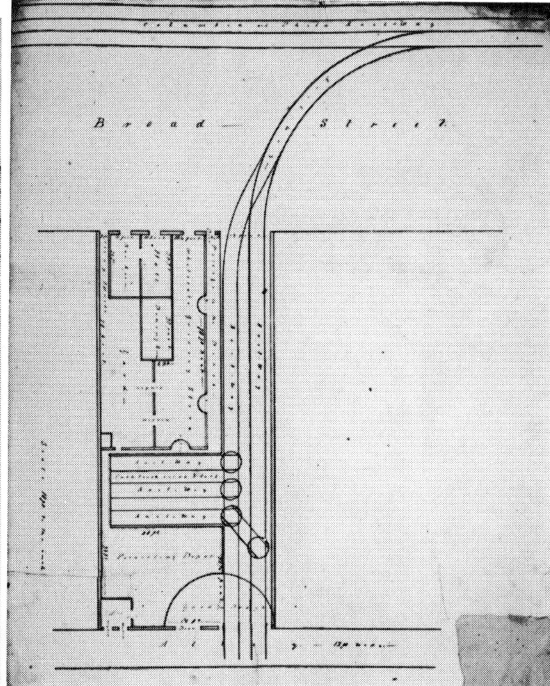

(Plate 49D) PLAN OF THE BROAD STREET DEPOT

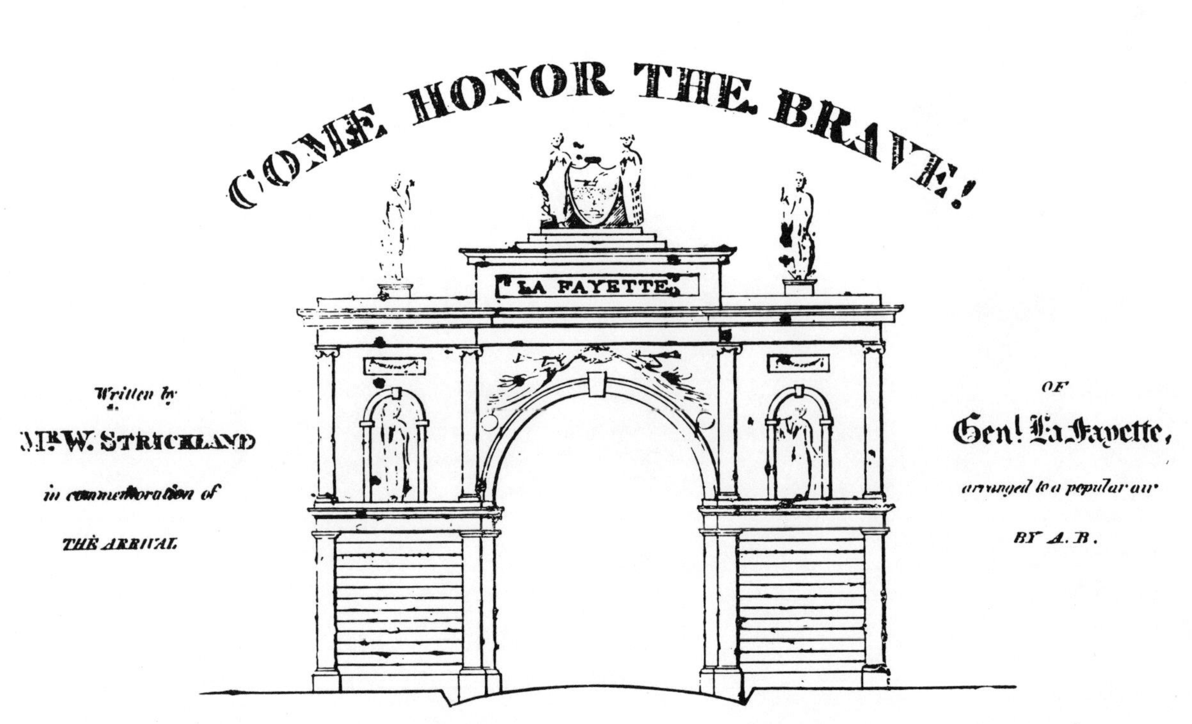

(Plate 50) TRIUMPHAL ARCH IN HONOR OF LAFAYETTE *Decoration on a piece of sheet music*

SUPPLEMENT

1. Additions to *William Strickland, Architect and Engineer, 1788–1854*
   (reprinted from the *Journal of the Society of Architectural Historians,* Volume XIII, Number 3, October, 1954)
2. The Philadelphia Exchange: William Strickland, Architect
   (reprinted from *Transactions of the American Philosophical Society,* New Series, Volume 43, Part 1, March, 1953)
3. Market Houses in High Street
   (reprinted from *Transactions of the American Philosophical Society,* New Series, Volume 43, Part 1, March, 1953)

ADDITIONS TO
WILLIAM STRICKLAND,
ARCHITECT AND ENGINEER, 1788 – 1854

(Philip Strickland Harper *of Chicago, great-grandson of the architect, has generously contributed funds for the printing of this supplement to publish some of the Strickland material which has been collected since the publication in 1950 by the University of Pennsylvania Press, Philadelphia, of* William Strickland—Architect and Engineer—1788–1854 *by Agnes Addison Gilchrist, which was also made possible by a subsidy from Mr. Harper.*)

I. Introduction

William Strickland, the pupil of Benjamin Henry Latrobe, began his career as a landscape painter, engraver and scene painter. For forty-six years he was a practicing architect and engineer. As an architect, his greatest contribution was as a planner of institutional buildings and designer of outstanding monuments of the Greek Revival in this country. Among the latter are the Second Bank of the United States, 1818–1824, and the Philadelphia Exchange, 1832–1834, in Philadelphia, and the Tennessee State Capitol, 1845–1859, in Nashville which was completed by his son after his death in that place in 1854.

During the past four years a great number of people have sent in photostats or transcripts of Strickland documents or references to Strickland material. More than a hundred and fifty items have been collected, all of which would have enriched the former study. I wish to thank all those who have contributed and to mention especially Louise Hall, Duke University; Henry Howard Eddy, Pennsylvania State Records Officer, and Hubertis Cummings of the Pennsylvania Historical Commission; Robert Smith and George Tatum of the University of Pennsylvania; Edward Riley of Colonial Williamsburg; Charles E. Peterson of the National Park Service; Miss Jeannette Eckman and Leon P. de Valinger, Delaware State Archivist.

The new material does not alter the over all picture of Strickland's career, but does point up three aspects of it:

The new material dealing with insane asylums and prisons shows that he was a pioneer in the design of institutional buildings, but not so successful in solving their problems as his younger contemporary John Haviland.

The second field of endeavor upon which the new material has cast light is in the design of steeples. His first architectural work was the Masonic Hall in Philadelphia for which his plans were approved in November 1808, when he was twenty years old. It had a Gothic Revival design, the most spectacular feature of which was the wood steeple, 180 feet high, which during the ten years that it stood added to the skyline of Philadelphia and was highly admired. Twenty years later Strickland designed the present steeple on Independence Hall which has become a national landmark. The new material adds three other steeples designed by Strickland (Figs. 24, 26, 28).

The third aspect of Strickland's career which is emphasized by the additional material is the fact that he did more work in the adjacent states of New Jersey and Delaware than was recorded in 1950.

The most glaring omission of Strickland buildings still standing in Philadelphia in the previous volume is that of the Mechanics Bank (Fig. 20) on the west side of South Third Street near Market which has inscribed on the inner plinth of the architrave, "William Strickland Architect J. Struthers Mason 1837."

More material on the training and position of his father John Strickland (Fig. 1) has come to light and is to be found in the doctoral thesis of Louise Hall, "Artificer into Architect," Radcliffe College, March 1954.

In the National Archives in Washington, D.C., there is much unpublished material dealing with the federal buildings designed by Strickland and especially their subsequent history of repairs and alterations; for example, the Second Bank of the United States which became a Custom House in 1844 and on which Strickland was employed to make the alterations at that time. There are records of the later alterations under the supervision of Isaiah Rogers when he was Supervising Architect in 1864–65, and of later repairs and alterations in 1879–81 when John McArthur was the architect in charge and Thomas U. Walter was employed by him as Clerk of the Works at $92 a month.

Some of the most important documents dealing with Strickland's work both as architect and engineer have been found in the Pennsylvania State Records Office by Dr. Eddy and Dr. Cummings. The latter is making a full study of the Pennsylvania Canal of 1825–1836. Hundreds of volumes of ledgers and letters and contracts, as well as surveys and sketches which give the detailed history of this State Canal and Railroad are preserved in the Pennsylvania State Land Office. These are in the custody of Warren J. Daniel who generously permitted me to use the material and provided me with many photostats of the Strickland letters and sketches contained therein.

For the personal life of Strickland from 1820 to 1823 the most informative document is an account book now in the Pennsylvania State Records Office. There are a few sketches in this small volume. The most interesting is the sketch of Fort Hamilton, so named because this fort was erected on the banks of the Schuylkill on the property of William Hamilton, who is best known for his country house Woodlands, still standing in West Philadelphia. The fort (Fig. 3) was erected as part of the fortification of Philadelphia in 1814. After the war was over, the fort remained unused until the Hamilton family petitioned for its removal. (Cf. "Minutes of the Committee of Defence, 1814–1815," *Memoirs of the Historical Society of Pennsylvania*, Vol. 8, Philadelphia, 1867.)

There have been several drawings by Strickland which have come to light. The most interesting is the well-rendered façade of a country house which is in the Stauffer Collection in the Print Room of the New York Public

Library (Fig. 8). It has a dome and low central porch and is the most ambitious design for a residence which has been found. As was the current practice of the architects of the early nineteenth century, at each window curtains are shown half of magenta and half of yellow. No identification of this drawing has been made.

Five drawings by Strickland were found in the Meredith Papers in the Historical Society of Pennsylvania. They are signed but undated (Fig. 14). They appear to deal with the alterations of the Academy building on Fourth Street in Philadelphia.

Another drawing which is now in the Arthur Sussel collection in Philadelphia and formerly belonged to Carl Drepperd, is a meticulously executed watercolor of the façade of Dr. Rush's house in Philadelphia (Fig. 9).

Mr. de Valinger and Miss Eckman told me of the present location of the survey of New Castle, Delaware, which was executed by Strickland, Mills and Peter Lennox under the supervision of Benjamin H. Latrobe. In the Delaware Archives in the State Records Office in Dover Mr. de Valinger found a letter from Strickland giving the estimate for the proposed Sussex County Court House (Figs. 17, 18).

Undoubtedly more material will be noted continuously as more people study the first half of the nineteenth century. Some of the professional letters of Strickland which have been brought to my attention are printed herewith. Mrs. Nell Savage Mahoney, who has long been gathering material for a biography of Strickland, has many Strickland letters in her possession. Mrs. Joseph Carson of Philadelphia also has Strickland letters. Carl Williams of Philadelphia knows of many unpublished Strickland buildings in New Jersey.

II. Three Designs for Insane Asylums

The first insane asylum in this country was erected in Williamsburg, Virginia, in 1769–73. The first asylum to introduce the reforms of Pinel and Tuke which date from 1792, was the Friends Asylum outside Philadelphia, designed by Strickland in 1815 and completed the following year. The plan introduced all the most forward-looking devices for the care and healing of "Persons deprived of the use of their reason."

Some of those features were the separate rooms for the patients in the two wings of the building. Another was the use of iron sashes on the windows so that the patients did not have to be chained and neither did the windows have to have iron gratings which give a prison-like appearance to many insane asylums. The design also took into consideration the theory that the most demented were best cared for in darkness as being more soothing than the daily change from daylight to night and so some of the rooms were without windows. These were heated with hot air and ventilated through openings in the ceilings so that the fetid smell which was formerly associated with the insane would be obviated.

Another feature to assure the good care of the patients was the large, comfortably planned central building for the people in charge and the well-planned offices in the basement.

An insurance survey was made on January 3, 1817, when the building was first completed, for the Philadelphia Contributionship by John G. Evans. It is preserved in the files of the company and is here published for the first time. It adds to our knowledge of this pioneering building, which is still in use, but much altered, and contains many details of interest about the materials and construction of the asylum and also of the barn which was on the property. The barn had three walls of stone and the south side of wood, a disposition of building materials which might be considered by those who are interested in solar heating.

The importance of insurance surveys as a source of architectural history cannot be too much stressed. While little of superficial stylistic form is recorded, the basic factors of plan, construction and materials are. For instance, in this survey one learns that the roof was slate, the gutters of copper and the downspouts of tin. The walls were of stone 22 and 18 inches thick and battlemented. There were plain marble mantels on the first floor and mantels with pilasters on the second floor. The flooring was of yellow pine common boarding throughout save in the garret where the floor was of white pine.

I have surveyed a Building belonging to "The Contributors to the Asylum for Persons deprived of the use of their reason" situated on the South side of a road leading from Frankford to the old York road about five miles from the City & about 2 miles west from Frankford, viz A Centre building 60 feet square & three stories high, two wings each 100 feet by 24 feet—two stories high—the walls of stone 22 & 18 in thick The lower story of the Centre building—divided into 4 rooms & two passages through the middle, intersecting each other at right angles—divided by stone walls—The floor of yellow pine Com^{n} boards—base only round, single architraves to the doors and windows, marble mantels to the fire places, plain, & marble hearths—doors double framed,—the 2nd story divided in 5 [6 in margin] rooms com^{n} yellow pine floor, base round, single architraves & mantles with pilasters, & marble jambs—the 3rd story divided in seven rooms—floor of yellow pine, base round single architraves to the doors & moldings to the windows—plain wooden mantles—& plain inside shutters to the windows—the Glass in the lower & 2nd stories 9 by 12 in sash double hung—Glass in the 3rd story 6 by 8 in, sash of cast iron—& a single sash of wood outside & hung.—The garret divided in 8 rooms—floor of white pine, plain base round, all the rooms plaistered—4 dormer windows in roof—plain & ridged.—Open newel stairs leading from the passage below into the garret—with ramped rail of poplar—skirted up the wall—(large)—all the doors of plank & 5/4 in boards — —

The wings are divided into a long passage—& ten rooms on each floor—division walls of stone—the floor of yellow pine com[n] boards—plain base round—the rooms & passage — — door frames of scantling & doors of plank—with a small wicket in neach—Iron sash in all the windows, with a single wooden one outside glass 6 by 8 in—the Iron sash below is glazed & the wooden one above—straight stairs at the extreme end of each wing leading into the 2d story,—kitchen, Ironing room, bake room, wash house & store room below-the two first with yellow pine floor, base round—single architraves, mantle shelf & dressers—with doors.—the other floor of mortar—& well secured from fire—all the joist—& the floor between the Joist are plaistered from the cellar to the garret—throughout—& the rafters of the wings—Brick eaves, Copper gutters on them—& slate roof on the whole building—& battlement walls—outside shutters to all the windows in the lower & second stories—the whole painted inside & out—newly built—two sash over each door of the Cells one of Iron the other wood—the latter glazed.—a door at the [second page of survey] the entrance from the centre building into the passage of the wings—with side lights & sash over.—panneled below the sash and the whole well built, & very secure from fire.—the pipes to convey the water from the roof are of tin.—

1 Mo. 3rd 1817

John G. Evans

$9000 at 4% $360

Also Surveyed their Barn.—38 feet by 45 feet stone walls on three sides & the south side of wood.—roof hipped & covered with Cedar—divided below into, passage & stalling & place for hay & grain above & a threshing floor of yellow pine—ledged door & shutters—those outside painted—a wooden gutter & trunk to the eve. ———

1 Mo. 3 1817

John G. Evans

$1000 at 5% cent $50———

Notations on survey

1) for Managers of Asylum
Edward Randolph

Rec[d] two Policies in lieu of those first issued & which have been lost or mislaid previous to 1818 our receiving them for Managers of Asylum Edward Randolph
9 Mo. 8th 1818

2) No. 3748, 3749—The Contributors to the Asylum—Survey

This survey is published through the courtesy of Charles E. Peterson who called my attention to its existence and of Jas. Somers Smith, Jr., Treasurer, The Philadelphia Contributionship for the Insurance of Houses from Loss by Fire, founded 1752, who furnished me with a photostat of the document.

In the New Almshouse in Blockley Township which was designed by Strickland for the City of Philadelphia in 1830 and completed by 1834, there was a ward for lunatics which was in use for over a hundred years.

In 1835, the Pennsylvania Hospital determined to build a Female Department for the Insane in West Philadelphia at Market and 49th Street. This was latterly known as Kirkbride's in honor of the great Philadelphia doctor who was connected with the institution and who did so much for the healing of the mentally deranged.

The plans of the Hospital were prepared by Isaac Holden, an architect who came from Manchester, England, in 1823, and practiced as an architect and builder in Philadelphia with his brother, from 1826 to 1828, when they returned to England.

The new building in West Philadelphia was so far completed as to be ready for occupation on the first day of the year, 1841. The period of construction had extended over four years and six months. The amount expended was $265,000 . . . .

For the purpose of obtaining some information of the history of the plan made by Isaac Holden, a letter of inquiry in relation to it was addressed to his son, John Holden, of Manchester, who stated in reply: "As to the hospital referred to I have always understood that the plan was obtained on a limited competition, one of the competitors being the late John Haviland and one other I believe named Strickland. I have a strong idea that the windows were made with iron sash bars instead of as was usual at that time—wood bars and iron outside bars in addition. I do not remember ever hearing what model or system he studied, but I should hardly think he had any information beyond what he could gather in America. I have compared the view of the old part of the Hospital with a drawing in my possession and they agree, and I assure you it is a great satisfaction to me to know that a building designed and (erected?) by my father so long since is in existence and still doing good work. I may say that after returning to England in 1838 the two brothers commenced practice in Manchester and one of their earliest works was the county lunatic asylum at Prestwick, near Manchester. I would have been much pleased could I have given you further information but unfortunately your request comes too late, as my father (Isaac) died in 1884, and my uncle in 1890.

This quotation is from Thomas G. Morton and Frank Woodbury, *The History of the Pennsylvania Hospital, 1751–1895*. Philadelphia, 1895, p. 165 & note; ill. opp. Courtesy of Louise Hall.

While Strickland was not successful with his plan for the Female Department of the Insane of the Pennsylvania Hospital, in 1835 he did design another insane asylum which was begun in 1842. This was for the Insane Asylum for the State of Pennsylvania the foundations for which were laid on the west bank of the Schuylkill between Gray's ferry and Carr's gardens and between the Philadelphia and Baltimore railroads and the Darby road, which site was south of the Hamilton estate of Woodland.

The report of the plan and the work completed which was made by Strickland on June 14, 1842 follows and gives a good idea of the general design and more particularly of the labor-saving devices such as the funnels for the used clothing so that it might be dropped directly to the cellar and the dumb waiters which would convey the food from the kitchens to the various floors. This asylum was designed to house 300 patients and so was on a much larger scale than Strickland's first design of an asylum, that of the Friends' asylum which had rooms for only 40 patients.

The heating and the plumbing both concerned Strickland greatly and for the latter he used a spring on the grounds to keep the conduits clean and so "prevent the escape of effluvium throughout the whole establishment." One of his first concerns were the culverts and diagrams of them and a plan of their location he added to his report.

Further research in the Pennsylvania State Records will explain why this first design for a State Insane Asylum was not carried out and the forthcoming study of John Haviland will doubtless tell why the state changed the site of its first asylum to Harrisburg and employed Haviland to make the design in 1848.

Dr. Henry Howard Eddy, Pennsylvania State Records Officer, found the following document among the papers of the Records office:

Auditor General's office Harrisburg May 26th 1845. This is to Certify that the foregoing are true copies from the Originals on file in this office— Witness my hand & seal of office the day and year aforesaid— John A. Purviance Auditor General

To The Commissioners for the building an Insane Asylum for the State of Pennsylvania—

Gentlemen

In obedience to the resolutions of the board passed on the 7th ultimo, directing the Architect to report as soon as practicable what amount of work has been done by each contractor under the contracts entered into by the board for the building the Asylum, and also requesting the Architect to report the details of the plan adopted by the Commissioners, so that the same may be incorporated in a report to be prepared for the Legislature of the State.

I have now the honor to submit for your consideration a precise and particular estimate of the cost of the workmanship and materials now forming a part of the foundations of the building, as well as a detailed description of the plan adopted by the Commissioners.—

These foundations are laid upon a beautiful site of elevated ground on the west side of the river Schuylkill between Grays' ferry and Carr's gardens and between the Philada and Baltimore railroads and the Darby road, and is elevated above the level of the river and of the City of Philadelphia and her most extensive and useful public works.—

In plan the building consists of a central projection and main wings, flanked by Verandahs upon each of the returning wings.—The principal front is toward the N.E. and is 467 ft. in length:—The returned wings are each 236 ft. these, as well as those of the front, are 3 stories in height; —The Centre building and verandahs are four stories, each with a quadrangular pitched, roof and the whole to be covered with Pennsylvania Slate over a bold projecting eve.—

The wings alone contain the dormitories, for each class of the Insane and they are calculated to accommodate 300 patients:—They are situated on each side of a Gallery or Corridor 10 ft in width; dimensions of the chambers 7 ft by 10 ft and from 11 to 12 ft in height and the ceilings of them all to be arched with brick; Each chamber is to be ventilated by a flue rising to the roof, and an open sash over each door way which is opposite to each of the windows on the front and rear.—

The warm air is to be introduced by flues from 8 furnaces to be constructed in the cellar story, and passed into the corridors of each separate story, these to be regulated by dampers placed 8 ft. above the floors.—

The Sash of all the windows are to be of cast Iron fixed upon central pivots in the sill and head and so arranged as to open 6 in on each side by the whole height of the window; the glass to be glazed in the cast iron frame, and a wooden frame surrounding the window sustains the whole. —In the arrangement of all the *Corridors* or *passages* they are made to have a free communication with the open air at each end; the one end entirely clear of the rear of the centre building; the other communicating with the verandahs, which are to be used as play rooms and for games and exercise either in fair or foul weather. These are each 50 ft. square and will be lighted and ventilated with moveable sash.—

In most of the Asylums for the insane there are defects in these particulars, especially in the direct connection of the corridors with the main or central building; In the plan which you have adopted this defect is entirely obviated and the introduction of the verandahs on each of the external angles of the building has been found highly useful in the management and economy of that excellent institution, the Asylum at Worcester in Connecticut.—

The Cellar Story is to be 5 ft above the surface of the ground and 6 feet below it. This story to be surrounded by an area 7 ft in width with sloping banks in every direction.—

The Kitchens and wash rooms are situated in each wing immediately under the dining and bath rooms of the upper stories:—

The water closets as well as the bath rooms have their drops into culverts of large dimensions which are to be arched over beneath the cellar floor and a fine spring of water will be introduced, under a rapid descent, to keep the conduits clean.—

The furnaces for the generation of hot air are to be placed in this story, two for each wing and the flue from each contains a cast iron smoke stack of 10 in. in diameter, they will be constructed for burning anthracite coal and supplied with air to be heated through openings leading from the outside of the building.—

The cellar story also contains all the necessary store rooms, drying rooms, laundry, bakery family dining rooms as well as rooms for domestics and upon the return wings a sufficient number of rooms, say 20 for the males and a similar number for the females, are to be constructed and set apart for the special accommodation of noisy and violent patients: In each of these wings three distinct classes of patients can be accommodated and from the position of the returned verandahs at the extreme ends of the building the most noisy will not interfere with the quiet of the inmates of the main building.—

The Basement Story on the first floor is divided into rooms ranged along the sides of the corridors and extending from a centre building through wings which terminate at verandahs.—

The Centre building is 95 ft by 52 and contains on the principal entry hall two rooms of 18 ft square each side of which is intended for the use of the superintendent as parlors, offices, Library and Apothecaries' shop:—In the second story the same arrangement of rooms is intended for the officers resident in the Asylum such as two parlors, stewards' and attendents rooms:—a reception chamber for visitors and other rooms intended for the better class of convalescent patients:—all the other stories are similar in their arrangements and fixtures as those just described, and the right and left wings are completely seperated in the rear, by the projection of the centre building.—

A Supply of water may be derived from a beautiful *spring run* which flows through the whole extent of the premises which may be dam'd up at a small expense and the water power used to fill the tanks which are to be placed under the roofs of the verandahs and centre building, from which the water may be conveyed to every section of the building for bathing and other purposes.—

All the fixtures for washing and drying clothes are to be in the cellar story of the verandahs immediately under the tanks or reservoirs, and *funnels* will be made at every Stairway from the different stories and wards into which soiled articles are to be thrown down into receiving rooms and from thence into the wash rooms.—

Dumb waiters are to lead from the dining rooms of each story directly into the Kitchens below, in which fixtures of the most approved construction are to be placed for steaming, boiling, baking, etc.—

One of the chief merits of the plan, now entered upon, consists in the location of all the chambers and rooms, where *hot* or *cold* water is to be used over the *sewers or culverts* which are found beneath the cellar story along with the rear walls of the building, so that all the waste water from the interior, the yards, roof, and from the Indian spring flows through the culverts upon a rapid descent, which at once will cleanse and prevent the escape of effluvium throughout the whole establishment:—These conduits are sufficiently large to allow a man to pass through their whole extent, and from the situation of the building on the site, the ground falls off in every direction towards the spring run which empties itself into the river Schuylkill on the eastern boundary line of the farm.—

To the Northwards of the site of the building the grounds furnish many advantages afforded by dense woods and shrubbery bordering upon a rocky formation descending in various places precipitously towards the stream of water from whence the building is to be supplied, through which, at a small expense walks may be laid out by clearing away the underbrush without any expense in planting trees for the purpose of landscape gardening, and on the southern and Eastern portions of the ground, where the building is situated, I do not know a view, from any portion of the citys' limits, which can compare with the one now under consideration;—There is every object to gratify the minds as well as the eyes. The quiet as well as the bustling picture of natural and artificial life.—

The Architecture of the principal front is of the plainest possible character; without mouldings, columns pediments architraves or cornices,—It is simply *a plain rubble stone structure*, to be dashed up with gravel mortar in a strict rustic style, and with Tuscan proportions.—All the wood work of the exterior as well as that of the interior is to be varnished and not painted: The dormitories and passages are to be finished in rough sand plastering without cornices or mouldings or any decoration whatever, and the cost of the whole building, including the furniture and contingent expenses, with the purchase of the land, will not exceed the amount appropriated by the Legislature.

Respectfully submitted
by your obdt servt
William Strickland
Architect

Philadelphia June 14th/42.

H. R. Brodhead & Co.

Estimate of the Lumber furnished for wheeling plank, centering, Carpenter's shop, Blacksmith's shop, Lime house &c, for the use of the building of the Pennsylvania Asylum for the Insane, as per bill.— $1,095.52

Clyde & Kennedy

Estimate of the workmanship & materials furnished by Clyde & Kennedy 2054 perches @ $1.59.— $3,265.86
Excavations in foundations of Culverts and walls = 650 cubic yards @ 30 cts. $ 195.00

Saml. Copeland

Bill of the Lumber and Carpenters work done in assisting the Architect to lay out the plan of the building on the site of Pennsylvania Asylum for the Insane including Axes nails, measuring lines, rods &c—As per bill of workmanship $100.00

Benner & Cox

Excavation of Cellar & Culvert pits = 4069 Cubic yds @ 15 cts = $610.35

Thomas McCulley

Measurement bill of the Carpenters work done in the construction of a Carpenters shop, Blacksmith's shop and Lime house for the use of the building of the Pennsylvania Asylum for the Insane.— As per days work $325.00

Parker Keim & Sherrell

Bill of the Ironmongery; such as nails, hinges padlocks &c used in the building of the Carpenter's Shop, Blacksmith's shop and Lime house on the site of the Pennsylvania Asylum for the Insane As per bill $25.09

Benner & Cox

Estimate of the Workmanship performed in excavating the culverts and cellar of the building of the Pennsylvania Asylum for the Insane.—(plan showing position of culverts)

Excavation in the Culvert pits of the N.W. return wing and in the N. wing of the main building.—	2180 cubic yds
Excavation of the cellar of the return wing and centre building.—	1589 cubic yds.
Excavation of the Cellar of the S.E. wing.—	300 cubic yds.
	4069 cubic yds @ 15 cts

William Strickland
Architect

N.B. The above amount of Cubic yds of Excavation is a full estimate.—The banks having caved and washed to a great extent from frost & rain.—

Clyde & Kennedy

Estimate of the Workmanship and materials furnished by Clyde and Kennedy in the building of the Pennsylvania Asylum for the Insane.—

Culvert under the N.W. wing	1028.
Culvert under the N. wing of the main building	404
Foundation walls of N.E. front and verandah	500.
west wing wall and covering culvert	122.
	2054 perches

Excavation in foundation of culverts & walls = 650 cubic yds done by Clyde and Kennedy @ 30 cts pr cubic yard.—
Quarried Stone perched up at the Quarries = Dimensions = 26 ft × 25 × 4 = 104 perches
William Strickland
Architect.

N.B. The above amount of perches is laid without mortar, and a large amount of rocks in the quarries is laid bare and cleared off and in reddiness for blasting—

III. Strickland Documents

1. Letter Oct. 1, 1816 to Nathaniel B. Boileau, Secretary of State of Pennsylvania, concerning Pennsylvania State Capitol, Harrisburg.

This letter was found by Henry Howard Eddy, State Records Officer in the Division of Public Records of the Pennsylvania Historical and Museum Commission, Harrisburg. It is interesting to compare with the letter of Feb. 24, 1817, *Strickland* p. 50, in which Strickland offers to erect the Capitol for $180,000 and to have it ready for the 1818–19 session and for a compensation of five dollars a day, a great reduction from the Oct. 1, 1816 letter in which he asks for 5% of 300,000 or $15,000. Stephen Hills won the competition and the corner stone was laid May 31, 1819. The building was opened on January 2, 1822.

Nathaniel B. Boileau Secretary of State
Sir,
The following is a description of the accompanying ground plan and Elevation for the State Capitol at Harrisburgh together with the terms for executing the centre building and connection thereof with the offices already erected.—
The Design of the centre building embraces 120ft. front by 135 feet in depth, including the Portico, which is a semi circle of 60 feet in Diameter composed of six Pillars 4 feet Diameter of the *Ionic Order* supported by a flight of steps 13 feet high—
The Ground plan exhibits the arrangment of the House of Representatives and its connection with the committee rooms, Library, Transcribing office, and the circular Hall or Vestibule, together with the interesting passages to the colonade connecting the wings to the centre.—
The Dimensions of the chamber of Representatives is 74 ft by 50 on a semicircular plan calculated to contain upwards of 100 members with all possible convenience.—
The committee Rooms 32 ft by 18 situated adjacent to the chamber of Representatives—
The Library and transcribing rooms of the same dimensions situated in front—
The Hall or Vestibule 45 feet in Diameter containing a flight of Stone steps leading to the Senate Chamber and rooms belonging thereto in the second Story being the same plan with the lower floor, this Hall or vestibule is surmounted by a Dome and sky light.—
The Senate Chamber is immediately above the Chamber of Representatives, and of the same plan 70 ft by 40 ft arched in the ceiling and lighted from the skylight and sides of the room.—
In the center of the colonade connecting this building with the wings, are appropriate Statues, emblematic of Liberty and Justice.
The centre building is composed of two Stories of 22 feet each, a dome and skylight rising 40 feet. The whole supported by a basement of 13 feet in height making the total elevation 75 feet, from the Terrace upon which it stands.—
In designing the State Capitol I have endeavoured as far as possible to preserve the character of the Offices already erected, by adopting the proportion of the *Ionic Order* in its leading features, at the same time keeping these Offices subordinated in the general arrangment of the front, in order to effect which the upper line of the Colonade is upon a level with second stories, presenting a grand avenue or covered way connecting the whole, by which means all business with the Capitol and Offices of State, may be transacted without being exposed to the weather.—
The nescessity of a strict compliance with the Architecture of the Wings is obvious, as any deviation in order or style would tend to injure the appearance of the whole structure, being beautifully situated, and calculated to produce grandeur of effect.
The capitol and buildings connecting the wings already erected, according to the accompanying ground Plan and Elevations, can be executed of such materials as are on the spot for 300,000 Dollars, and in consideration of the time necessary to finish this Edifice in a substantial and durable manner, requiring 4 or 5 years depending on the ease or difficulty of procuring materials or workmen, I will superintend the execution of the design now offered on the usual terms of 5 pr cent on the cost.—
I have the honor to be
most respectfully
Harrisburgh Octor 1. 1816—
Your Obdt servt
William Strickland
Archt
Philada

On the outside of this letter is the following notation: "1816, Oct. 1) Proposals for building the State Capitol at Harrisburg by William Strickland of Philadelphia ——
2 Copies sent to the Legislature Decr 1816———J. F."

2. Excerpt from Immanuel Church Record Book, Vol. I, 1822, telling of Strickland's contributions to the remodelling of the Church.

Photostatic copy of Immanuel Church Record Book, Vol. 1, pp. 103–104. Courtesy of Judge Richard S. Rodney.

To those, whose zeal and activity effected the rebuilding and enlarging of the Church, the present occasion was deeply interesting.—But two years ago, the Church was in almost ruinous condition;—now it was finished in a style of neatness and simplicity,—and even elegance,—that reflected the hightest credit on the Congregation;—the pulpit, reading-desk, chancel, pews and the whole interior of the Church, were arranged and furnished with much taste.—The exterior—with tower and spire rising to the height of One hundred and thirty feet,—the former furnished with a fine clock placed there by the Trustees of the New Castle Common, and showing a dial-plate on each side.—the latter surmounted with a beautifully gilt cross, ball and vane,—presented a strong contrast to the former appearance of the Church and produced the most pleasing emotions.—

It is but an act of justice to notice in this place the important services rendered by Mr. William Strickland of the City of Philadelphia, Architect.—He furnished the plans for the improvement and enlargement of the Church; and when his professional avocations permitted; superintended the repairs at different times, and whenever consulted assisted with his advice and directions. All his services were gratuitously bestowed. He presented to the Church, a marble slab of the value of ten dollars,———which is placed in the West Side of the Tower, and records the date of the Church and the year of its enlargement.

3. Letter Sept. 15, 1828 to James A. Hillhouse of New Haven, Conn., giving Strickland's views on the design and heating of a residence. Sterling Library, Yale University, New Haven. Courtesy of Roger Hale Newton.

Philada. Septr. 15th 1828

Sir,

I have just finished a plan and South Elevation of your house—You will percieve I have made a few alterations in your ground plan which I hope will please you—The fire places will be best placed on the inner sides of the Drawing and Dining rooms being recessed and backed by heaters in the Hall—This arrangement will be advantageous on two accounts, first in getting rid of the projection of the Breast of the chimney stack in these rooms, which always produces a bad effect in breaking the cornice of the Ceilings besides taking up 2 feet of their breadth. Secondly the flues will be concentrated and brought out of the roof of the building in the best place for appearance.—The Stair Way is in a better position for privacy and convenience to the Dining room and Kitchen—I have never thought of beauty in a Stairway; indeed it is difficult to produce this effect in small buildings without too great a sacrifice of room and comfort.—I think the closets are out of the way and yet convenient—They may be well lighted from the passage leading into the small room on the North west angle of the building.—I do not think you would like these articles placed in the main hall of the building.—In the South front elevation I have drawn a Pediment which is better in point of effect than the attic you speak of.—If an attic were made there would be a necessity for Parapet walls above the springing of the roof which would make your house look too much like a *cube*, besides exposing it to leaks in the gutter behind the wall—In this country we ought to guard against producing lodgements for the snow or rain on our roofs, for it is from these circumstances that our public and private buildings are brought to speedy dilapidation. A simple Pediment pitch on the South and North fronts will look best, containing two neat dormant windows on each flank for lighting the Garret story—The flues of the Library and small West room are to be carried out of the Roof as those of the Dining and Drawing rooms;—This will produce symmetry on both fronts.—The sills of the windows are to be level with the top of the washboard.

I have put down the dimensions of the several details on the plan and Elevation, and I believe the scale will point out those that are not marked.—Should you require any further information if you will drop me a line I will endeavor to furnish you with a speedy answer—

Yours very respectfully
William Strickland

James A. Hillhouse Esqr.

P. S. I have directed the parcel of Drawings as you directed to the care of Mr. Lawrence New York.

4. Letter Mar. 27, 1837 to Wm. D. Waples, Building Commissioner, Sussex County Court House, Georgetown, Delaware, giving description and estimate of Court House.

   Delaware Archives, State Records Building, Dover, Del. Courtesy of Leon P. De Valinger, Archivist. Building completed in 1840. Altered in 1914 by Brinckloe and Canning with "Columns to be stock, taken from Hartman-Sanders Co., or equal . . ." Specifications, Office Board of Trustees. Courtesy of Mrs. Hess, Secretary of Board.

Philadelphia March 27, 1837

To

Wm. D. Waples Esqr

Dear Sir

Agreeable to the Request Contained in your Letter of the 16 Instant I have made all haste in designing & drawing the plans of a Court house and fire proof offices for the County of Sussex. I think I have made a *Convenient Plan* for the Hall Stairway and other interior arrangements for the Court Room and Jury rooms. If I have not been so happy in the front:—Your limits as to the funds are the basis of the Brick Appearance, and I could have wished to have introduced a few Columns and some other decorations, on the exterior but was afraid on account of the smallness of the sum to be appropriated.

I have drawn an Iron Gallery in front on the Court Room lobby floor for the use of the Cryer of the Court, Or for any purpose of disclaiming to a Multitude beneath, it is intended to project about 3 feet from the front of the long window and immediately over the door of entrance in the basement Story—I thought you might want a Clock and have therefore introduced one in the base of the Cupola which is very Conveniently placed in front over the Stairway which are double and Commodious

As you may at Some future day want a Gallery in the Court Room you can Continue the stairs to a level with the ceiling of the Jury rooms which will not be more than 12 feet in height and you will perceive that you can have a large Gallery over these Rooms, as the Court Room is 21 feet in height

My charge for these plans and estimate is $60.

With Great Respect Sir
I am yours very truly and Sincerely
William Strickland

Estimate of the Cost of Building a Court house and fire proof offices 60 feet Square According to the accompanying plans & Elevations, viz.

Digging and foundation 120 cubic yds.......$	24.00
Building Stone = 150 perches including freight—laying trim and Sand............	450.00
Bricks—350,000 @ 10$ including laying lime and Sand.......................	3500.00
Lumber for floors, Roof, framed Scaffolding &c.	1800.00
Carpenters Work	2300.00
Plastering Work and Materials.............	520.00
Painting and Glazing.....................	450.00
Ironmongery, nails, Straps, Spikes &c........	380.00

Zinc 3900 Supr. feet at 14 cts including Solder and putting on	546.00
Copper 750 feet of Copper for Cupola	275.00
Stone window sills 28	112.00
Stone steps front and Back doors	60.00
Total cost	10,417.00

Add 5 per cent for Contigencies
William Strickland
Architect
Philad[a], Nov[r] 22[d] 1842.—

5. Letter Nov. 22, 1842 to the Vestry of St. Peter's Church giving bill for designing and superintending the construction of the tower and steeple of St. Peter's.

Transcript of a letter in the Vestry minutes for Dec. 13, 1842 from the typed copy of the Vestry Minutes in the Rector's Office. Courtesy of the Rector, the Rev. Mr. Evans.

Dr the Vestry of St. Peter's Church
To Wm. Strickland, Architect
For professional services in constructing Tower and spire $250.

Gentlemen

I beg leave to present to you my bill for professional services in the construction of the St. Peter's Steeple. I have felt pleasure in reducing my charge against the Church to the one half of the accustomed Architect's fees and have only to regret that circumstances do not allow me the higher satisfaction of dispensing with the charge altogether——

I am very respectfully and truly yours
signed Wm. Strickland
Philad[a], Nov[r] 22[d] 1842.—

6. Letter Dec. 9, 1844 to Judge Blythe, Customs Collector for the District of Philadelphia, telling of repairs and alterations made in changing the Second Bank of the United States into a Custom House.

Washington, National Archives. General Records of the Department of the Treasury (MS). Strickland to Blythe, Philadelphia, Dec. 9, 1844. Courtesy of Charles E. Peterson.

This letter shows that Strickland was employed to adapt the Bank building which he had designed in 1818 to be used as a Customs House when it was bought by the Federal Government in 1844. This was the second time that Strickland had redone the building. The former time was in 1836–37 when the ownership of the bank passed from the Second Bank of the United States to the United States Bank of Pennsylvania. This and the other papers preserved in the National Archives show that this building received major repairs about every twenty years. We don't expect people to look as they did the day they were born when we meet them sixty years later. Houses also go through the natural processes of decay and repair, alteration and addition. The date of the original design of a building does not tell the whole story of what is presently visible. Therein lies the fascination of architectural history: to learn what we are looking at when we see a building.

To
Judge Blythe, Collector of the District of Philad[a]

Sir

When it became necessary to put the former U. S. Bank building in order for the purposes of a Custom House I found that the whole of the interior as well as the exterior required a thorough cleansing and repair, particularly in the items of carpentry, masonry, painting & glazing.

It is now upwards of nine years since the building has had any repairs whatever, which neglect has rendered it imperative in you to incur a much heavier expense than otherwise could have been foreseen:—Upon the removal from the Old Custom House into the new one there was necessarily many new arrangements to be made in the Desks and Counters——The building had to be finished in almost every particular for the conveniences of the Officers, and you are well aware Sir, that the old building had no furniture at all, at least none fit for the proper uses of the new one.

There was an absolute necessity for additional carpenters work, making Desks, Counters, Shelving &c. all of which had to be done before & while the various officers were in the transaction of their ordinary business——The whole house had to be cleansed & white washed in the upper Story, and in the business rooms of the principal floor the walls and ceilings painted with two coats for the proper restoration of light and cleanliness——This item alone has cost upwards of $1300——at the fair rates per measurement and the City prices——

[In the Harrisburg Account book, there is figuring giving the total interior area of this building which may date from this period.]

Many of the grates and fire places had to be renewed——The marble columns and architraves of the principal business room required scrubbing with pummice Stone, to remove the dust of accumulated years, and for this purpose Scaffolds & ladders had to be used.

The Gas pipes were out of order as well as many of the locks and keys throughout the building.

The external portions of the premises, such as the coppering of the roof, Terraces, Steps and pavements required a thorough overhauling and amendment for the preservation of the building——no superfluous expenditure has been incurred in these items——the repairs have been but partially carried out, and as you have requested me to stop all further proceedings tending to increase the expenditure until the proper sanction from the Treasury and owing to the coming on of the winter season I have given orders to the workmen accordingly——

The whole amount of the jobbing above mentioned exclusive of furniture, has cost about $3500——and when the Carpenter & painters have finished the room now fitting up for the use of the Surveyor, all will be done that is immediately necessary.

In conclusion Sir permit me to draw your attention to the importance of making such alterations as will render the Cellar Story available for storage of Spirits and wines, which can be done at an expense of about $600——The Space in the Cellar is equal to 9000 superficial feet which would when filled bring in an income of at least $1000 per annum. This portion of the building cannot be made to serve the purposes of the Inspectors & appraisers, nor for the storage and safe keeping of sample goods; this can only be properly done by the purchase of a lot of ground in the immediate neighbourhood, and by the construction of stores upon a fire proof plan suffciently capacious for the officers of this important branch of the Custom house——

Respectfully Submitted
by your Obd Servt
Signed William Strickland
Architect

Philadelphia Dec. 9, 1844

IV. Illustrations

Fig. 1. John Strickland, Sr., (1757–1820) by Thomas Sully, 1809. Courtesy of the owner, Lois Harper Wyman, Cincinnati.

Fig. 2. William Strickland, bronze bust by Gevelot. Library, Tennessee State Capitol, Nashville. This bust was exhibited in the Paris Salon of 1836. Photograph by Wiles. Courtesy of Fiske Kimball.

Fig. 3. Plan of the Parapet of Fort Hamilton, 1814. Drawing in the Strickland account book, State Records Office, Harrisburg, Pa. Courtesy of Henry Howard Eddy. This fort was erected above the Schuylkill near Woodlands, the country house of William Hamilton.

Fig. 4. Original Plan of the Western Penitentiary, Pittsburgh, Pa., as constructed by W. Strickland, 1820–27. It was remodelled by John Haviland in 1833. *Report on Penitentiaries* by William Crawford, London, 1835, Appendix, Pl. 3, opp. p. 14. Courtesy of Henry Howard Eddy.

Fig. 5. Elevation of the Western Penitentiary, Pittsburgh, Pa., as erected by Strickland. As above, Fig. 4, Pl. 4.

Fig. 6. Baltimore in 1752, aquatint by Strickland, 1817, from the drawing by John Moale, Maryland Historical Society. Courtesy New York Public Library.

Fig. 7. Prospective View of the City of Cairo, *c.* 1838. Lithograph by A. Hoffy after the drawing by William Strickland. Courtesy Knox College, Galesburg, Illinois, and the City Art Museum of St. Louis. Photograph by Piaget Studio, St. Louis.

Fig. 8. Elevation of a country house with dome, water color by Wm. Strickland. 7⅞ x 11 inches. Stauffer Collection. Courtesy New York Public Library.

Fig. 9. Dr. Rush's Mansion, Nineteenth and Chestnut Streets, Philadelphia. Water color drawing by Wm. Strickland. 11¾ x 15½ inches. Courtesy of the owner, Arthur J. Sussel, Philadelphia.

Fig. 10. Ceiling of Crosby Hall. Water color drawing signed: W. Strickland Archt., London, Feby 14th/38. "Shewing the timbers of the roof constructed of oak in a low pointed arch,—In plan it is formed into eight divisions in length and four in breadth, each of which principal compartments is again subdivided by moulded styles into four smaller divisions or pannels.—From the points of intersection hang pendants terminating in octagonal ornaments, each pendant forming the center of 4 arches.—The spandrils being pierced with trefoil headed niches.—The frieze consists of pierced quatrefoils in square pannels surmounted with an embattled cornice.—Length of Hall 55 ft. breadth 28 ft."

Fig. 11. Crosby Hall,—Bishopgate Street, London. Water color, London, Feby 10/38. "North doorway forming the entrance into the Council Chamber from great St. Helens court. This doorway has a low pointed arch inscribed in a square head and sheltered with a weather cornice; above it are three square windows separated by chamferred mullions of stone, the iron sash is walled in flush with the cross bars.

"The annexed sketch represents all the parts of the northern entrance in Crosby hall which is much dilapidated and weather worn, but, still the reeds and coved mouldings retain much of their original boldness and relief.

"This entrance to the council chamber projects from the oriel of the hall and is now used by a packing box maker.

"Glo. That it may please you to leave these sad designs
To him that hath more cause to be a mourner,
And presently repair to Crosby place;—
Richard III."

Fig. 12. Locomotive of "Great Western Railway from London to Bristol W. Strickland Archt & Engr. London, Feby. 6/38."

Figures 11, 12, and 13 are from the sketch book entitled "Sketches of Roman Architecture," Tennessee State Library, Nashville. Photographs by Steve Hood.

Fig. 13. Ground plan of a church at Gay and Fayette Streets as yet unidentified. Signed: William Strickland Archt & Engr. Portfolio of Strickland Drawings, Tennessee State Library, Nashville. Photograph by Steve Hood.

Fig. 14. Longitudinal section of a church. Signed: William Strickland Archt. One of five Strickland drawings recently found among the Meredith papers. Courtesy of the Historical Society of Pennsylvania.

Fig. 15. Ground plan of a project for an office building to be erected at Sixth and Walnut streets, Philadelphia, *c.* 1836. Courtesy Historical Society of Pennsylvania.

Fig. 16. Meriwether Lewis, Esq. Aquatint by Strickland after drawing by St. Menim, *Analectic Magazine*, Vol. 7, p. 328, April 1816. Sketch believed to be only extant likeness of Capt. Lewis in 1816. Courtesy New York Public Library.

Fig. 17. Sussex County Court House, Georgetown, Delaware. Designed by Strickland, 1837, completed 1840. Old photograph found by Leon de Valinger, State Archivist. Courtesy Delaware State Archives, photo No. PB #131.

Fig. 18. Sussex County Court House, Georgetown, Delaware. Present state after remodelling in 1914 by Brinck-

Fig. 1. John Strickland, Sr., (1757–1820) by Thomas Sully, 1809. (Courtesy of the owner, Louis Harper Wyman, Cincinnati)

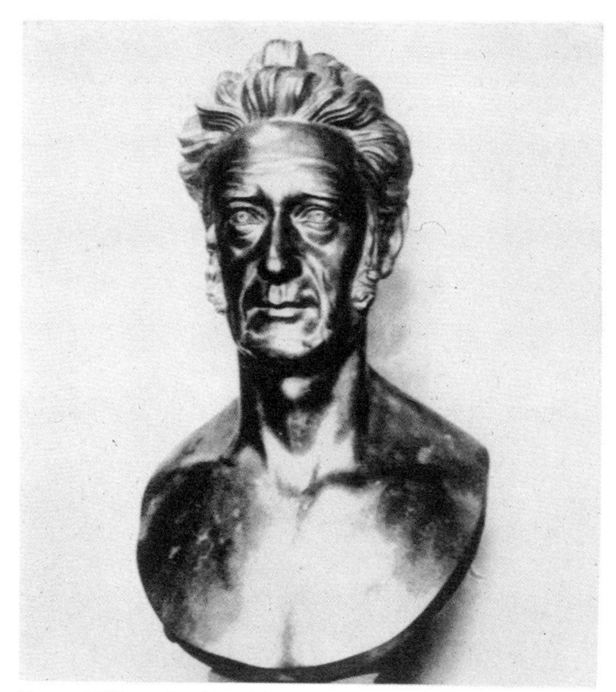

Fig. 2. William Strickland, bronze bust by Gevelot, 1836. Library, Tennessee State Capitol, Nashville.

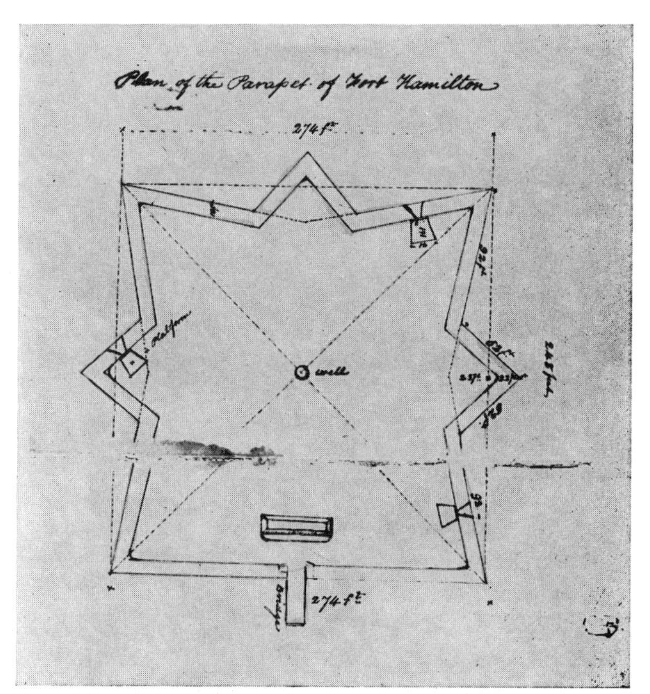

Fig. 3. Plan of the Parapet of Fort Hamilton, 1814. (Courtesy of Henry Howard Eddy, Pennsylvania State Records Officer)

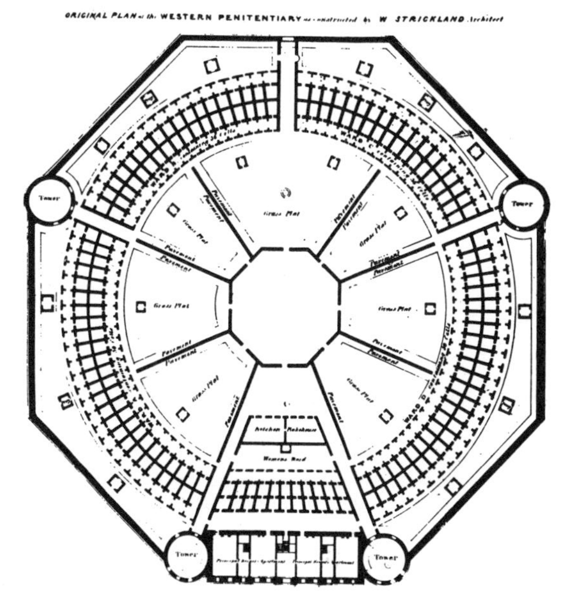

Fig. 4. Plan of the Western Penitentiary, Pittsburgh designed by Strickland, 1820. (Courtesy of Henry Howard Eddy, Pennsylvania State Records Officer)

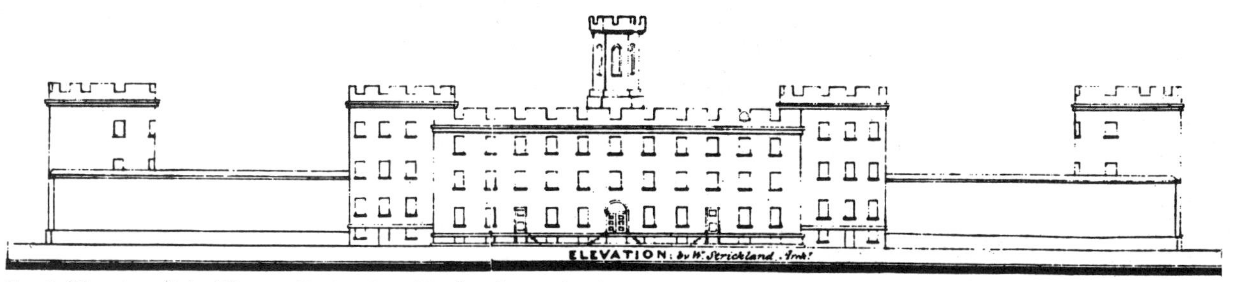

Fig. 5. Elevation of the Western Penitentiary, Pittsburgh completed 1827. (Courtesy of Henry Howard Eddy, Pennsylvania State Records Officer)

FIG. 6. Baltimore in 1752, aquatint by Strickland, 1817. (New York Public Library)

FIG. 7. Prospective View of the City of Cairo after drawing by Strickland, *c.* 1838. (Courtesy of Knox College and the City Art Museum of St. Louis. Photograph by Piaget Studio, St. Louis)

FIG. 9. Dr. Rush's Mansion, Philadelphia. Water color sketch by Strickland. (Courtesy of the owner, Arthur J. Sussel, Philadelphia.)

FIG. 8. Water color of a Country House by Strickland. (Stauffer Collection, New York Public Library)

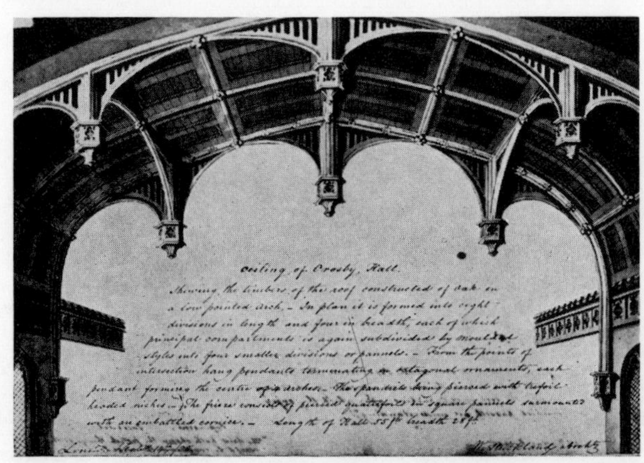

FIG. 10. Ceiling of Crosby Hall, London, Feb. 14, 1838. Strickland Sketchbook. (Tennessee State Library)

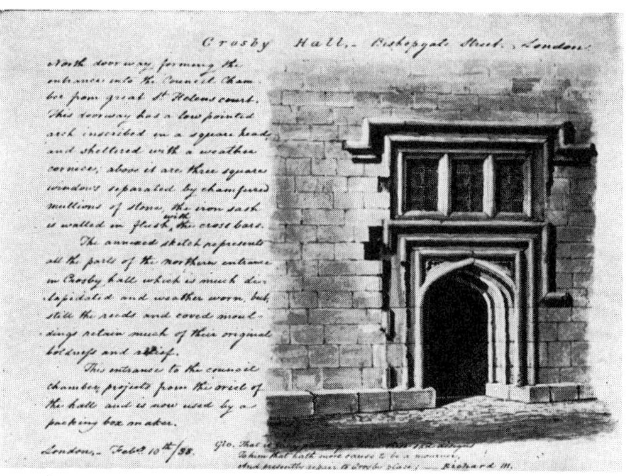

FIG. 11. North gateway of Crosby Hall, London, Feb. 10, 1838. Strickland Sketchbook. (Tennessee State Library)

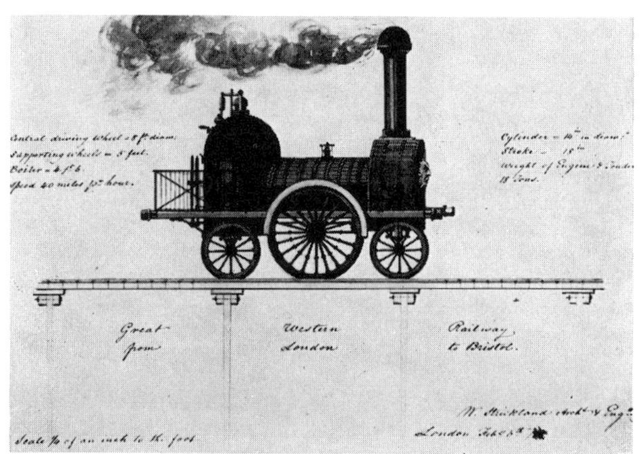

FIG. 12. Locomotive of the Great Western Railway, England, Feb. 6, 1838. Strickland Sketchbook. (Tennessee State Library)

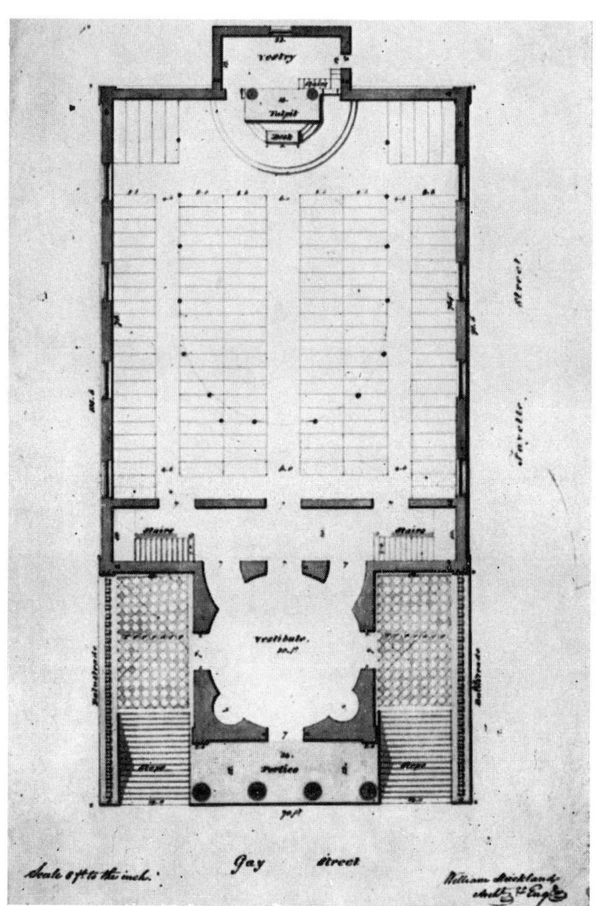

FIG. 13. Ground plan of a church. Strickland Portfolio. (Tennessee State Library)

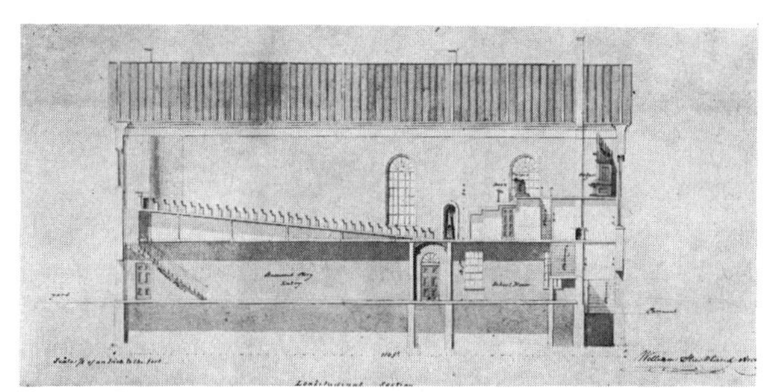

FIG. 14. Longitudinal section of a church. Meredith Papers. (The Historical Society of Pennsylvania)

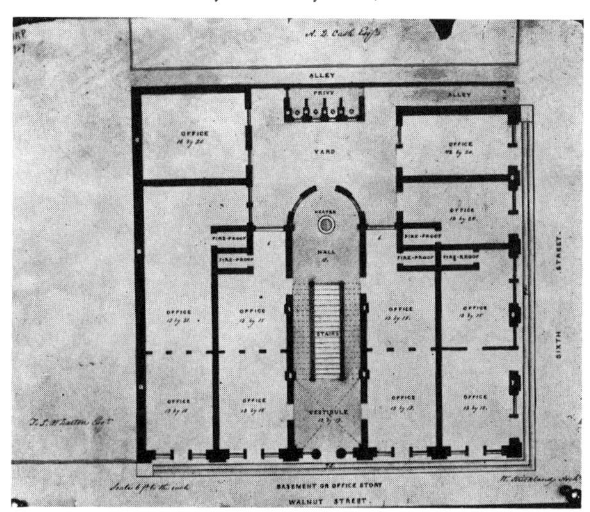

FIG. 15. Ground plan of a project for an office building at 6th and Walnut Streets, Philadelphia. (The Historical Society of Pennsylvania)

FIG. 16. Meriwether Lewis, Esq. Aquatint by Strickland after St. Menim, 1816. (New York Public Library)

FIG. 17. Sussex County Court House, Georgetown, Delaware, 1837–40. (Delaware State Archives)

FIG. 19. Philadepphia Bank, 1836. Old photograph before 1863. (Seymour Adelman Collection)

FIG. 21. Sepulchral Monument of William Lehman, d. 1829. Harrisburg Cemetery, Harrisburg, Pa. (Courtesy of Hubertis Cummings)

FIG. 18. Sussex County Court House, Georgetown, Delaware. Remodelled 1914. Photograph 1953

FIG. 20. Mechanics' Bank, Philadelphia, 1837. Photograph 1950.

FIG. 22. Sepulchral monument in memory of Alfred Theodore Miller, 1840. Laurel Hill Cemetery, Philadelphia. Photograph 1953.

FIG. 23. Immanuel Church, New Castle, Delaware. Built 1703. Water color view of church in 1804 from Latrobe survey. Enlarged detail. (Delaware State Archives)

FIG. 25. Philadelphia Exchange, 1832–34. Codman photograph of the 1890's, showing Strickland Tower demolished 1900. (Metropolitan Museum of Art)

FIG. 27. St. Peter's P.E. Church, Philadelphia. Designed by Robert Smith, 1758–63. Lithograph after painting by R. S. Smith, April 1, 1842. (New York Public Library)

FIG. 24. Immanuel Church. New Castle, Delaware. Remodelled with tower and steeple by Strickland, 1820–22. Photograph 1953.

FIG. 26. St. Augustine's R.C. Church, Philadelphia. Cupola added by Strickland, 1829. (The Historical Society of Pennsylvania)

FIG. 28. St. Peter's P.E. Church, Philadelphia. Tower and Steeple added by Strickland in 1842. (The Historical Society of Pennsylvania)

loe and Canning, Inc., architects, Wilmington, Del., and Easton, Md. Photograph by author, 1953.

Fig. 19. Philadelphia Bank, 1836, SW corner Fourth and Chestnut Streets, demolished. From Minutes of the meeting of the Trustees of the Bank, May 10, 1836: "resolved to tear down present building and erect one fronting on Chestnut Street according to William Strickland's plan." Courtesy of Nicholas B. Wainwright. Old photograph of Bank before 1863, courtesy of Seymour Adelman Collection.

Fig. 20. Mechanics' Bank, south side of Third Street between Market and Chestnut, Philadelphia. On the inner plinth of the architrave is the inscription "William Strickland Architect J. Struthers Mason 1837." An early view of this bank is in Moses King, *Philadelphia and Notable Philadelphians,* New York, 1901, p. 80. Courtesy of Charles E. Peterson. Photograph by author 1950.

Fig. 21. Sepulchral monument of William Lehman, died 1829, Harrisburg Cemetery, Harrisburg, Pa. It was originally in the Zion Lutheran Burial Ground which was where the Pennsylvania Railroad station and tracks are now. Courtesy of Hubertis Cummings.

Fig. 22. Sepulchral Monument in memory of Alfred Theodore Miller, son of Matthew T. and Caroline Miller. Born Feb. 7, 1840. Died Sept. 8, 1840. Laurel Hill Cemetery, Philadelphia. Sculpture by Pettrick. Monument designed by Strickland and executed by Struthers. *Guide to Laurel Hill Cemetery,* John Notman, Arch. & del. Philadelphia, 1844. Courtesy of George B. Tatum. Photograph by author, 1953.

Fig. 23. Immanuel Church, New Castle, Delaware. Built 1703. Water color view of church in 1804 from the Latrobe survey of New Castle, Record Office, Wilmington, Del. Courtesy of Miss Jeannette Eckman, Leon de Valinger. Photograph courtesy of Delaware State Archives, No. C & T #81.

Fig. 24. Immanuel Church, New Castle, Delaware. Steeple and transepts (lengthened an additional 12 ft. in 1860) by Strickland, 1820–1822. Courtesy Albert Kruse, Charles E. Peterson, Judge Richard S. Rodney. Photograph by author, 1953.

Fig. 25. Philadelphia Exchange, 1832–34. Codman photograph of 1890's showing Strickland tower which was demolished in 1900; present tower by Louis Hickman. Courtesy of Charles E. Peterson and Clay Lancaster. Photograph courtesy of Abbott L. Cummings, American Wing, Metropolitan Museum of Art, New York.

Fig. 26. Cupola of St. Augustine's R. C. Church, Fourth near Vine, Philadelphia. Corner stone 1796. Built by Nicholas Fagan, 1799–1801. Front added 1826 and cupola designed by Strickland in 1829. Burned in anti-Catholic riot of 1844. *Memoirs* of the Catholic History Society of Phila., I (1887), 169. Courtesy of Charles E. Peterson. Lithograph by Geo. Lehman, published by C. G. Childs, 1830. Courtesy of the Historical Society of Pennsylvania.

Fig. 27. St. Peter's Church, Third and Pine Streets, Philadelphia. West view, April 1, 1842, R. S. Smith paint., J. H. Richards, lithotinted. St. Peter's was designed and built by Robert Smith, 1758–63. Cf. Charles Peterson, "Notes on Robert Smith," *Historic Philadelphia (Transactions of the American Philosophical Society,* New Series, Vol. 43, Pt. 1), p. 120. Print in Stauffer collection. Courtesy of the New York Public Library.

Fig. 28. St. Peter's Church, Philadelphia with tower and steeple designed by Strickland in 1842. Vestry minutes courtesy of the Rector, Mr. Evans. Photograph by Ph. B. Wallace. Courtesy of the Historical Society of Pennsylvania.

V. Strickland Bibliography Since 1950

Davis, Louise, "Stripped to the Buff, Tennessee's State Library Makes a Hit," *The Nashville Tennesseean,* Feb. 8, 1953. With color illustrations. Tells of the restoration of the library room in the Tennessee State Capitol designed by Strickland.

Gilchrist, Agnes Addison, "Before Our Time—The Bankers Build," *The American-German Review,* June 1951, pp. 22–23.

———"William Strickland: Architect of the University: 1829," *The General Magazine and Historical Chronicle,* University of Pennsylvania, 54: 1, autumn 1951, pp. 50–59.

———"The Philadelphia Exchange: William Strickland, Architect," *Historic Philadelphia (Transactions of the American Philosophical Society,* New Series, Vol. 43, Pt. 1, March 1953), pp. 86–95.

———"Market Houses in High Street," *ibid.,* pp. 304–312. In this was published the letter found by Louise Hall of Duke University, in the library of the American Philosophical Society, written by Strickland on July 4, 1834 to the Committee on Markets of the City of Philadelphia.

Mahoney, Nell Savage, "A Strange Will Indeed!" *The Nashville Tennesseean Magazine,* March 5, 1950. This tells of two writs served against Strickland during 1850 while he was in Nashville.

Moore, Mrs. John Trotwood, "The Tennessee State Library in the Capitol," *Tennessee Historical Quarterly,* 12: 1, March 1953.

Newcomb, Rexford, *Architecture of the Old Northwest Territory* (Chicago: University of Chicago Press, 1950). P. 87 notes Strickland entered plans in the competition for the Indiana State Capitol.

Smith, Robert C., *John Notman and the Athenaeum Building.* The annual address of the Athenaeum of Philadelphia, 1951. Illustrates and describes the Strickland drawings entered in the competition of 1839 and which are still preserved in the Philadelphia Athenaeum.

THE PHILADELPHIA EXCHANGE: WILLIAM STRICKLAND, ARCHITECT

THE PHILADELPHIA EXCHANGE: WILLIAM STRICKLAND, ARCHITECT

AGNES ADDISON GILCHRIST *

By 1831, when it was decided to build an Exchange building in Philadelphia, the pattern of American civilization, as we know it today, was already being established. The colonial period was over, not only politically, as it had been for fifty years, but also spiritually. A new generation had grown up which recognized the potential power of the United States. Andrew Jackson was President; the spoils system was initiated; the west was being opened up as fast as roads, canals and, by the end of the decade, railroads could be built. Emigrants were coming in ever larger numbers. New industries were being started. Boom years were coming with extension of credit and an over-supply of paper money only to be briefly stopped by the depression of 1837.

Fig. 1. Early photograph of the Philadelphia Exchange. Historical Society of Pennsylvania. From A. A. Gilchrist, *William Strickland,* Phila., Univ. of Penna. Press, 1950.

Philadelphia participated in the national growth and prosperity. A newspaper article which appeared on May 14, 1831, stated that it was estimated that 1,600 new buildings would be erected in the city during the summer and it continued:

> Philadelphia is truly the Athens of America: in its public institutions, in its benevolent and charitable societies, in its literary reputation—in its site, the beautiful regularity of its streets—its buildings both public and private—in every particular, except in the dust and dirt, the noise and bustle, which attends an extensive shipping, we are superior, without a doubt to every other City in the Union.[1]

There were Philadelphians then as now who regretted the demolition of historic landmarks. *The Philadelphia Album* on July 16, 1831 lamented the destroying of the old building at 43 Market Street where Benjamin Franklin had his post office and bookstore. Then as now, the newspapers recorded the growth of Russian power and applauded her enemies, at that time the Poles, for whom, owing to Kosciuszko, the Philadelphians felt a special sympathy.[2]

THE NEED FOR AN EXCHANGE

Since Philadelphia was a busy port and there was great local pride, it is not surprising that a group of financiers and merchants organized themselves into a society for the building of an Exchange. In the middle of the eighteenth century there had been a bequest for the building of an Exchange but it had never been car-

* Fiske Kimball, Director of the Philadelphia Museum of Art; Edward Riley, Chief Historian and Charles E. Peterson, Resident Architect of the Independence National Historical Park Project, have permitted me to use their notes, which help I wish to acknowledge with thanks and have indicated in the footnotes.

[1] *The Philadelphia Album,* 156, Sat., May 14, 1831.

[2] *Ibid.,* May 21, 1831, "The Poles Have Gained a Complete and Signal Victory over Their Russian Adversaries." Kosciuszko was in Philadelphia during the Revolution and again from December 1796 through 1798.

ried out.[3] Charleston[4] had an Exchange building in 1761, built by the Horlbeck brothers for the cost of £44,016 16s 8d and which with changes is still standing. New Orleans had Exchange buildings, although its Merchants Exchange which also included the Post Office was not built until 1835–36 with James Dakin as architect.[5] The Baltimore Exchange designed by Benjamin Henry Latrobe and Maximilian Godefroy was opened in 1820.[6] Town and Davis designed the New York Exchange in 1825–27, which burned in 1835.[7] Boston's Exchange, designed by Isaiah Rogers, was not completed until 1842.[8]

The purpose of an Exchange building is to provide a meeting place for merchants to barter or sell their cargoes and merchandise. Venice was content with the Rialto, the covered bridge over the Grand Canal. The first Exchange building in Europe was in Antwerp built in 1531. Thomas Gresham who knew the Antwerp Exchange well, offered to build one in London, which he financed by the rents from shops on the second floor. It was formally opened by Queen Elizabeth in 1571. It burned in the Great Fire and was replaced by the Royal Exchange by Edward Jerman of 1668 which in turn was burned in 1838 to be replaced by the present Exchange by Tite.[9] In the eighteenth century an Exchange was built in Edinburgh, but the guidebooks of the period comment that the merchants continued to do their business on the street corner as formerly.[10] Thomas Cooley in 1769 won the competition for the Exchange in Dublin for which sixty-four architects submitted plans. It is now the city hall.[11] The Exchange in Copenhagen with its fascinating tower of twisted tails was opened in 1619.[12] By the end of the eighteenth century most commercially important cities had an Exchange.

The Philadelphians who were Trustees of the Philadelphia Exchange in 1831 were Stephen Girard, Robert Ralston, Joseph P. Norris, James C. Fisher, and Joshua Longstreth.[13]

THE SITE

Their first problem was to determine upon an appropriate site. The block chosen was bounded by Dock, so named because formerly there was a creek which came up there where small vessels unloaded fire wood at the dock, Walnut and Third Streets.[14] It was well placed, not far from the banks and most convenient to Stephen Girard's own bank building on Third and not too distant from the water front [D, IV].

The hundredth anniversary of the birth of George Washington was chosen as the day for the laying of the corner stone. There was a ceremony at 12 noon when the large block was placed twenty feet below the surface of the ground. It had carved on it the following inscription:

February 22d. Anno Domini 1832

Building Committee Joshua Lippincott
Ashbel G. Ralston
John Sites
Elwood Morris—Clerk of Works
John K. Kane—Solicitor
William Strickland—Architect
John Struthers—Marble Mason
John O'Neill—Carpenter
Joseph S. Walter & Son—Bricklayers
David Henderson—Marble Quarrier
Leiper & Crosby—Stone Quarriers

Poulson's American Daily Advertiser reported that

> When the masons had completed their work, the following neat and happy address was delivered by Mr. John K. Kane, to a numerous and respectable audience.—Fellow Citizens.—The edifice, whose deep and secure foundation we have assembled to witness, is dedicated to the uses of a commercial Exchange for the city of Philadelphia. Accustomed as we are to the rapid and silent advance of every thing about us, from the simplicity which characterizes a new settlement, to the refinements of splendour and of wealth, it has been a subject of frequent surprise that the commencement of such a structure should have been delayed so long. Yet there are even now those living amongst us, who perhaps may remember when the site which it is to occupy was the shore of a sluggish and winding stream.

Later in his address, Kane projected his thought forward 150 years into the future, to 1982, "when the building which we have founded shall stand among the relics of antiquities, another memorial to posterity of the skill of its architect,—and proof of the liberal spirit, and cultivated taste, which, in our days, distinguish the mercantile community." [15]

On March 8, 1832, the Board of managers of the Exchange addressed a Memorial to City Councils regarding Footways surrounding the Exchange and petitioned that the grade from Third to Dock be evened.[16]

By the end of the year, at the annual meeting on December 6, 1832, the Board of Managers reported to the

[3] *Souvenir history of the Philadelphia Stock Exchange,* 1903. In May 1754, James Hamilton, retiring Mayor offered the city £150 to build an Exchange (Peterson).

[4] Ravenel, Beatrice St. Julien, *Architects of Charleston,* 39–43, Charleston, Carolina Art Assn., 1945.

[5] *Norman's New Orleans and environs: 1845,* 157–161.

[6] *The stranger's guide to Baltimore,* 32, 1852.

[7] *The Family Magazine,* 402, New York, Feb. 1836.

[8] Kilham, Walter H. *Boston after Bulfinch,* 36, Cambridge, Harvard Univ. Press, 1946.

[9] Wilson, Effingham, *Description of the New Royal Exchange,* London, 1844.

[10] *Views of Edinburgh,* 1787.

[11] *The life of James Gandon, Esq.,* ed. by Thom. J. Mulvay, Dublin, 1846.

[12] Portfolio on Exchanges, Art Division, New York Public Library.

[13] Scharf, J. T., and Thompson Westcott, *History of Philadelphia* **1**: 634–635, Phila., Everts, 1884.

[14] Deed Book A M, p. 239—June 2, 1832 Robert Ralston *et al.* sells site to Philadelphia Exchange Co. (Peterson).

[15] Hazard, S., *Register of Pennsylvania* **9**: 128, 1832.

[16] *Ibid.,* 120.

FIG. 2. North façade of Philadelphia Exchange—(1947). Courtesy of Charles E. Peterson.

FIG. 3. Woodcut of Third Street façade of Philadelphia Exchange. Drawn by Ed. Glenn. Hist. Soc. of Penna.

Stockholders of the Philadelphia Exchange Company on the progress made on the building, part of which report which follows was printed in a Philadelphia newspaper.

Twelve months ago the site on which this beautiful structure stands, comprising an area of fifteen thousand feet or more, was encumbered by an uncouth mass of buildings angular, unsightly, misshapen, a proverbial deformity in our symmetrical city. Since then the incubus has been removed, 700,000 bricks forming the huge chaotic mound, have been displaced, individually handled, and now form a portion of our sub-structure. The very cleansing of the soil, from this foul rubbish, cost no less a sum than $3000. About the 10th of March, (barely nine months ago,) our masons commenced these substantial foundations, and behold in that short period 2,200 perches of stone and 900,000 bricks have been laid, besides thousands of cubic feet of marble then in the quarry, hewn and fitted to give brilliance and beauty to our edifice for untold ages.

All our contracts, even to the roofing copper, have been made. Of 28,000 cubic feet of marble, (the whole quantity required) 12,000 cubic feet and upwards have been delivered. 250,000 bricks more will be all that are needed. In the mean time, the season of the year has arrived, when it is proper to suspend the prosecution of our masonry, but we have already attained the full altitude of our second story—the lintels are over our windows.

Nor do we allow the winter to stop our progress—materials are in the hands of the workmen, the preparations of which, for their respective positions, will be complete by the opening of the spring, and six weeks after the work is recommenced, it will be ready for roofing, a temporary covering serving in the interior, to preserve it from injury by the weather. By extraordinary exertions, the Post Office may be located in its destined apartments in May, but it will probably be July before the whole building is fairly under cover.[17]

The work on the Exchange proceeded as planned through 1833 and the Post Office opened in its new location on June 25. By November the roof and tower were completed and the cap stone set in place, which event was celebrated by a banquet for the 140 men employed on the building. At that dinner many toasts were drunk including one proposed by J. R. Chandler, "William Strickland, the architect of the Merchants' Exchange. He will realize the boast of the ancient emperor. He found us living in a city of brick, and he will leave us in a city of marble." [18]

EXTERIOR DESIGN

That William Strickland was chosen to be architect for the Exchange in preference to John Haviland,[19] was perhaps because of the friendship of two of the Board of Managers. Robert Ralston [20] in 1826 when Strickland was desirous of obtaining the appointment as architect of the United States Naval Asylum, wrote the Secretary of the Navy on November 1, saying in part:

Three large buildings, the Orphan Asylum, the Indigent Widows' and Single Women's Asylum, and the Mariners Church have been constructed and erected under his direction, in each of which, I have had to make all the payments, and consequently have derived information which enables me to bear testimony to the skill, good judgments, punctuality, and fidelity of Mr. Strickland.[21]

John K. Kane,[22] the solicitor of the company who was chosen to give the address at the laying of the corner

[17] *The Daily American Advertiser,* Jan. 3, 1833 (Riley).

[18] Hazard, *op. cit.,* **12**: 293, 1833.

[19] English architect who settled in Philadelphia, designed the first Franklin Institute building, 1825, now the Atwater Kent Museum and the Eastern Penitentiary, 1825-1832, and became world famous as a prison architect.

[20] In 1826 Ralston was appointed Saxon consul in Philadelphia. Lingelbach, William E., Saxon-American relations 1778–1828, *Amer. Hist. Rev.* **17**: 538-539, 1912.

[21] Records of the Department of the Navy, Office of Naval Records and Library, P N—Naval Asylum, Phila; construction. The National Archives, Washington, D. C. (Mr. Peterson directed me to this material.)

[22] Kane was president of the Beef Steak Club of which Strickland was a member. In October 1833, at a dinner at Kane's house, 191 Walnut Street, at which Strickland was present, William Kneass read a poem. MS. copy by Strickland Kneass, 1911. Kane also wrote Strickland's obituary for the American Philosophical Society, the original MS. copy of which is in the Society's Library

stone was one of Strickland's closest friends and would have encouraged his selection.

At that time, Strickland was just completing the U. S. Mint at Juniper and Chestnut and the U. S. Naval Asylum on Grey's Ferry Road and working on the Almshouse in Blockley Township. He had designed the much admired steeple on Independence Hall [23] and his plan for the Second Bank of the United States had established his reputation as an architect [24] [C, IV].

After the site for the Exchange had been chosen and Strickland had been appointed architect, he published a *Prospectus of a Plan for . . . an Exchange* to encourage the sale of shares in the Philadelphia Exchange Company.[25] He also made a water color drawing of the proposed Exchange which was widely known through the mezzotint which John Sartain made from it. The Dock Street façade was built in all essentials as it was shown in the drawing. The most notable change was that a weather vane was put on top of the tower instead of the female figure holding a trident. In the drawing the antefixes are indicated only on the curved portico, but when it was built the antefixes were continued on the flat faces of the western façade. The general design of a basement story with plain openings in the curved section and openings flanked by columns with water leaf capitals on the sides; the tripartite windows on the flanks; the Corinthian portico on the second story with stairs on either side leading to tall doors and the long windows with rectangular blank insets above under the circular portico; and the circular tower with tall narrow windows; all these features were carried out.

The sides of the building are severely plain, but harmoniously rhythmic based on a three-part design which moves both horizontally and vertically. There are three tiers of tripartite openings which give a strong vertical feeling. These are tied together by three bands of masonry. The platform of the porticos is continued around the building by a projecting band above the lintels of the ground floor openings. There are three courses of masonry below the main story windows and four above and a full entablature crowning the whole. The second story is accentuated by having openings three courses higher than the top story and by having the dividing piers ornamented with simple cap moldings. The horizontal divisions are equally rhythmic. Each opening has three lights, one wide and two narrower. These form three units: at either end there is a tripartite opening flanked by wide bands of masonry; in the center, there are three tripartite openings set closer together equidistantly (fig. 2).

The Third Street façade is also imposing with the heavy basement, Corinthian portico *in antis* with four columns and two pilasters, flanking sides with tripartite windows and crowning pediment (fig. 3).

[23] Hazard, *op. cit.* 1: 152–154, 1828.

[24] Gilchrist, A. A., *William Strickland,* Phila., Univ. of Penna. Press, 1950.

[25] Copy in Free Library of Philadelphia, Ridgway Branch.

FIG. 4. The New Tower of the Royal Exchange in London, 1821. Engraving by Rawle in the *European Magazine.* New York Public Library.

It is likely that Strickland when asked to produce a design for the Exchange thought of the various Exchange buildings which he had seen in this country: the Baltimore [26] Exchange designed by his teacher Latrobe with a central dome and the New York Exchange [27] by the firm of Town and Davis with a circular tower. Joseph Jackson suggested that the circular tower of Town and Davis may have influenced Strickland.[28]

[26] Strickland engraved a plate entitled "Ancient View of Baltimore" for Messrs. Coale and Maxwell of Baltimore in 1817 while the Exchange was under construction.

[27] Strickland may have been in New York in 1828 to see James Lloyd who acted as agent for James A. Hillhouse of New Haven. Strickland made designs of a house for Hillhouse that year. Drawings and letters are in the Sterling Library, Yale Univ., New Haven.

[28] Jackson, Joseph, *Development of American architecture,* 88, Phila., David McKay, 1926.

FIG. 5. Pavilion in the park of Klein-Glienicke near Potsdam; architect K. F. Schinkel, 1836. Courtesy of Ernest Nash.

However, Strickland had been in Great Britain in 1825 and seen the Exchanges in Dublin, Edinburgh, and London.[29] At that time the Royal Exchange had a circular tower (fig. 4), a new one which was currently much admired. It was designed by George Smith, Surveyor to the Mercers' Company in 1821 because the old tower by Jerman was found to be in a perilously dilapidated condition and in danger of falling.[30] These two examples in New York and London may have predisposed Strickland to favor a circular tower.[30a]

Before making any plans, Strickland must have carefully studied the site with its rising ground and commanding position at the intersection of Dock and Walnut. As he stood looking at it from Dock Street, he saw at the end of Dock one of the most handsome buildings in Philadelphia, Girard's Bank, designed by Samuel Blodgett in 1795 [31] to house the First Bank of the United States and which was itself modelled on Thomas Cooley's Exchange in Dublin. The portico of that building has Roman Corinthian columns. Strickland's water color of the Exchange also shows Girard's Bank and he must have considered how his building could be harmonized with the older building. To use the Corinthian Order was the answer.

However by 1832, architectural ideas had changed since the end of the eighteenth century. Behind all architectural design there is a determining idea. By 1830, the idea was that Greek architecture provided the best models for modern architects. Greek architecture was best known at that time through "the rare and costly old English work of Stuart and Revett." [32] Strickland, himself is reported to have said repeatedly to the pupils in his office "that the student of architecture need go no further than the *Antiquities of Athens* as a basis of design." [33] In this instance, Strickland followed his own advice and turned to chapter IV of the first volume of the *Antiquities* published in 1762 and found the model that he needed in the Choragic Monument of Lysicrates. The capitals and antifixes are meticulous copies of the Stuart and Revett plates (fig. 6) and the circular tower of the Exchange is an adaptation of the monument itself [34] (fig. 7).

INTERIOR PLAN

The plan for the Exchange had to provide for the Exchange room, for the reading room, for the post office, for a coffee shop and for offices to be rented out for revenue. The area of the rectangular building is 95 × 114 feet with the circular portico extending another 36 feet. There was a basement story under ground built of brick. No ground plans or views of the interior as it was originally have been found. In January 1835 a description and view of the Exchange was printed in the *Family Magazine*. The part concerning the interior plan follows:

> A hall passes through the centre of the building from Dock to Third Streets, and another likewise communicates with this from the north side. The basement story [the ground floor] is fifteen feet in height—is arched throughout, and has twelve doorways on the Third street front and flanks. On the right or north side of the hall is the Post Office, seventy-four by thirty-six feet, and on the left are several insurance offices and banks, and the session-room of the chamber of commerce. Two flights of stairs, one on each side of the hall, ascend to the second floor, at the head of these is the entrance to the Exchange Room, which is on the east front, extending across the whole building, and occupying an area of 3300 superficial feet. The ceiling extending to the roof, is of the form of a dome, and supported by several marble columns. Its pannels are ornamented with splendid fresco paintings, representing Commerce,

[29] Strickland, William, *Report on canals, railways, roads and other subjects*, Phila., 1826.

[30] Wilson, *op cit.*, 48.

[30a] The circular cupola on Latrobe's Bank of Pennsylvania, 1799, may have also influenced Strickland's design.

[31] Gilchrist, A. A., The bankers build, *Amer.-Ger. Rev.* **17** (5): 22, 1951.

[32] *Saturday Courier*, Phila., Mar. 29, 1834, from a notice of the French translation of the *Antiquities of Athens* by M. Hittorf of Paris who "has acquired a distinguished reputation by his discovery of the extent to which the Greeks employed colors in ornamenting the interiors and exteriors of their edifices." At present we are discovering the extent to which the Greek Revival architects employed color in their interiors.

[33] MS. memoir of Horace Sellers (Fiske Kimball).

[34] Thomas Jefferson wrote to Robert Mills on March 3, 1826 suggesting the use of the Lantern of Demosthenes as it was then called, for a tower. Latrobe noted it in his journal. Addison, Agnes, William Strickland, *Pa. Mag. Hist. Biog.* **67** (3): 278, 1943. But Strickland was the first architect to use it. Schinkel in 1836 in the second, smaller pavilion in the park of Klein-Glienicke near Potsdam also used the choragic monument as a tower on the circular colonnaded garden structure (fig. 5). Sievers, J., *Karl Friedrich Schinkel: Bauten für den Prinzen Karl von Prüsser*, 112–123, Berlin, 1942.

Wealth, Liberty, etc. beautifully executed, appearing to have as striking a relief as sculptured work. On one side is a book containing a list of daily arrivals and clearances of vessels. On the right is an extensive reading-room, to which admission is gained by subscription and the payment of an annual tax. The rooms upon the right side of the hall of this floor are appropriated for the meetings of stockholders, brokers, etc. The attic story is of the same height as the basement, containing six large rooms, occupied by library associations, artists, etc.[35, 36]

[35] *The Family Magazine,* 290, New York, Jan. 17, 1835.

[36] The following description of the interior in 1848 is to be found in the insurance survey of the Philadelphia Contributionship No. 7442 printed in Gilchrist, Strickland, 86.

"I have Surveyed the Exchange Building belonging to 'The Philada. Exchange Company' situate on Third, Walnut, & Dock Streets. Being 90 feet on Third Street. by 150 feet to Dock Street including the semicircular basement or first story & Portico, thick brick walls faced with marble. Fronting on Third Street from the second story is a portico with four large marble columns fluted & two anties all with richly carved marble capitals. On the Dock Street front is a semicircular portico with Eight columns & two Anties all with capitals &c. as those on Third Street. The first story is divided into Eleven rooms & two halls, one room large, & occupied as the Post office, the other rooms as Public & private offices, seven marble mantles, of neat patan [?], moulded base round, windows cased, & inside shutters to all these. Cornices, fire proof closets with iron doors in seven rooms, the floors of 5/4[in] yellow pine, laid on mortar, the whole of the basement floor is arched under. In the halls is marble wash board, stucco cornice & floored with Italian marble flags. In the large hall are two flights of marble stairs, right & left with large continued hand rail of mahogany & large turn'd ballusters & an opening though the 2nd floor about 12 by 14 feet surrounded by rail & ballusters of the same kind. All the door ways on Walnut Street, Third & part of Dock Street have each two plain marble columns with carved caps. Those on the other part of Dock Street are plain marble folding sash doors, Glass 6½ & 8½ by 15"; a vestibule with each also with folding sash doors. Glass in the windows 12 by 18". Brick partition walls dividing all the rooms.—The 2nd Story is divided into six rooms, large Hall & Exchange room, one a reading room, two marble mantles, moulded base, windows cased with double architraves, Glass 13 by 18 & 14 by 20" with panneld inside shutters, the other 5 rooms are occupied as Offices, with marble mantles & neat wash boards, inside Shutters & Stucco cornice. In the Hall is a continuation of the Stairs from the first Story—with mohogany rail & turn'd ballusters to the 3rd Story. In the Exchange room are two marble mantles, moulded base, windows cased, & inside shutters, four large columns of marble with carved caps, similar to those of the Porticos, supporting the roof & ceiling a part of which is a semicircular dome & part flat with a stucco cornice round. The walls & ceiling of this room are ornamented with Fresco painting, outside doors large & folding. The columns in this room also support a circular Lantern of wood, 40 feet high, neatly finish'd outside with Eight columns of wood & with carved capitals, carved roof, covered with copper, ornamented with carved work vane &c. sashes round. The entrance to this room from the Hall has an arch'd head, side lights, venetian door way, & close folding doors. 4 large fluted columns with carved capitals, brick partitions, between the reading room & the North west room, is a flight of open newal stairs such as before described leading to the 3rd Story. The 3rd Story is divided into Seven rooms, & passage, the floor of 5/4" yellow pine, moulded base, windows cased & pannel'd inside shutters. Those rooms are occupied for public & private purposes, in one is the Magnetic telegraph, operating machine. In this Story is one flight of winding Stairs leading to the Garret, & connecting with a circular Stairs in the Lantern leading to the top of the Same with painted rail, close String & square ballusters. Garret formed in the centre running East & west & plastered stud partitions, floor rough white pine boards, *groved,* two flat sky lights in the roof, the whole of which is boarded & covered with copper.

"In the cellar are two Furnaces, safely built in brick work, one for the use of the Post office, & the other for warming the Exchange room, the heat from which passes up through a hollow cast iron column in the hall of the first story into the room, covered by a marble curb with a brass revolving ventilator. A smaller one in the Post office of iron. Marble cornice round the whole building, copper gutterd & pipes.

7 Mo. 3rd 1848. John C. Evans
Surveyor

"Liberty of Magnetic Telegraphs in Insured Building. It is expressly understood that this Insurance is not to apply to, nor is the Company to be in any wise responsible for any injury, that may be done to the Fresco or Ornamental painting in the premises hereby Insured.

"Policy No. 7442. Drs. 10.000. at 3 per Cent Drs. 300.—

Agreed to be correct.

John C. Martin
For Phila Exchange Co.

"A Furnace in the Cellar (South West Corner) for warming the room above which appears safely constructed.

November 11th 1851 D. R. Knight
Surveyor"

ITALIAN ARTISTS EMBELLISHED THE EXCHANGE

Although the ceiling decoration of the Exchange Room is described, the artist is not named in this account. He was in *The Guide to the Lions of Philadelphia,* 1837 (p. 41) fortunately. He was Nicola Monachesi, born in Italy at Tolentino in 1795. He went to Rome to study at the Accademia di S. Luca under Gasparo Landi where he gained the first prize for painting. In 1831 Monachesi came to Philadelphia, became an American citizen, and remained until his death in 1851. He early obtained commissions from Stephen Girard, Mrs. Rush, and Joseph Bonaparte. In 1832 he decorated St. John's Roman Catholic Church, then the Cathedral, with frescoes which are said to be the first real frescoes, that is painted on wet plaster, in this country. In 1834 he painted frescoes in Matthew Newkirk's house, which later became St. George's Hall. He did frescoes and altarpieces for the Roman Catholic churches of St. Mary, St. Joseph, St. Augustine, and St. Philip. In 1841–42, he exhibited a large painting of the Murder of Jane McCrae.[37] In the Philadelphia Directories, his address is given as 156 Pine Street and he is listed as a Portrait painter.

Two Italian sculptors worked on the Exchange. William Strickland proposed a toast to them at the dinner celebrating the cap stone.[38] They carved the capitals and their skill was so admired that they were permitted to sign their work. It is still possible to read on the narrow band between the top of the fluting of the

[37] *Cyclopedia of painters and paintings,* ed. by John Denison Champlin, Jr., 3 (2) : 283, N. Y., Scribners, 1887.

[38] Thieme and Becker, *Lexikon* **2**: 489, 1908.

FIG. 6. The Monument of Lysicrates. Engraving from Stuart and Revett, *Antiquities of Athens,* vol. I, chap. 4. Detail of capital and antefix. New York Public Library.

FIG. 7. The same. New York Public Library.

columns of the Dock Street portico and the Corinthian capitals the following inscriptions: "Petrus et Philipus Bardi de Carcaria Fecurunt 1832." They were brothers who came from Carrara in Tuscany which since Roman times has been famous for its marble quarries and stone carvers. Peter, in 1818 at the Academy of Carrara, did a relief of Joseph as the Interpreter of Dreams. He was noted for his ornamental sculpture and returned to Carrara to become a professor in the Academy there.[39]

All the men connected with the building were skilled and had worked with Strickland on other buildings he had designed. John O'Neill had been carpenter of the tower of Independence Hall. Joseph Walter, the father of Thomas the architect of Girard College and the present dome of the Capitol in Washington, had worked on the second Bank of the United States. John Struthers[40] had also as well as on the Naval Asylum and the Mint. The workmen did such excellent work that at the Cap stone banquet, Strickland proposed another toast to "The artizans, mechanics and working men engaged in the building of the Philadelphia Exchange. Their good conduct and orderly deportment have been

[39] On the inner plinth of the rotunda is carved "W. Strickland, Architect J. Struthers Mason" as also on the Second Bank of the United States and the Mechanics Bank, 22 S. Third St. The plaque on Struther's shop at 360 High Street is now in the Historical Society of Pennsylvania. In 1837, Struthers donated the marble sarcophagi which contain the remains of George and Martha Washington at Mount Vernon, Va.

[40] Hazard, *op. cit.* **12**: 293, 1833.

as remarkable as their skill and excellence of workmanship." [41]

EARLY HISTORY OF THE EXCHANGE BUILDING

On January 2, 1834, when the building was almost completed, the Board of Managers held a meeting at which they decided to hire a superintendent of the Exchange and Reading Room at a salary of $1,500 a year and announced the appointment of Joseph M. Sanderson. They also announced the lease of the room on the ground floor to the Post Office for ten years and that the basement and second-story rooms were completely rented and part of the cellars and the third story. The rents already assured were $9,800 a year and another $1,500 was expected making an annual revenue of $11,-300. The land had cost $75,000 and the estimate for the building was $159,435.

At that time, there was one problem which had not been solved. That was where to place the privies. It had been decided to have none within the building, but to use the ground between the Exchange and Mr. Gowen's wine shop on Third and Dock, but it had become evident that situation for the privies was "entirely inadmissible, because of the immediate vicinity of the Post Office to which all classes of our citizens *female* as well as male would be obliged to resort." The solution was to buy the lot at No. 60 Walnut Street which extended 138 feet back along Pear Street and place the privies there.[42]

On March 22, 1834 the Merchants Coffee House on Second next the Bank of Pennsylvania burned down. The Philadelphia merchants had conducted their business there for many years. Fortunately, the Exchange was sufficiently finished to permit it to be used for business the following day, March 23. During the following weeks many people visited the building, including the ladies who were specially invited to view it.[43]

The Philadelphia Exchange Company had a meeting on April 5, 1834 with John R. Neff in the chair and Richard Price as secretary. It was then determined that one o'clock should be the hour of High Change and all those wishing to do business should be there five minutes before. On the same day there appeared in the papers a letter signed "A Merchant" which said in part:

As regards the Philadelphia Exchange, I hope that every individual in the city and county who does anything like a wholesale business, whether he be a merchant, manufacturer, dry goods merchant, grocer, broker, shipmaster, builder, or lawyer, or retired capitalist, will consider it his duty to be present *for at least 5 minutes* of each day at one o'clock—if business requires.[44]

The Notebook of Francis Gurney Smith (owned by Mrs. H. B. Dupont)[45] adds the following bits of information about the Exchange. The weather vane was put up on October 31, 1833. The clock in the Exchange Room was started Wednesday June 18, 1834. Gas was introduced into the reading-room at the Exchange on Saturday April 2, 1836.

By June 22, 1835 the Philadelphia Exchange Company was able to obtain a mortgage for $60,000 from the city.[46]

McElroy's Philadelphia Directory for 1837 lists the following Marine Insurance companies as having offices in the Exchange building which by then was always referred to as the Merchants Exchange: Union, office No. 6; Delaware No. 3; United States No. 5; Atlantic No. 4 and also the American Insurance Company as being at the N. E. corner. William Strickland, architect, is listed at 31 Exchange and J. A. C. Trautwine, architect, at 24 Exchange.

The 1837 Guide to Philadelphia gives a picture of the Exchange and comments of it that "It serves the purpose of a commercial and financial center of the city." It notes that there is a bar on the ground floor and after describing the principal story concludes, "The building is surmounted by a cupola, which affords a commanding view of the commercial part of the city and the river." [47]

The Dock Street front of the Exchange was the headquarters for the omnibus lines in Philadelphia and the same guidebook in describing another sight in Philadelphia in 1837, the Fairmount Waterworks, notes, "A stranger may take passage in an omnibus at the Merchants' Exchange, and reach the water works in half an hour." The Guide for 1849 lists all the city omnibuses and how often they left from the Exchange. At that date the omnibus for Girard College left every 15 minutes and the fare was 6¼ cents. The Western Rail Road also passed in front of the Exchange and William Strickland was the engineer in charge of laying the tracks which came from Market Street, along Third and down Dock in front of the Exchange.[48]

[41] Desilver's *Philadelphia Directory and Strangers' Guide* for 1835 and 1836 contains a map by J. Simons of "Philadelphia as it is in 1834" Published by C. P. Fessenden which shows the ground plan of the Exchange and the shop of James Gowen, wine merchant at 69 S. Third St. next to it. The article on the Exchange in *The Family Magazine*, Jan. 17, 1835, has an illustration showing the Exchange and Girard's Bank, which view the article calls, "one of the most imposing for architectural display of which Philadelphia can boast. We would respectfully recommend, however, the demolition of Mr. Gowan's wine store, which is the only object that detracts from the beauty of the picture."

[42] Hazard, *op. cit.* **13**: 12–13, 1834.

[43] *Ibid.*, 208.

[44] *Ibid.*, 238.

[45] From Mr. Peterson's notes.

[46] *Journal of Select Council*, Jan. 5–July 2, 1863, App. p. 204 (Riley).

[47] Americans of that period had a positive mania for climbing monuments, towers and cupolas. Perhaps they were curing themselves of vertige in anticipation of the skyscraper. Desilver, *op. cit.* in describing the Old State House or Hall of Independence advised, "Its top is surmounted by a steeple, to which every citizen has ready access, and from which, in a clear day, may be enjoyed one of the most splendid views in our extended country, of which no stranger should omit the gratification."

[48] *Journal of Select Council*, 126, 1835/36.

Later views of the Exchange show recumbent lions of marble guarding the outer stairs to the Exchange Room, but the early views do not. It appears that about 1838 they were placed there, the gift of John Moss (1774–1847), a Philadelphia merchant.[49] They were imported from Italy and are copies of the lions by Canova in St. Peter's in Rome. The lions are now at either side of the steps leading toward the river from the west entrance of the Philadelphia Museum of Art.

Strickland was in Rome in 1838 [50] and may have had something to do with importing the statues of the lions. On his return from Europe, Strickland was appointed engineer of the Asphalte Company of the United States [51] and on February 21, 1839 presented a Memorial to Common Councils recommending the use of "Asphaltic blocks for paving the streets." [52] In this connection, it is interesting to read the description of the Exchange which appeared in the Philadelphia Guide for 1849, especially the part which follows: "the eastern front being circular, embellished with a portico recessed, with columns in the Corinthian style, having a fine piazza paved, or rather covered, with asphalte, with beautiful patterns formed of pebbles." [53]

The Post Office remained in the Exchange for thirty years until a separate building was completed in 1862 on Chestnut Street [54] next to Strickland's bank which was then the Custom House, and it remained there until the Drexel Building superceded it and the Post Office moved to Ninth and Chestnut. Postage stamps were first sold in the Post Office in the Exchange in 1847,[55] but the idea of prepaying for letters took several years to become established as a description of the Post Office in 1849 shows.

> It [the Post Office] is admirably arranged throughout. Strangers wishing letters will apply at the first window in the western entry having a sign with *Paid Letters* over it. Here also are received letters on which the postage is desired to be paid. The window in which all unpaid letters are dropped is on the outside of the building.[56]

LATER HISTORY OF THE EXCHANGE BUILDING

Until the Civil War, the Philadelphia Exchange was admired as one of the fine buildings in the city and it was used as it was originally intended. During the war, the first Exchange company dissolved. The Corn Exchange of 1866 and the Philadelphia Stock Exchange of 1875 took its place. Then too, the Greek Revival was no longer the admired style of architecture. The French Baroque became fashionable. The Post Office of 1862 had a mansard roof or as contemporary writers called it a "mashed attic." By 1867, when a survey was made of the Exchange for the Philadelphia Contributionship Company, the interior had been greatly changed. The Rotunda had been divided and two offices put in, many of the rooms were subdivided and water closets had been installed.

From then on the building ran down steadily until in 1900 when the Philadelphia Stock Exchange decided to move from the east wing of the Drexel Building and to move back into the Exchange Building, the Building Committee permitted the architect, Louis C. Hickman, who was retained to supervise the alterations, to rebuild the interior completely, the roof and the tower and found his work "entirely satisfactory." [57]

The building became reoriented after its purchase by the Hallowell Estate on March 22, 1922, partly owing to the growth of the city to the west and the Third Street entrance became the main entrance and the Dock Street portico the back—the Hallowell Estate operated the building as the Produce Exchange. The lions were removed, the outside stairs were pulled down; market sheds put up instead and, on the north, a gas station.

In 1952 the Exchange was taken over by the National Park Service to form part of the Independence National Historical Park Project. The intention is to restore the exterior as nearly as possible to its earlier appearance and to return the lions to their former positions beside the outer stairs.

In the last thirty years, as the building itself has become more delapidated, architectural historians have become increasingly aware of its architectural importance. Joseph Jackson wrote of it.

> This structure, which still survives although thoroughly ruined by modern additions . . . was the finest structure of its kind then in the country and really marked the beginning of a new era in architecture in America. . . . Strickland . . . set off an otherwise flat structure with a copy of the choragic monument to Lysicrates. This was a daring innovation, placing one structure upon another, but the effect was found to be attractive, and the building has remained until lately, one of the best examples of the period when American Architecture had released itself from British tradition.[58]

Rexford Newcomb had high praise for the Exchange Building in his essay on Strickland and Shakleton, whom he quotes, is lyrical in his eulogy.

---

[49] *The Philadelphia Bulletin,* Nov. 24, 1937. "Pedigreed Lions Guard City Art" by Sanford A. Moss (Fiske Kimball).

[50] Strickland, William, Sketches of Roman Architecture, a portfolio of watercolors in the Tennessee State Library, Nashville.

[51] *Journal of Common Council,* 167, 1838/39.

[52] *Ibid.*, Feb. 21, 1839.

[53] *A hand-book for the stranger in Philadelphia,* 47, 1849.

[54] *Smith's hand-book and guide in Philadelphia,* 56, 1870.

[55] Baker, Charles R, Post office buildings of Philadelphia. *Phila. Hist.* **2** (9). The post office had been at 109 Chestnut Street before moving to the Exchange.

[56] *A hand-book,* 1849, *op. cit.,* 96.

[57] *Souvenir history of the Phila. Stock Exchange,* 1903 (Peterson).

[58] Jackson, *op. cit.,* 206–207.

In the design the architect gives us a unique and original composition—the main rectangular mass, with its lovely *in antis* portico, fronts Third Street, but at the rear where Walnut runs into Dock Street, a semi-circular colonnaded rotonda, flanked by admirable steps and surmounted by a cupola patterned after the Choragic Monument of Lysicrates, makes a pretty termination that capitalizes its site most magnificently; "a classic structure," remarks Shakleton, "perfect in mass and detail, an up-standing, forth-facing, audacious building, looking out from its sweeping curve with such graceful bravery as gives a veritable Victory of Samothrace air." [59]

The final summing up of the architectural importance of the Philadelphia Exchange as it is judged by mid-twentieth century critics is best given by quoting in part what Talbot Hamlin writes of it in his volume, *Greek Revival Architecture in America.*

But it was undoubtedly in the Exchange . . . that Strickland achieved his Philadelphia masterpiece . . . in every detail of the design the quality of each part is stressed, and yet the whole is brought into the most perfect unity. The windows of the rectangular part are wide, the motion horizontal, the wall surfaces simple; and this, the simpler part of the design, is by itself one of the most charming examples of that true aesthetic functionalism which underlies so much of the best Greek Revival work. But this alone is not enough; in addition horizontal lines lead inevitably to the climax of the building, the superb curved colonnade of the front, with its conical roof and its delicate lantern founded on the Choragic Monument of Lysikrates. Here each part of the composition falls so naturally into place that even the purists can find little to criticize in the derivative nature of the detail. Not only as a building, but also as a piece of city decoration, the Philadelphia Exchange takes its place as one of the great creations of American architecture.[60]

[59] Newcomb, Rexford, William Strickland. *The Architect,* 455, July 1928.

[60] Hamlin, Talbot, *Greek revival architecture in America,* 79–80, N. Y., Oxford Univ. Press, 1944.

EARLY VIEWS OF THE PHILADELPHIA EXCHANGE

In the Historical Society of Pennsylvania: [61]

Drawings:

1. Wash drawing signed W. Strickland Architect et pinxt not dated, probably done in 1831 or 1832 before the completion of the building because of differences: the female figure on the tower; the square post to support the lamps by the outer stairs; the omission of the scrolls by the lamps and the antefixes on the flat parts of the western façade.
2. Pen and ink and charcoal drawing. Unsigned and undated. Used as a model for an engraved fire insurance policy.

Engravings:

3. Mezzotint by John Sartain after Strickland.
4. Lithograph by J. C. Wild, published by Chevalier, 1838.
5. Line engraving by Davis after Bartlett, 1839.
6. Colored lithograph of J. T. Bowen, 1840.
7. Lithograph by George Lehman.
8. Reproduction of a wood cut of Third Street front, drawn by Ed. Glenn, figure 3.

Photograph:

9. Early photograph taken in nineteenth century before changes, figure 1.

In the Atwater Kent Museum of Early Philadelphia:

10. Lithograph by A. Köllner.

In Harper Collection of Stricklandia in Old Custom House:

11. An illustration from *Gleason's Pictorial,* May 6, 1854.

Illustrations in Magazines and Guides:

12. *The Family Magazine,* January 17, 1835, p. 290.
13. *A Guide to the Lions of Philadelphia,* 1837, p. 41.
14. *A Hand-Book for the Stranger in Philadelphia,* 1849, p. 47.
15. *Smith's Hand-Book and Guide in Philadelphia,* 1870.

[61] There is also a portfolio of views not listed here, including a Talbot type dated Aug. 16, 1849.

MARKET HOUSES IN HIGH STREET

MARKET HOUSES IN HIGH STREET

AGNES ADDISON GILCHRIST*

IN 1682, when Thomas Holme, the surveyor for William Penn, made the plan for Philadelphia, the proposed capital city for the newly granted colony of Pennsylvania, only the names of the axial streets were given: Broad Street and High Street, the latter running east and west from the Delaware River to the Schuylkill River. From the founding of the city, High Street was used for markets; at first outdoor markets and later market houses were built in the center of the street, until, by 1858 when the name was officially changed, eleven blocks of High Street had market houses. Nine market houses were to the east of Broad Street from Water to Eighth Street and two market houses to the west of Broad, from Fifteenth to Seventeenth Streets. In 1745 market houses were erected in South Second Street and later in Callowhill, Spring Garden, and other streets outside the original boundaries of Philadelphia. However, High Street remained the most important market area and early in common parlance was called Market Street as is shown by an advertisement of Samuel Grisley, a wine merchant, who stated that his store was in "High-Street commonly called Market Street" which appeared in the *Pennsylvania Gazette,* June 8, 1758.[1] About a hundred years later, R. A. Smith in his guide to *Philadelphia as it is in 1852* commented upon confusion afforded the stranger in the city by having the main street legally of one name and commonly called by another name.

This confusion was abolished by the Ordinance passed September 1, 1858, when the name was legally changed to Market Street. However, an ironic anomaly came into being the next year with another ordinance which ordered the demolition of the market houses down the center of the street. In 1854, the Northern and Southern Liberties were incorporated into the city and with the new boundaries and increased size of the city; the increase of traffic and new methods of transportation; and above all with economics of marketing food changing from simple sale from producer to consumer to the more complex one of wholesaler and retailer, High Street was no longer the effective marketing center of the city. That the name of the street was changed to Market Street, the year before the market houses were all demolished affords another example of the commemorative character of much legalization.[2]

The High Street markets had a good reputation. Both natives and visitors praised the abundance and high quality of the meat and produce sold in them. Benjamin Franklin, who lived just off High Street, wrote to Mrs. Mary Hewson on May 6, 1786, ". . . Considering our well-furnished, plentiful market as the best of gardens, I am turning mine, in the midst of which my house stands, into grass plots and gravel walks, with trees and flowering shrubs . . ." (A. H. Smyth, *Writings of Benjamin Franklin,* **11**: 511, N. Y., Macmillan, 1906).

The first permanent market building to be erected in High Street was the arcaded ground floor of the Court House built in 1709 [E, II]. This building continued the mediaeval practice of combining the market and the Court. Architectually, it echoed on a reduced scale the handsome market houses of England and Scotland, many of which are still standing such as at Shrewsbury and Ross. A more pretentious colonial market of the same type which has been preserved is The Brick Market in Newport, R. I., designed by Peter Harrison in 1761.[3]

* My special thanks are due Professor Louise Hall, Duke University, who found the Strickland letter among the Peale-Sellers Papers in the Library of the American Philosophical Society. Charles E. Peterson, Resident Architect, Edward Riley, Chief Park Historian, and Dennis C. Kurjack, Supervising Park Historian, all of the Independence National Historical Park Project gave information; also Walter Knight Sturges of the Avery Library, Columbia University. Miss Catharine Miller of the Historical Society of Pennsylvania; Barney Cheswick of the Ridgway Branch of Free Library of Philadelphia; Mrs. Ruth Duncan, American Philosophical Society Library; members of the staff of the New-York Historical Society and the New York Public Library at 42nd Street and the Free Library of Philadelphia all aided in the search for material and illustrations.

[1] *Penna. Mag. Hist. and Biog.* **13**: 487, 1889.

[2] Other examples of commemorative legislation are the Doctrine of the Immaculate Conception, 1854 and the Infallibility of the Pope, 1870.

[3] In the Stauffer Collection of the Historical Society of Pennsylvania there is an item entitled "FAC-SIMILE of the Original Plat of the Lots assigned to William and Laetitia Penn drawn 23rd of 12th month 1698, and recovered 4th of 9th month 1882 by W. F. Boogher. (Copyrighted.)" This shows the Bell Tower at Second and High with "The Cage" beside it and in the middle of High Street between Second and Front a rectangle 30 feet wide with the Prison at the west end 24 feet long, the Prison Yard 80 feet long and "A Plat designed for the Court House 46 feet." Mr. Peterson kindly sent me a photostat of this. Since I have neither seen the original nor know anything of the accuracy of W. F. Boogher, I cannot assess the value of the "FAC-SIMILE." There has been much confusion about the early history of the Court House, which has been dated 1698, perhaps partly because of this Plat and partly because of Gabriel Thomas, *Historical and Geographical Account of Pennsylvania,* 1698, who wrote of Philadelphia, p. 37, "Here is lately built a noble *Town-House* or Guild-Hall, also a *Handsome Market House* and a Convenient *Prison.*" There may have been an early Court House near Front Street as shown on the Plat, but the *Colonial Records of Pennsylvania* do not mention it. Therefore, I begin with the well-documented Court House of 1709. It was the scene of many historic events, for example the death of Queen Anne, whose Coat of Arms was on the façade, and the accession of George I was announced from the balcony in 1714. In 1740 George Whitefield preached from the balcony and tradition says that his voice could be heard in Camden across the Delaware. The Court House was the seat of government both for the city and

The Court House ground floor arcaded market and the subsequent market houses of the eighteenth and early nineteenth centuries had brick piers for supports. The market houses built after 1834 had iron columns for supports. The first markets continue a type of construction which had long been in use in England and in the Low Countries.

The *Minutes of Common Council* for January 2, 1720, give in some detail this type of construction:

> The Method of Building the Market Stalls being Often and Long Debated at this Board, Alderman Redman now proposes and Agrees to Build Thirty Stalls with all Expedition, after the Modell now exhibited and proposed with this Addition, Vizt. to carry the Brick pillars three foot higher, to Arch the Roof and plaister the same, Which Stalls he is to ffinish and ffind all materials According to an Estimacion now brought in by George Claypool and Thomas Redman. . . .

which estimate was for the

> Sum of ffour hundred pounds to be paid in three several payments, Vizt. the Sum of two hundred pounds immediately, the Sum of One hundred pounds at Raising the Roof, the Sum of One hundred pounds more at the ffinishing thereof.

The conservative pattern of market house construction is illustrated by the Ordinance of February 11, 1822—For rebuilding the Jersey Market House [F, II], in High between Front and Second Streets, and for other purposes. In Section I, it states

> . . . said Market house to commence within fifteen feet of the West line of said Front street, to continue along the middle of said High street, to within ten feet of the East line of said Second street.—The columns of said Market house shall not be less than eight feet high, and in no instance, regard being had to the necessary levels, more than ten feet high, the width or breadth of said Market house shall be the same as those already erected in High street.

This form of market house with gable house, brick supports, and plastered ceiling was in the European tradition begun in the late Middle Ages and found useful and acceptable until the nineteenth-century building practices felt the impact of the Industrial Revolution and the increased production of iron. This impact was felt at varying dates in different localities. The Councilmen of Philadelphia became aware of structural iron in the 1830's and so when there was a need for a new market in High Street west of Broad, the ordinance passed to authorize it, demanded the second type of construction, that with supports of structural iron.

Section II of the Ordinance of June 5, 1834, authorizing "a market house to be built and erected in High street, along the middle thereof, between Schuylkill Eighth and Seventh streets," that is between Fifteenth and Sixteenth, reads as follows:

> Sect. II. It shall be the duty of the city commissioners, under the direction of the committee on markets, to offer a premium of fifty dollars for such plan as may be approved and adopted by the said committee—provided, that the said market house shall be erected with iron columns.

The notice which was printed in the newspapers was even more explicit.

> Premium
> For a Plan of a Market House
>
> City Commissioner's Office
> Philadelphia, June 4, 1834
>
> By an Ordinance of Councils, enacted June 5th 1834, it is made the duty of the City Commissioners under the direction of the Committee on Markets, to offer a Premium of Fifty Dollars, for such plan as may be approved by said Committee, provided the said Market House shall be erected with iron columns. It is contemplated to cover the roof of said Market House with metal and consequently it may be of a low pitch.
>
> The Market House will be 336 feet in length including the Porticoes, and it is to be placed in the middle of High street, between Schuylkill Seventh and Eighth streets.
>
> Drawings and descriptions of a Market House will be received at this office until Saturday, July 5, next ensuing.
>
> By the Board
> A. Traquair, President

There were a number of men in Philadelphia at that time who were practicing architects. Nine of them competed two years before in the competition for the Girard College buildings, by name: William Strickland, Thomas U. Walter, W. Rodrique, John Haviland, George Strickland, William B. Crisp, R. W. Israel, Y. J. Stewart, and Mr. Jenks of Germantown. Another Philadelphia architect was Isaac Holden who built the Tobacco Warehouse at Dock and Walnut. How many of these architects made plans for the Market House is not known, but the description and estimate offered by William Strickland is preserved in the Peale-Sellers Papers in the Library of the American Philosophical Society and is now published for the first time.

> Philadelphia July 4th 1834
> To the Committee on Markets,
>
> Gentlemen,
>
> The accompanying design of a Market house which is intended to be entirely composed of cast and wrought iron is submitted to your notice with a view of introducing into our city this novel mode of building;—There is perhaps no better object of Architecture than a Market house for an iron construction, and no better site than the centre of Market Street to exhibit its delicate but strong and durable properties.
>
> The design contains all the necessary diagrams and notes which are calculated to explain the simplicity and convenience of the plan for the purposes of a Market house, where cleanliness and the greatest possible space for the exposure and sale of provisions is to be had in a much superior degree to any other material or mode of structure.
>
> I have accompanied the plans with an estimate of the cost of the superstructure, omitting the curbing and brick paving, in order that you may judge of the expense of such

the colony until the State House, now known as Independence Hall, was completed in 1735. Both historically and architecturally, the Court House deserves a special study. Its affiliation with English Market houses and a comparison with other colonial markets would make a good topic of research in architectural history.

a building compared with the present Market houses with wooden shambles, and brick piers.

Estimate

52	Cast Iron columns each 8 in. in diameter and 10 ft. in length	$1872.--
48	Cast iron Shambles, made in four sections—diam. 6 ft. the brackets or supports included	$3552.--
768	Cranes & hooks suited to each Column & Shamble	$1440.
50	Rail iron ties from Column to Column longitudinally	$ 520.
24	wrought iron rafters extending across the Market from Column to Column, each 28 ft. in length	$1488.
	Roof constructed with sections of Iron corrugated	$3080.
680	ft. of Cast Iron gutter	$1700.
		$13,652.

respectfully submitted
by Your Obdt. servt.
William Strickland

To/
Messrs Yarnall
Warner
Darragh
Jackson
W. Credy &
Eyre
Committee on Markets

P.S. If the shambles be made of wood, as they now are, instead of Cast iron as drawn in the plan, the whole cost will be diminished at least $3000.

It is probable that the City Commissioners decided to save the $3,000 and have the shambles of wood, for there is no further reference to cast iron shambles. The market house with cast iron columns and metal roof was built and before it was completed there were petitions for another market house west of Broad Street.

The Ordinance of October 1, 1835, provided that a market house should be built on High Street between Schuylkill Seventh and Sixth (that is between Sixteenth and Seventeenth as the streets were renamed in 1839). The first market house with iron columns was so satisfactory that the second western market was ordered to be built with iron columns also and of the same height and with the roof of the same elevation and projection.

One of the events of 1834 which affected the markets in High Street was the opening of the Columbia-Philadelphia Railroad which was part of the Canal and Railway System which connected Philadelphia and Pittsburgh. One track was completed in April and the second track was ready for use on October 6, 1834. There were daily trips each way with locomotive power and the cost was $3.00. The terminal was without the city limits at Broad and Columbia, so soon there was agitation for the railroad to be brought into the city limits. In December 1835 a Memorial was presented to the City Commissioners by the Philadelphia Board of Trade requesting that a railroad might be constructed from the terminal in Broad Street east on High Street to Third, then south on Third to Dock by the new Exchange and east on Walnut to the Drawbridge. "In conclusion, your memorialists take it for granted, that no locomotive will be permitted to enter the chartered limits of the city." The power on the railroad was to be "horses at a moderate rate of going." Until about 1850, the term railroad meant only what it said: a road with rails. It did not imply locomotive power as the term does now.

The need for continuing the railroad to the Delaware was so evident that an Ordinance was passed on December 24, 1835, for the building of the railroad and for new market houses from Third to Eighth Streets along High Street.

By February 11, 1836, the Committee on City Property was able to report that all was set to begin work in the spring on the railroad and the rebuilding of the market houses and that it had

> appointed William Strickland, as Architect, he having been selected as Engineer on the Rail Road; they also adopted a plan for a neat Market House, having the full width of those now in existence, without eave stands, and without the cumbrous and unsightly appearance that is now presented; together with the requisite inquiries in the contracts for iron columns, and the mechanical work necessary for their completion.
>
> Your Committee could not but feel a regret that any delay should be experienced, to a prompt removal of the present unsightly Houses, and of substituting new ones, possessing architectural beauty, with equal conveniences in their stead; but they could not reasonably refuse the recommendations of their intelligent Architect.

The architect, so flatteringly referred to, William Strickland, had recommended that the market houses remain standing until the railroad was laid. As part of the modernization of High Street in 1836, it was determined to demolish the first permanent building erected in High Street between 1708 and 1710, the old Court House which had stood west of Second Street which had served as the State House until 1735 when the new State House, now called Independence Hall, was ready for occupancy. There was some opposition to the removal of such a landmark. John Fanning Watson lamented that there was not much more. However, the progressive Commissioners carried the day and on September 1, 1836, an ordinance was passed for the "doing away with the Court House." It was demolished in March and April 1837.

There was some delay in obtaining sufficient cast iron columns for the construction of the market houses, but they were completed and generally admired as the following contemporary comments show. J. C. Wild, in his *Views of Philadelphia,* noted in 1838 that "The Markets excepting 'The Jersey' were removed last year, and light, airy, convenient and modernized ones were erected in their places." *A Guide to the Lions of Philadelphia,* 1837, commented on the markets that "The old buildings have been recently taken down, and new and more elegant ones erected on their sites." By the end of the 1830's in Philadelphia a new aesthetic, based upon an admiration for structural iron, was being formed.

Judging from Strickland's letter no building constructed entirely of iron had been erected in Philadelphia before 1834, but structural iron had been used at least a dozen years previously by Strickland himself in the rebuilding of the Chestnut Street Theatre which was completed in 1822. It was described as having cast iron columns secured with iron sockets from the foundation to the dome. Strickland also used iron columns for the supports of the piazzas on the wings of the United States Naval Home (1827–1829). John Haviland used structural iron in the rebuilding of the Walnut Street Theatre in 1828 in the same way that Strickland had used it in the Chestnut Street Theatre, for it was "supported in each story by Iron Columns that extend from the pit to the roof." Haviland used iron in the construction of the Eastern State Penitentiary. The records of Hopewell Furnace, Berks County, show that "in 1825–26, Hopewell supplied much of the cast-iron installations used in the cell blocks. . . ." [4]

These were notable buildings in Philadelphia and this use of structural iron must have been known by all the members of the City Councils. Probably they also knew of the increasing use of cast iron supports for market houses in England and on the Continent such as the Marché de la Madeleine at Veugny in 1824.

John Haviland in the first volume of his *The Builders Assistant* published in Philadelphia in 1819 under his discussion of building materials wrote the following about iron:

> Iron has been applied to many purposes unthought of in former times. The improvement and general introduction of cast iron bids fair to create a totally new school of architecture. It has already been occasionally employed in bridges, pillars, roofs, floors, chimneys, doors, and windows, and the facility with which it is moulded into different shapes will continue to extend its application.

In the 1830's Haviland gave substance to his prophetic statement that cast iron would "create a totally new school of architecture." His innovation is best described in his own words, taken from his improved and enlarged edition of *Biddle's The Young Carpenter's Assistant,* Philadelphia, 1837.

> A Bank has recently been executed by Mr. John Haviland, Architect, of Philadelphia, the author of this work, at Pottsville, Schuylkill co. Pa. and every feature of the front (not excepting the moulded cornices) are formed of cast iron, in imitation of marble; and it is believed to be the first and only example of this material being employed in the whole *façade.* The iron plates are cast in lengths and form corresponding with the size and jointing of the stone-work, backed in with masonry two feet thick, and secured to the same by wrought iron ties, two and three to each plate; when finished, the whole was well painted and sanded with white sand, which gave the surface a very beautiful and uniform texture of stone, free from gloss, and at the same time prevented its rusting. It is very much to be regretted that this valuable material is not more frequently used, as a substitute for the more perishable ones of wood, and expensive one of marble, or cut free-stone. Iron is not only more fire-proof, durable, and stronger, than wood, but also more economical and favorable to embellishment, than marble or cut free-stone. When duplicates are required, the labor of carved or moulded work in one pattern, answers for all.

[4] Kurjack, Dennis C., *Hopewell Village,* Washington, National Park Service Historical Handbook Series No. 8, 1950.

FIG. 1. Coat of Arms of Queen Anne from Court House (1709). Pen and ink sketch frontispiece of volume XXX, Stauffer Collection, Historical Society of Pennsylvania. Courtesy of Hist. Soc. of Penna.

The enthusiam of these architects, both of whom were well informed of the English advances in the diversified uses of structural iron, Haviland by being an Englishman by birth and beginning his architectural career under James Elmes and Strickland having investigated the manufacture of iron in England in 1825 for the Pennsylvania Society for the Promotion of Internal Improvements, must have influenced Philadelphians to take an interest in iron as a building material.

In Pennsylvania there were both coal and iron deposits and in Philadelphia itself there were founderies.

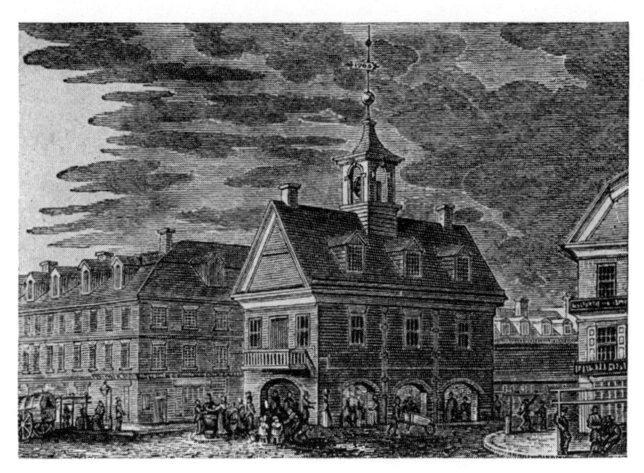

FIG. 2. Woodcut of the Old Court House from *The Casket,* June 1828. Courtesy of Hist. Soc. of Penna.

Fig. 3. Market Hall, Amersham, Buckinghamshire, England. Built in 1682 by Sir William Drake. The Philadelphia Market and Court House of 1709 was similar in design: arcaded ground floor with hall above; and in construction: brick with stone dressings. Courtesy of The National Buildings Record, London.

The I. P. Morris Company was founded in 1828. The Mars Works of Oliver Evans had two furnaces capable of melting five tons of iron. The Eagle Works of S. and W. Richards on the Schuylkill advertised casting, as did the City Iron Foundry. Among the first members of the Franklin Institute in 1824, James J. Rush and James Somerville are listed as Iron Founders and James Roland as an Iron Master.

Fig. 4. High Street Market looking west from Jersey Market, showing balcony of Court House and vista through market house to Fourth Street. Engraving by Thomas Birch, 1799. Courtesy of Hist. Soc. of Penna.

There must have been much experimentation with iron to convince the members of City Councils that the new market house should have cast iron columns and a metal roof. Perhaps they knew that Charles Bonnycastle of Charlottesville, Virginia, had obtained a patent on June 29, 1833, for a method of covering roofs with sheet iron.

An advertisement which appeared in *Poulson's American Daily Advertiser,* Saturday, July 19, 1834, shows how many metals were available for roofing at that time.

Roofing—1000 sheets Copper, suitable thickness for roofs.
1000 sheets Zinc, very superior for roofs.
Leaded Plate, of Truman's make, for roofs
Sheet Iron, prepared to order for roofs
Sheet Tin, best quality for roofs
A constant supply of the above for sale by
N. Trotter & Co.
36 north Front street

Fig. 5. The New Jersey Market of 1822 at Second Street. Lithograph by J. C. Wild, 1838. Courtesy of Hist. Soc. of Penna.

CONCLUSION

Market houses are purely utilitarian sheds and yet they reflect the architectural practices most clearly. In High Street in Philadelphia, the first permanent market was the arcaded ground floor of the Court House at Second Street. It faced east and had a balcony from which proclamations were made. It was built in the reign of Queen Anne and her coat of arms were carved in its façade (fig. 1) and it continued the mediaeval custom of combining courts and markets (figs. 2, 3).

The three subsequent market houses of the eighteenth century were also mediaeval in form and construction, that is simple gable-roofed sheds with brick piers and plastered ceilings. These were the market house which continued westward of the Court House in 1720 and the Jersey Market between Second and Front and the market between Third and Fourth built after the Act of March 23, 1786 (fig. 4).

The six market houses built in the first quarter of

FIG. 6. A demonstration by the Fire Companies at Fifth and Market showing the metal Market Houses of 1836–1837. Lithograph by Charles H. Spieler, 1882. (The accuracy of this lithograph made 23 years after the demolition of the Market houses has not yet been confirmed by a contemporary view of the metal markets.) Courtesy of Hist. Soc. of Penna.

the nineteenth century have more ornamentation and reflect in some slight measure the rebirth of homage to antiquity which stemmed from the Italian Renaissance. These traces of classicisms are not yet of Stuart and Revett Greek origin. The market houses to the west to Eighth Street had porticos supported by two round wood columns. The fish market of 1816 had a shad ornamenting its gable. The Jersey Market was rebuilt in 1822 and had a cupola at the Front Street end with cornucopias at either side of the gable spilling the abundance of Jersey produce (fig. 5).

The seven market houses built in the 1830's introduced structural iron construction on a large scale to Philadelphia and heralded a new aesthetic which prepared the way for technics and architectural design of the present century (fig. 6).

CHRONOLOGICAL LIST OF MARKET HOUSES WITH REFERENCES

1693

Bell Tower

Colonial Records of Pa. I: 388. August 9, 1693.

Agreed to have market where Second Street crosses High Street.

Resolved, that after the 12th instant, the markett and stalls be for the present removed to markett-hill, and be there kept until such time only, and no longer, as the Lt. Gov. shall cause the place where the second street crosses High-street, to be staked outt for the market place, and till a Bell-house be built and erected, and the bell hung in the sd place, and that notice yrof be given to all persons concerned, by the Clark of the market.

The Bell tower was evidently built before Oct. 1, 1693 when the Regulation of the Market was given. *op. cit.* I: 391

1709

Court House with Market on ground floor

Minutes of the Common Council 1704–1776, Phila., 1847 p. 52. Common Council 30 March 1708 to pass a law for building a Court House.

p. 58. Nov. 22, 1708, The Mayor and Joshua Carpenter are requested to consider what length and Extent may be proper for the building of the new Market House. And how much money may be required to finish the same.

p. 64. The building of the new Market House being thought by this Council to be of great service to the Town and Beneficial to the Corporation, 'twas put the rate how money should be raised for the doing thereof And it was voted that seven Aldermen shall contribute and pay double what the Common Councilmen should do.

p. 74. May 11, 1711, Ordered that a Shop may be Built under the Court House Stairs, to be Lett out to the best advantage.

Caspipina's Letters by a Gentleman who resids in Philadelphia [Jacob Duché], Bath, 1777. I: 8 (Description of High Street, 1771)

The principal street, which is an hundred feet wide, would have a noble appearance, were it not for an ill-conditioned court-house, and a long range of shambles, which they have stuck in the very middle of it.

The Casket, June 1828, p. 253. A view of the Court House and an article on it based on J. F. Watson's manuscript.

This once venerable building, long diverted of its original honours, had long been regarded by us and others, as a rude and undistinguished edifice. . . . Fully therefore, we entered into his feelings [J. F. Watson's] of gratification, at seeing its exterior lately refitted and repaired in a manner calculated to add to its future antiquity and veneration by its longer preservation and continuance.

This structure, diminuitive and ignoble as it may now appear to our modern conception, was the *chef* d'ouvre and largest endeavor of our Pilgrim Fathers.

The article continues that Watson has the manuscript papers concerning its building, that it cost £616 and Samuel Powel was the carpenter, that it had windows with leaden panes and a balcony in front with steps formerly on either side leading up to it.

Probably the engraving of the "Paxton Boys" 1764 which shows the Court House with such steps was a source for this tradition. Certainly by 1799 when William Birch made his engraving of the Markets and Court House, there was only the balcony as is seen again in Strickland's painting of Christ Church and Second Street (now in the H. S. P.) and in the woodcut in *The Casket* of 1828, and the oil painting by Russell Smith, of 1835 also in the H. S. P. The illustration in Watson's *Annals of Philadelphia,* 1898, p. 350, is an engraving of the pencil drawing by Edward William Mumford now in the Ridgway Branch of the Philadelphia Free Library, which is a reconstruction of Second and High when a Meeting House was at the corner.

Journal of Common Councils 1835–1836, p. 204. On August 11, 1836 a resolution was introduced for the removal of the old Court House and the Market Houses. On September 1, 1836, an ordinance was passed "for the doing away with the Court House" which was accomplished in March and April 1837.

1720

Minutes of Common Council 1704–1776, p. 187, January 2, 1720.

A "Modell" of the Market with thirty stalls to be built west of the Court House was approved and the estimate of 400 brought in by George Claypool and Thomas Redman. On August 29, 1720, p. 180, it was determined that "Some ffit person skilled in Building to oversee yesd Work" be appointed and George Claypoole was chosen, p. 184. By May 28, 1753, the roofs of the Western markets were out of repair, p. 566. Demolished 1837.

1759

The Markets were continued to Third Street. *op. cit.*, p. 644. Demolished 1837.

Only the one block of markets was built before the Revolution as is shown by the Map of Wm. Faden, Jan. 1, 1779

1786

The Municipal Law of Philadelphia—1701–1887, compiled by Charles B. McMichael, Philadelphia 1887. p. 113.

Act to empower wardens to extend market House in High Street from Third to Fourth street and continue westerly from time to time. Demolished 1836.

1789

Constitution and Ordinances of the City of Philadelphia, Hall and Sellers, Phila, 1790.

June 8, 1789. An Ordinance for the Regulation of the Market held in High-street in the city of Philadelphia, on the 4th and 7th days of the week, called Wednesdays and Saturdays.

By then the Jersey shambles were built with engine houses at the west end. Demolished 1822.

By the end of the eighteenth century there were three blocks of market houses as shown in Birch's engraving of 1799 and the map of 1794 dedicated to Thomas Mifflin, Governor of Pennsylvania, drawn by A. P. Folie and engraved by R. Scot and S. Allardice, that is from Front to Fourth streets.

1810

Ordinances of the Corporation of the City of Philadelphia by John C. Lowber, Philadelphia, 1812. p. 118. March 19, 1810. Additional Supplement to the of March 23, 1786 for building Market Houses "from time to time westerly from one street to another, in the middle of High-street."

Mease, James, *Philadelphia in 1811,* Phila. 1811. pp. 116–122. Markets from Fourth to Sixth streets in 1810.

The increased projection of the eaves over the pillars in the last part, is a great improvement as it increases accomodation and protection to the country people, and admits of a more advantageous display of their various productions.

In the new parts, the upright posts and cross pieces having hooks to suspend the provisions on, are required to be regularly taken down after market hours, and packed away under the stalls: a very proper regulation and strictly enforced.

The pillars of all the markets are of brick, and openings are left at proper distances to admit a passage between them. The footpaths are paved with the same material. Their breadth in the clear is about thirteen feet.

Map of the City of Philadelphia. Actual Survey by John A. Paxton, W. Harrison Sc't. drawn under the direction of J. A. Paxton by Wm. Strickland. Jan. 1, 1811. This map shows Market Houses from Front to Sixth Street. Demolished 1837.

1815

Ordinances of the Corporation of the City of Philadelphia: passed since 18 day June, 1812–1815. Chap. 198: An ordinance for building a fish market in High Street east of Water Street, passed March 23, 1815.

Wilson, *Picture of Philadelphia,* Philadelphia 1823, p. 69. The Fish Market. Water Street and Wharves. A new market house built 50 ft. in Market Street from east of Water running 150 ft. to river Delaware. Its center is 18 ft. including brick piers; its eaves project 7 ft. on each side, supported by turned columns, and of its kind, is an ornament to the city. It is well stored with the finny tribe, such as resort to its contiguous waters.

Map of Philadelphia of 1819 dedicated to Wm. Sansom shows markets to Sixth and the Fish Market at Water. Demolished 1859.

1821

Ordinances of the Corporation of the City of Philadelphia: passed since the 3rd Day of August 1820. Lydia Bailey, Phila. 1822. Passed March 29, 1821—An Ordinance for extending the Market House in High street from Sixth to Eighth streets. Which provided "that the said market houses shall be finished in the same manner, and corresponding with the market houses erected between Fourth and Sixth Streets."

An amendment to this Ordinance was passed May 3, 1821 directing that the market houses between Sixth and Eighth Street be built with "a plain and neat portico of the Doric order in conformity to a plan exhibited to Councils." Also that it include four more stalls by narrowing the passages and shortening the shambles. Demolished 1836.

1822

National Gazette and Literary Register, February 11, 1822 An Ordinance enacted 6 day February 1822

For re-building the Jersey Market House, in High between Front and Second streets, and for other purposes.

Sect. I Be it ordained and enacted, by the citizens of Philadelphia in Select and Common Councils assembled, That the City Commissioners be, and they are hereby authorised and required to rebuild or cause to be re-built, as soon as convenient after the passing of this ordinance, the Jersey Market House, in High Street, between Front and Second streets; and previously thereto to cause the said High street to be regulated so as to make its ascent from the river more easy, and also to cause the said street between the West side of Second and the East side of Water street, to be re-paved:—said Market house to commence within fifteen feet of the West line of said Front street, to continue along the middle of said High street, to within ten feet of the East line of said Second street.—The column of said Market house shall not be less than eight feet high, and in no instance, regard being had to the necessary levels, more than ten feet high, the width or breadth of said Market house shall be the same as those already erected in High street, and the said Market house shall be finished in the same manner, and corresponding with the Market houses erected in said High street, between Sixth and Eighth streets, except the East end, which shall be finished in conformity to a plan now exhibited to

Councils, to be certified by the Clerks of Council, and deposited in the Commissioners' office.

Wilson, *Picture of Philadelphia,* Philadelphia, 1823, p. 70
Jersey Market

On the east end is erected a fanciful cupola or rotunda, raised on doric columns, or pillars, in which is placed a clock with two dials, one on the east and the other on the west. The front on High street presents itself supported on each side by Ceres with her cornucopia or horn of plenty, having a most pleasing effect, and adds greatly to the beauty of the market house.

Map of Philadelphia—J. Drayton, 1824, shows markets to Eighth Street (also gives the designs of the paths in the public squares).

Demolished 1859.

1834

A Digest of the Ordinances of the Corporation of the City of Philadelphia and the Acts of Assembly relating thereto. Philadelphia, 1841, p. 216. Ordinance of June 5, 1834

57. sect. I. The city commissioners, under the direction of the committee on markets, are hereby authorized and required, to cause and procure, as soon as possible after the passage of this ordinance, a market house to be built and erected in High street, along the middle thereof, between Schuylkill Eighth and Seventh streets, beginning thirty feet west of the west line of said Schuylkill Eighth street, and extending westward to within thirty feet of the east line of Schuylkill Seventh street.

Sect. II. It shall be the duty of the city commissioners, under the direction of the committee on markets, to offer a premium of fifty dollars for such plan as may be approved and adopted by the said committee—provided, that the said market house shall be erected with iron columns.

Poulson's American Daily Advertiser, vol. LXIII, Friday, June 27, 1834, p. 1, column 6. Notice of the Premium to be offered for a plan for the market having iron columns and a metal roof. Full text appears in this article.
National Gazette, Saturday, April 4, 1835.

City Commissioners Office

Victuallers, Farmers and Gardeners. Stands and Stalls in New Market. Applications April 1835. Date of auction to be set. Ad. Traquair, Pres.

Demolished 1859

1835

A Digest of the Ordinances of the Corporation of the City of Philadelphia and the Acts of Assembly relating thereto. Philadelphia, 1841 October 1, 1835

An ordinance to construct a market house on High street between Schuylkill Seventh and Sixth. With iron columns and of the same width and design as the market already built west of Broad Street.

Journal of Common Councils 1835/36, p. 80

Budget for new market house $5,000.00

$4000.00 for 1836

p. 246. The new market house in High street between Schuylkill Seventh and Sixth streets will be shortly ready for occupancy and your committee would recommend that early measures be adopted for renting stalls.

Demolished 1859.

1835

Ordinances of the City of Philadelphia, 1834–1854, Philadelphia 1854, p. 520, chap. 559. December 24, 1835
An ordinance to construct a Branch of the Philadelphia and Columbia Rail Road from Broad Street to the River Delaware, and for the building of certain Market Houses.

Sect. I. Route of R.R from Broad along Market to Third along which to Dock along which to Walnut and so past Tobacco Warehouse to Delaware at Drawbridge Dock. R.R to be built with stone sills and iron rails.

Sect. III. Three miles an hour and no cars on Market days.

Sect. IV. New Market houses Delaware Third to Eighth.

Sect. VI. Appropriations of $40,000 for Committee on Highways to build rail road and $40,000 for Committee on City Property to build market houses.

Sect. V. And be it further ordained and enacted by the authority aforesaid, That it shall be the duty of the said committee to have the roof of the proposed market houses supported on iron columns, the width of the said houses not to exceed nineteen feet, the stalls to be erected in such manner and form as in the opinion of said committee will best adapt the same to public convenience and usefulness.

Journal of Common Council, Philadelphia 1835/36. p. 107
Part of a letter from William Strickland to Richard Price, Chairman of the Committee on City Property, dated February 4, 1836. I regret, as much as any citizen, the present unsightly appearance of the Houses in High street, and would wish them removed on that account, independently of their obstruction to the Railway, but my principle object in addressing you on this subject is for you to consider the propriety of permitting the *present buildings* to *remain until the Railway is finished,* and when that is done I am confident that there will be much less remorse in parting with the old buildings *altogether,* or, in the erection of new ones in their stead.

Strickland also promised that the rail would be laid by the first of July 1836.

p. 134. The Committee on Public Property reported Strickland's desire for a delay and agreed to it. It also announced that William Strickland had been appointed architect of the markets since he was already acting as engineer of the Rail Road.

p. 147. The Committee reported that the market houses would be built as soon as iron columns could be procured. The cost for each block of market house was to be not over $6,000.

Demolished 1859.

1836

Journal of Common Council of Philadelphia 1835/36

p. 204. August 11, 1836, there was a discussion of the removal of the old Court House and it was ordered that a new Market should be built by Feb. 1, 1837.

The Ordinance for doing away with the Court House was passed September 1, 1836.

pp. 214–215 Ordinances relating to Market Houses provided that a cupola be built on the west end of the market house between Second and Third streets with a "publick" clock with two dials, one facing east and one facing west.

This ordinance was repealed June 22, 1837.

1859

Journal of Select Council of Philadelphia Nov. 11, 1858–May 5, 1859

Act of Assembly—4 February A. D. 1859
Section I. The Select and Common Councils of the City of Philadelphia do ordain, That the Commissioner of Markets is hereby directed and required forthwith to contract with any party offering to remove the market buildings in Market street west of Broad street, at an expense to the city not exceeding one dollar for the taking down and removal of said buildings, which amount is hereby appropriated for that purpose: Provided, That the materials of every description be removed under the direction of the Commissioner of Markets to such places as he may designate.

April 14, 1859

An ordinance to authorize the Commissioner of Markets to take down and remove certain Market houses on Market street, and to sell certain materials and to rent stalls to 1 October 1859

p. 613 Appendix No. 186 An Ordinance

To provide for the expense of removing the market sheds from Market Street

Select and Common Councils appropriated $2000. for the removal of Market sheds East of Eighth Street, provided that not more than $300. be expended for the removal of any one square of said Market sheds.